DISCARD

DR. JOHNSON & FANNY BURNEY

DR. SAML. JOHNSON.

Engraved from an original Drawing
by N. Gardiner.

Publish'd Nov.r 15th 1786, by Wm. Richardson, 174. Strand.

DR. JOHNSON & FANNY BURNEY

Being the

JOHNSONIAN PASSAGES FROM THE WORKS
OF MME. D'ARBLAY, *Frances Burney d'*

WITH INTRODUCTION AND NOTES

BY

CHAUNCEY BREWSTER TINKER
Assistant Professor of English in Yale College

———

"For we shall go down hand in hand to posterity"
Johnson to Miss Burney

———

GREENWOOD PRESS, PUBLISHERS
WESTPORT, CONNECTICUT

Originally published in 1911
by Moffat, Yard & Co., New York

First Greenwood Reprinting 1970

Library of Congress Catalogue Card Number 70-98806

SBN 8371-3067-0

Printed in United States of America

To

A. EDWARD NEWTON
Johnsonian

PREFACE

This book represents the first complete collection
of the Johnsonian material in the works of Miss
Burney. It is remarkable that no such volume has
appeared before; for, apart from Boswell, there is
no account of Samuel Johnson more lifelike and pic-
turesque than Miss Burney's. Yet, although practically all the other Johnsonian material has been
edited with scrupulous care, Miss Burney's account
has been allowed to remain scattered through the
pages of two voluminous diaries and hidden in the
now-forgotten *Memoirs of Doctor Burney*.

I have included in this work all the reminiscences
of Johnson in Miss Burney's various works, with the
exception of repetitions and of a few passages in
which his name is only casually mentioned—passages
in which he does not actually appear at all. The
present extracts are, therefore, within the limits of
their subject, not a volume of selections, in the strict
sense of that term; they form, rather, a complete
treatise. In my endeavor after completeness, I have
even transcended the avowed subject and included
also some passages dealing with such intimate
friends of Johnson as Boswell and Reynolds.

The text followed in the body of the work is that
of the earlier impression of Mrs. Barrett's edition
of the *Diary and Letters* (London, 1842); but minor

changes in spelling and punctuation have been made
in the interests of consistency. In the extracts from
the *Early Diary* and the *Memoirs of Dr. Burney,*
the text is, in each case, that of the first edition of
the work. To this statement there is exception to be
made of one selection from the *Memoirs* which has
been somewhat condensed; this change is duly mentioned in the proper note. I have done what I could
to supply dates, but my attempts have often failed.
Miss Burney was confessedly careless respecting
dates, so that the utmost ingenuity (which the present editor certainly does not possess) can hardly
hope to do more than correct some few, and to supply some few that are wanting.

My thanks are due to Messrs. George Bell and
Sons, who have kindly permitted the use of the selections from the *Early Diary.* When I have used a
note from that work, or from any other edition of
Miss Burney's works, I have, I believe, acknowledged the source. Many of the illustrations are from
the invaluable collection of Johnsoniana in the possession of R. B. Adam, Esq., of Buffalo, New York,
to whose kindness the editor has been so frequently
and so deeply indebted that he can make no adequate
acknowledgment of it here.

LONDON, *July, 1911.*

INTRODUCTORY ESSAY

" HARRY FIELDING, too, would have been afraid
of her; there is nothing so delicately finished in all
Harry Fielding's works as *Evelina!*" So spoke
Samuel Johnson, not *ex cathedra,* to be sure, in the
Mitre Tavern, but from his easy-chair in the library
at Streatham. And although the pronouncement may
appear casual on the face of it, yet it cannot be regarded as other than a serious literary opinion of the
Great Dictator; for it is true of Johnson's critical
dicta that, unlike those of some of his successors, they
invariably emanate from general principles and
settled convictions. In other words, Johnson certainly meant what he said. The remark represents
an established opinion, not a sudden enthusiasm for
the achievement of a dear friend. Indeed, it would
hardly be fair to say that Miss Burney was a friend
of Johnson's when she wrote *Evelina.* Johnson had,
it is true, been more or less intimate with Dr. Burney
and his children ever since the days of the *Dictionary,*
but all this time Fanny had been to him nothing more
than an undistinguished detail in the family background. It was *Evelina* who introduced Miss Fanny
Burney to Dr. Johnson. Chance had thrown them
together once before, as the reader of the following
pages may see for himself, but the meeting had apparently not left upon the mind of Johnson the

vaguest impression. Even after he had come to know her through *Evelina*, he saluted her rather as a new-found literary acquaintance than as the daughter of an old and loving friend. He, like the rest of the world, had been ignorant of the author when he had read the novel: " Why, madam, why, what a charming book you lent me! " he had said to Mrs. Thrale, who knew the secret of the authorship, and he had presently extracted the whole story from that lady; whereupon he, again like the rest of the world, fell into a passion of curiosity concerning the maiden-author. It is clear that it was enthusiasm for the book that produced the acquaintance, and not friendship that produced the enthusiasm. There was something puzzling in the existence side by side in one person of the timorous maiden and the keen-sighted observer of manners that very naturally fascinated the intellect and challenged the emotions of Johnson, producing, though late in his life, a friendship as deep and true as any in that long life of ardent friendships. But had *Evelina* appeared a decade later, the introduction just described could never have taken place, and Samuel Johnson would never have known " little Burney."

It is certainly a misfortune of the following reminiscences that they have so much to say of *Evelina*. We may tell ourselves again and again that in recording the compliments, delicate and coarse, bestowed upon her book, the young author intended them only " for the eyes of two or three persons who had loved her from her infancy," and yet it is probable that, even in pardoning her, a majority of us will smile at her unrivaled diligence in this kind of work; or when Dr. Johnson insists upon comparisons with Fielding (to Fielding's utter confusion), we may be permitted to take them *cum grano salis. Evelina,* in truth, still possesses distinction, a certain prim attractiveness which time will probably only enhance; the book has always had numerous readers and even more numerous admirers (admiration and perusal sometimes existing quite independently), but it has not yet eclipsed *Tom Jones* or even *Amelia.* It is perhaps a little difficult to account for the rank which one instinctively gives the novel. In respect of plot, though distinguished by a unity and a movement uncommon in eighteenth-century fiction, it is yet both crude and conventional in structure. The modern reader whom scores of novelists have trained into an intuitive respect for the demands of probability cannot but be amused at the happy ubiquity of a character like Lord Orville; whenever there is need—or excuse —for his presence on the scene, the reader may be sure that he will not be wanting: at Ranelagh, at Vauxhall, at the ball, in the playhouse, in city and in country alike, lo! there is Lord Orville in their midst. Other work in life he appears not to have than to meet Evelina at the right—or the wrong—time, and to advance the plot. A similarly unskilful manipulation may be found in the general working out of the story; in its larger aspects the plot is a somewhat mitigated form of the ancient story of the missing heir and of his restoration to long-lost parents. But, as in *Joseph Andrews,* the mystery of the birth is doubled by the introduction of a second heir (also missing), a Mr. Macartney, who is made to fall in love with a woman whom the reader is for a time allowed to suppose his sister. By a careful readjustment of brothers and sisters at the end, each Jack is permitted to have his Jill; wealth and high rank, as a result of marriage or sonship, are bestowed on each, and the delighted reader exclaims with Sheridan,

> Hence may each orphan hope, as chance directs,
> To find a parent where he least expects.

At the plot of *Evelina,* too, I venture to think, posterity must be pardoned for an indulgent smile.

It is, however, much easier to bestow praise upon the delineation of character in this story. It is the farcical element in *Evelina* that has been most freely and frequently praised: Johnson loved to talk of the Smiths and the Branghtons, and of impossible old Mme. Duval (for whom, in spite of her vulgarity and worldliness, one cannot but feel a touch of affection) ; Macaulay praised her for " her variety of humors," but would allow her little more; and even Mr. Dobson appears still to prefer the " broad " treatment of the farcical personages to the quieter characterizations. There are probably no more famous scenes in the book than the ducking of Mme. Duval and the attack of the monkey upon Beau Lovel's ear; and, though we may wonder how a young woman like Miss Burney was able to describe such scenes, it must certainly be admitted that they are successful—

so successful, in truth, as to challenge comparison with some of the lesser scuffles in the pages of Smollett. It is surely a fact of significance that critics have chosen to speak of Mme. Duval and the Branghtons rather than of the hero and heroine, Evelina and Orville, who absorb more of our time and attention. But there have been readers who felt differently. Orville and Evelina were, and are still no doubt, the chief attraction to many a devoted reader who thinks of Duvals and Branghtons merely as obscuring that fine old issue whether the hero can be brought to unite himself in matrimony with the heroine; but the critics appear to have been rather too willing to allow the lovers to be thus obscured. It was hardly to be expected, even by Dr. Johnson, that Miss Burney should equal Fielding in the depiction of an agreeable rake, Sir Clement Willoughby, or surpass Richardson in the depiction of a perfect man, Orville. When all is said, it is to be feared that the comparative indifference of the critics to these gentlemen means that Orville is a prig and a bore, and that Willoughby, obviously more likeable than the peer, is, nevertheless, only an echo.

But the chief distinction of *Evelina* has yet to be mentioned. Whatever we may think of its plot or of its farcical characters, or of its hero and its rake, we must admit that it possesses an interest truly unique in its intimate revelation of the mind of young womanhood. It is remarkable that this characteristic has not been more enthusiastically discussed by those who wish to praise *Evelina,* for this novel contains the first

great analysis in English literature of the mind of a
young woman, produced by a young woman. There
is nothing in earlier English literature quite com-
parable with it; for apt comparisons we must go to
Miss Austen or Miss Brontë, and even then the wonder of it is hardly diminished. But if there is no
earlier woman's achievement that can be fairly compared with this story, there is of course a man's
achievement which completely overshadows it, and
that is the work of Richardson. The parallel between
Pamela's constant " scribbling " and Evelina's devotion to her correspondence is too obvious to have
escaped notice; it is too obvious, indeed, to enable the
reader to regard *Evelina* as quite free from a rather
conscious imitation of *Pamela*. There is at times
in Miss Burney's heroine a suspicion of servility, a
fluttering admiration of rank, which one might wish
away; but when, as a last letter, Evelina records,
" This morning, with fearful joy and trembling gratitude, your Evelina united herself for ever with the
object of her dearest, her eternal affection," then the
likeness to Richardson's heroine almost evokes a cry
of pain. But there is nothing merely repetitious in
the fine portrayal of maidenly simplicity, of bewildered innocence in its first contact with the disillusion-
izing world, its *mauvaise honte,* its all-embracing faith
in the simple maxims of the nursery. Here, at last,
there is perfect knowledge. Here is a figure to oppose
to the colorless stupidity of a Narcissa or to the
studied cleverness of a Lady Teazle.

And yet I cannot but feel that in testing *Evelina*

by the standard of its great predecessors, the chief
interest of the comparison is to reveal the elements in
Richardson's young women to which Miss Burney, as
a young woman speaking for her kind, was willing
to give, as it were, her official sanction. And thus the
chief interest of *Evelina* is likely often to remain just
what it was in 1778, an interest in Miss Burney herself. " She is herself the great sublime she draws,"
wrote Sir Joshua Reynolds to Mrs. Thrale, and
despite all protest to the contrary, it is probable
that the worth of *Evelina* will be ultimately measured
by the truth of its portrayal of young womanhood—
that is to say, by the truth of its portrayal of Miss
Burney.

That most of what went into the characterization
of Evelina came from Miss Burney's knowledge of
herself is not, I imagine, likely to be very strongly
denied. Evelina is of course her idealized self. She
had, to be sure, no Orville, much less a Willoughby,
but under similar circumstances she would have done
—who can doubt it?—precisely what Evelina did.
Miss Burney gave to Evelina her own passion for
recording her life, her own abounding modesty, something, though not full measure, of her sanity and her
keen penetration into character, and above all, something of her own pride. There is, I take it, no real in-
consistency between Miss Burney's intense pride and
her intense modesty. The link between them was her
sensitiveness. Of this she seems to be fully conscious herself; for in speaking of a certain " high
lady " at Bath, she says,

" Characters of this sort always make me as
proud as they are themselves; while the avidity
with which Mrs. Byron honors, and the kindness
with which Mrs. Thrale delights me, makes me
ready to kiss even the dust that falls from their
feet."

So extreme was her sensitiveness that she could hardly
endure to overhear the mention of her name; at the
voice of praise she almost swooned—but it was from
delight. She herself speaks of praise as a " delicious
confusion." When the victim of such adulation, she
must have felt that now more than ever it were rich
to die. But destructive criticism assumed to her the
proportions of cosmical disaster. And yet withal she
knew her deserts; she knew the kind of company in
which it was her right to move. She is often described as filled with a horror of the limelight, a
sitter in corners, content to be a quiet observer of
others. And this is, in a measure, true; but her favorite station was a corner in the salons of the Great.
To realize this we have but to remind ourselves of
some of those whom she might fairly call friends,—
her King and her Queen; Burke, the greatest of
England's statesmen, and his enemy Warren Hastings; the greatest of actors and the best-loved of
painters, bluestockings like Mrs. Montagu and Mrs.
Ord, Mrs. Vesey, Mrs. Thrale, Mrs. Cholmondeley,
and Mrs. Delany. A policy of complete self-
effacement is surely inconsistent with such a host
of acquaintances as that. These are not the friends

of a recluse. The true recluse of the following pages is not the author of *Evelina,* but Mr. Crisp of Chessington, whose first meeting with Johnson affords some interesting contrasts with Miss Burney's. Miss Burney's pride and modesty are most likely to be understood if we conceive of both as a sensitive dread of not living up to what is expected of a proclaimed genius. Praise distressed her because praise is almost always a challenge, and Miss Burney had a young woman's dread of a challenge. It was much easier to disclaim ability than to "talk for victory." Miss Burney's ability to justify the enthusiasm of her friends was so exclusively confined to her hours of solitude that there are times when her modesty seems a studied affectation, the ostentatious humility of a Miss Esther Summerson, rather than the inexperience of an Evelina. These meek young women who are for ever retiring to their "chambers," to escape the voice of the flatterer or to record his words in interminable letters, seem at times possessed of a remarkable sanity which detects the market value of this favorite virtue. They exhibit a surprising facility in contracting successful engagements, in publishing novels (though without fame or fortune), or an almost Boswellian faculty for scraping acquaintance with the distinguished folk of their time. It is all very innocent; and in Miss Burney, at least, there is enough sincerity to give her pages an authentic note of guilelessness, unfrequent in eighteenth-century literature, a characteristic which blends pleasantly with real literary skill. The pages of the Journal

here laid before the reader are simple, unpremeditated
even, at times, casual, after the very best manner of
occasional composition; but underneath it all there is
art. Miss Burney was by no means inexperienced
with her pen. She began writing diaries at the age
of fifteen, but, by her own confession, she had been
for five years before this an inveterate scribbler of
romances, all of which came to a timely end in flames.
These years of practice had given her ease and rapid-
ity of style, and the ability and habit of seeing things
in the large. This unpremeditated skill (if I may be
allowed the expression) may perhaps be more easily
discerned if the reader will compare with some one
of the earlier of Miss Burney's records the gay and
careless chatter of her younger sister Susan, here
given in the Appendix. Both accounts have the
charm of naïveté, but the latter is totally deficient in
the experienced craftsmanship that so delightfully
characterizes the former. Not that there is any trace
of self-consciousness. In Fanny's record there is art,
but it is unstudied, such unstudied art as may result
only from long practice. Thus I believe that we may
find in Miss Burney's diary, not only a truer portrait
of herself than is to be discovered in *Evelina,* but a
style and, indeed, a dramatic skill surpassing any
that can be found in her novels.

And first of her style. Lord Macaulay, with that
magnificent ease which has been alternately the disgust
and despair of his successors, distinguishes three
totally different styles. The first is her natural style,
" perspicuous and agreeable "; the second displays the

stiffening influence of Johnson, and was perhaps produced under his immediate influence; the third represents a " new Euphuism," in which pomposity has gone mad. Now this analysis, touching the high points in the development of Miss Burney's style, is like much of Macaulay's work, most useful, and yet, if accepted as literal truth, somewhat misleading. It is a late day to be saying that Lord Macaulay's criticism is lacking in chiaroscuro; but, commonplace as is the observation, it is yet necessary to give one more illustration of it here. Miss Burney did not suddenly adopt a new style when she came to the composition of *Cecilia;* she did not submit that work to the revision of Samuel Johnson; it is not even true that in *Evelina* she exhibited a charming simplicity of style which she thereafter unaccountably corrupted. In short, there is no impassable gulf fixed between her earliest and her latest style. To begin with the matter of " agreeable perspicuity," *Evelina* is by no means a well of simple diction undefiled. There are sentences in it that display so prim a sense of decorum that they already indicate a strong tendency towards the pomposity of the *Memoirs of Doctor Burney.* Here are three specimens from *Evelina* which would have no unfamiliar ring if found in her latest work, and might, indeed, easily be mistaken for quotations from it:

> " Indeed, had you, like me, seen his respectful behaviour, you would have been convinced of the impracticability of supporting any further indignation."

"Can you wonder I should seek to hasten the
happy time . . . when the most punctilious
delicacy will rather promote than oppose my
happiness in attending you?"

"Suffer, therefore, its acceleration, and generously complete my felicity by endeavouring to
suffer it without repugnance."

Sentences such as these show that Miss Burney's
passion for dignity of language was from the beginning in danger of becoming inflamed. The more
prominent she became, the more did the sense of her
importance exhibit itself in this false dignity of diction which issued at last in mere bombast. The
reader who is interested in this gradual development
toward an unfortunate conclusion may follow it from
Evelina through *Cecilia, Camilla,* and *The Wan-
derer,* to the delicious absurdities of the *Memoirs;* he
will find in it no sudden breaks; but rather a development as natural as it was unfortunate. It is such a
result as might normally be expected from a lady
whose innate tendency to formality was fostered in
the dull pomposities of the court of King George III.

I have said so much of Miss Burney's style in
Evelina and other books not represented in the following pages, because I believe that it is in the pages
of the *Diary* alone—and in its earlier pages at that—
that Miss Burney's work is seen at its best. Here she
is simple; here her style flows swift and limpid.
There is no affectation of dignity in this pleasant converse with her sisters, no suspicion of pomposity in
this spirited account of Dr. Johnson. Here she is

what she is " by art as well as by nature." In respect
of style, as in so many respects, the *Diary* emerges as
Miss Burney's supreme achievement.

If the Journal, then, is superior to Miss Burney's
works of fiction in this, it is also, I believe, at least
equal to them in dramatic quality. When we have
taken into account all other aspects, it perhaps re-
mains the chief distinction of the *Diary* that it exhibits a sense for a dramatic scene which goes far to
justify Mrs. Thrale in her conviction that Miss Burney's genius should be devoted to the service of the
Comic Muse. The author grasps life with the in-
stincts of a novelist, and although plot is necessarily
absent from her work, she exhibits a series of scenes
that fairly deserve the much abused adjective
" dramatic." We are unfortunately accustomed to
speak of any scene that reads brightly and easily as
" dramatic." Boswell's *Life of Johnson,* for example, is almost always so described; but in spite of
all its superiority in other ways, that marvelous
biography is not dramatic in the same sense as are
the following selections. Here and there in Boswell,
no doubt, in passages like the famous account of the
Wilkes dinner and the conversation with King
George, there are scenes as truly dramatic as any
in the present volume; but the general aspect of Boswell's *Life* is not *dramatic.* Whoever is satisfied with
that adjective as a description of the great biography
has either never read it, or is but ill acquainted with
the drama. If, in the infinite variety of that great
book, there can be said to be any strict method, its

unit is rather the sentence, the Johnsonian pronouncement, than the dramatic scene. One recalls the *Life*
as a series of trenchant utterances, now magnificent,
now trivial; one recalls the *Diary* as a succession of
glimpses into Mrs. Thrale's drawing-room. Boswell
is too concerned with the demands of literal truth to
permit himself to " write up " a scene after the manner of the author of *Evelina*. His book is the greatest piece of realism in English; Miss Burney's is
only a book of dramatic sketches. And in this one
respect, I cannot but think that Miss Burney has surpassed the incomparable one himself, and this for the
very simple reason that her lesser task gave her the
greater freedom in the treatment of her material.
Be this as it may, you will find it difficult to discover anywhere in the vast mass of Johnsonian reminiscence anything which, for dramatic vividness, sur-
passes the scene in which the Streathamites discuss
Johnson's kitchen, or that which describes the quarrel with Pepys, or the conversazione in which Dr.
Johnson announces that he prefers Burney to Siddons.
Or, to pass for a moment beyond the strictly Johnsonian material, where is there a neater specimen of
dialogue than that scene in which two ladies, summoned by a bluestocking to partake in high literary
converse, reveal their genuine interests by flying at
once to the congenial subjects of clothes? Surely it
has not its superior in *Evelina*.

> " ' How disagreeable these sacques are! I am
> so incommoded with these nasty ruffles! I am
> going to Cumberland House—are you? '

" ' To be sure,' said Mrs. Hampden; ' what else, do you think, would make me bear this weight of dress? I can't bear a sacque.'

" ' Why, I thought you said you should always wear them? '

" ' Oh yes, but I have changed my mind since then—as many people do.'

" ' Well, I think it vastly disagreeable indeed,' said the other; ' you can't think how I'm encumbered with these ruffles! '

" ' Oh, I am quite oppressed with them,' said Mrs. Hampden; ' I can hardly bear myself up.'

" ' And I dined in this way! " cried the other; ' only think—dining in a sacque! '

" ' Oh,' answered Mrs. Hampden, ' it really puts me quite out of spirits.'

" Well, have you enough?—and has my daddy raved enough? "

Now, with all this dramatic quality, is Miss Burney reliable? May we depend upon the scenes which she represents us as essentially truthful? How far is her charm due to a skillful manipulation of facts? It is a question to be asked. It is, therefore, not very reassuring to be told that Miss Burney's accuracy is by no means unassailable. She was careless about dates. She often prefers, with true feminine instinct, to mention the day of the week rather than the day of the month. Even then, it is often difficult to follow the order of events through the week. Later in life, she showed a shocking carelessness in dealing with her own records—" ancient manuscripts " she

calls them—which is most reprehensible. She cut,
tore, and destroyed,—" curtailed," to use her own
words, " and erased of what might be mischievous
from friendly or Family Considerations." In addi-
tion to all this, new sources of error and confusion
appear in the work of her first editor, Mrs. Barrett,
the only editor of her *Diary* who has had access to
the original manuscript, a lady who, far from ascer-
taining and correcting Miss Burney's errors, seems to
have shared some of Miss Burney's indifference to
mere detail. But this critical distrust may easily be
caried too far. When we have made all necessary
allowance for error, Miss Burney's slips and omis-
sions remain of the slightest importance. It is quite
true that she has not the accuracy of a Boswell; but
it is because we have a Boswell that her errors are so
very negligible. In his pages we have, in all conscience, a sufficiency of details and dates—more than
in any other biography in existence. We go to Miss
Burney's records for something else, for intimate
scenes from Johnson's daily life with the Thrales;
and, in this respect, we may feel comfortably con-
fident that our record is truthful. The question of
the accuracy of such a record is a large matter, and
it is not to be permanently settled by the enumeration
of a few unimportant errors in chronology, or even
by producing evidence that the author late in life
occasionally made verbal changes that are obviously
for the worse. The question of the truthfulness of
the whole portrayal of Johnson can only be tested by
the standard of witnesses of acknowledged reliability.

The world will be ready to admit that we have one such witness in Boswell. Now the life described by Miss Burney differs somewhat from the aspects familiar to the reader of Boswell. The latter naturally saw more of his hero on dress parade; Miss Burney saw more of him in what the world might then have called "the agreeable relations of domestic privacy." But in the general characterization of Johnson there is an almost startling agreement with Boswell, which, in the minds of any but the most skeptical, will go far toward furnishing a sufficient proof of Miss Burney's authenticity. Certainly this was the impression in the eighteenth century; "How well you know him," writes Mrs. Thrale, "and me, and all of us." Large matters like the general truthfulness of a portrait, I repeat, must be tested in large and general ways. In the present case, we find in Miss Burney's Johnson the same formal courtesy of address, the sudden bursts of ferocity, the contradictions, the *argumenta ad hominem,* the humor, the pronouncements, the wealth of anecdote and reminiscence, and the appeal to first principles, that we find in Boswell's record of Johnson's conversation. The words may (conceivably) be the words of Miss Burney, but the voice is the voice of Johnson.

Now, the question of inaccuracy aside, is there any animus in Miss Burney's work that is likely to distort her account of Johnson? She was not, like Mme. Piozzi in her *Anecdotes,* eager to vindicate her own conduct, and therefore not over anxious to do justice to Johnson's.   She was not, like Hannah More, determined to " mitigate " Johnson's " asperities."   She might perhaps have been capable of the latter sin, had she been consciously preparing her record for the press; in fact she once actually deplores the publication of Johnson's *Meditations,* " too artless to be suited to [the world]," and becomes disastrously artificial in her account of Johnson inserted in the *Memoirs of Doctor Burney.*   But in the *Diary* her account is neither marred by mitigations, nor tainted by suggestions of malice.   It is the account of one who saw sympathetically, and therefore saw clearly, of one who was concerned simply with telling the truth to two sisters who were themselves acquainted with Johnson, and who were certainly unlikely to be deceived by a policy of " mitigation."   It is undoubtedly true that Miss Burney is occasionally inaccurate in her dates; in her record of Johnson's conversation it is extremely probable that her memory sometimes played her false, and that, like Boswell, she found herself obliged to draw upon her imagination for a Johnsonian phrase; but in the larger matter of general truthfulness, her record, when compared with other records of Johnson, will be found not only loving, but accurate, not only brilliant, but reliable.

And now with trembling quill and an adequate sense of my own unfitness, I come to the point where it is necessary to say something of the great protagonist of the following pages—if, indeed, anything more can safely be said! So much has been written

of Samuel Johnson that it would now be unwise, if
it were possible, to avoid the commonplaces of criticism. Johnson is, we have been frequently told, the
most completely preserved of any figure in our history. It is unlikely that any one, even in this day of
"personal interviews," will be inclined to dispute it.
I touch upon the matter now only by way of pointing
out that this familiarity with Johnson in the end
breeds no contempt. Posterity may follow Johnson
into the gloom of his solitude, may intrude into his
very confessional, and even scrutinize his final agony
as he lay through long weeks waiting for death; but
the completeness of the revelation (and who could
be found to covet a similar one for himself?),
though it has led many to patronize, has caused few
to sneer. It is the slow death of his works—destined
perhaps to include even the *Lives of the Poets*—
simultaneously with the perfect preservation of his
reputation that has puzzled the critics, and driven
them to explain away Johnson's greatness by the fame
of the books which record him. It is Boswell, we
are often told, that made Johnson great. Mr.
Thomas Seccombe, for example, is at a loss to find
other explanation for the greatness of the man than
"the extent and accuracy of our information about
him," and intimates that the bird of immortality is
capricious in its perching, and the critic leaves the
reader of the *Bookman* to infer that there is, when all
is said, something accidental about Johnson's immortality. I should be sorry if the present volume
contributed to spread this notion. I consider these

reminiscences, for reasons that I have brought forward, a capital specimen of the personal record in literature; but I am far from thinking that this, or any book like it, accounts for the greatness of Samuel Johnson. We cannot dispose of the miracle of the Great Dictator by expatiating on the perfection of works about him; for, if we could, it would next be necessary to inquire whence came this invincible impulse to record the man, an impulse which men and women felt alike. Why, as Carlyle asked long ago, did Boswell, among all the great men whom he knew, fasten upon Johnson? In all this biographical activity, what was the *causa causans?*

It is easy to say that Boswell's choice of Johnson as a biographical subject was owing to the latter's literary eminence, and this is partly true. But whence, we must ask again, came Johnson's literary eminence? Why was he the acknowledged Dictator? There was certainly no sufficient explanation of this in his literary works. It is, indeed, sometimes supposed that readers in the eighteenth century hung over the pages of *Rasselas* and the *Rambler* with a breathless rapture; but this is far from true. Those books were of course more widely and enthusiastically read than they are to-day, but they were commonly recognized by Johnson's friends, and by Johnson himself, for that matter, as no sufficient explanation of his fame. Fanny Burney herself had difficulty in reading *Rasselas* because of its " dreadful " subject, a subject which Miss Hannah More found " as cheerful as the Dead Sea." Lady Mary Wortley Montagu was

bored by the *Rambler,* " who follows the *Spectator*
with the same pace that a pack-horse would a hunter."
Johnson himself found it, as modern readers do,
" too wordy." So that even in 1778 it was difficult
to give a satisfactory explanation of Johnson's acknowledged supremacy. The puzzle was already
stated. It was hoped that the publication of the
Lives of the Poets would establish his fame once for
all; but, splendid as was that achievement, it was not
sufficiently great to account for his reputation. Certain of the biographies were received with a storm of
merited protest; some were completely negligible;
others gave evidence of distorted critical standards;
and yet others betrayed evidences of haste and of in-
adequate preparation. Johnson himself realized that
the work was no satisfactory representation of the
powers that were in him. But even had it been so,
even had it satisfied the most eager demands of his
admirers, it would still be not an *explanation* of his
supreme position but an *illustration* of it. His fame
had been long since established, and was now hardly
susceptible of sudden change. Here was an author
whose fame already transcended that of all his works
combined, who filled those close to him with a desire
to do justice to his personality in written records of
it, a personality that stimulated hatred as well as love,
but left nobody indifferent. There is, it would therefore appear, no hope of falling back upon Johnson's
position in the literary world as an explanation of his
fame; and yet the conviction persists that he is really
a figure in English literature. Even Mr. Seccombe

has written a book called the *Age of Johnson*. It is
evident that Johnson represents more than Johnson
achieved; that he stimulated more than he wrote.

There is a principle in the history of modern literature which I think will help us. It has not, so far
as I am aware, been definitely formulated, though it
is unconsciously employed by all discerning critics.
Modern literary history, we are coming to see, consists of something more than the *belles lettres* which it
contains. With the rise of what I may call the personal record in literature—biographies, diaries, and
letters—there has entered literature a new interest
which tends quite as often to centre in the individual
who creates as in the book created. It is an interest
which is stimulated not so much by felicities of style,
or excitement of plot, or brilliant imagination, as by
an acquaintance with the secret places of some great
man's mind. It is the desire of knowing the whole of
a giant personality, its weakness and its vagaries, its
passion and its pride. It desires to ransack the very
holy of holies and find out its secret. It was this interest that Johnson himself felt in literature. "Sir,"
he would say, "the biographical part of literature is
what I love most." Now it is most important to
notice that such an interest as this may exist quite
independently of our appreciation of an author's
books. Johnson himself felt a profound interest in
men like Savage, whose poetry he held in low esteem.
And if such an interest be sufficiently diffused, it may
result that a man attains a position in literature not
by what he has himself contributed to it, but by a

kind of transcendental force which he exerts upon it
by virtue of what he was. The literature of the
nineteenth century is fertile in examples of what I
am trying to describe. Take the case of Byron. He
is unlike enough to Johnson, in all conscience; yet
there is the very problem in his case that we are considering in Johnson's. Upon what is based the enduring fame of the man? Who now reads Byron?
The dramas are forgotten, and the early Oriental
tales are grown a little shabby. Even *Don Juan* seems
too long. And the lyrics, fresh and fervid as they
yet are, nevertheless fall below the best productions
of Shelley, Keats, and Wordsworth. Yet there is
the star of the man's fame burning on; distance does
not dim its radiance nor reduce its magnitude. Byron
has lived; only Childe Harold is dead. He, like
Johnson, has survived not so much because of a purely
literary achievement as by virtue of a remarkable
temper of mind, an ardor, an attitude toward life, a
force and a fire. What is the secret of his influence?
His works alone will never explain it, and fortunately
or unfortunately, he had no Boswell. What was it
that fired the imagination of Goethe? Was it
Manfred that Goethe loved, or *Cain?* or was it that
bright, perverse spirit who created these, his lesser
selves? However we may try to escape the conclusion, are we not forced to assert at last that his reputation springs to-day, as it did a century ago, from his influence upon other men rather than from his books?
That fire did not spring from books alone which
kindled a new school of poets in Spain and in Italy.

The note which is heard to-day in the rending har-
monies of Tschaikowski, that is the genuine voice of
Byron, that and not the mocking cry which too often
echoes that voice in Byron's verse. The English poet
speaks to-day with greater authority in Russian music
than he ever spoke in English verse. His spirit is
still at work among us, producing greater works than
any that were actually done in his own name, and
that miracle will continue until another supreme
patron of the philosophy of revolt shall usurp his
dominion, and rule his disciples in his stead.

Now this same high potential which Bryon had,
was Johnson's in large measure. Whenever this
dynamic power makes its appearance, it operates in
remarkable and unusual ways. It may divert the
whole stream of literature into new channels, as did
Byron, or confine it in old ones, as did Johnson. It
may color the very language and style of authors,
causing other men's work to have the ring of a quotation. It makes small men large, breaks down fears
and prejudices in timorous minds, suddenly exalting
them to levels which they have never reached before,
and which indeed they are by nature unable to reach.
It impels them to accomplishments of which they
had deemed themselves incapable. Above all, it sets
in motion a whole current of feelings and ideas
that swells as it moves away from its source. Pre-
sumably the greatest authors have always this ability,
but there are other orders of genius who possess it
in apparent independence of the highest literary skill.
The main interest of these men is always in literature,

but they are sometimes incapable of producing it without a medium, for their work is rather with men than with books. Thus such men become a type. They bear, as Oscar Wilde said of himself, "a symbolic relation to their age," and those who fail to find in them an author may amuse themselves by the attempt to discover there an era. Of these men is Samuel Johnson, and this is the secret of his fame.

Let us now consider some of the ways in which Johnson infused his genius into his age. To begin with, he was generally recognized as an author whose influence transcended that usually exerted by authors. Here let me quote a contemporary eulogy of Johnson which puts into heroic couplets what I am trying to say:

By nature's gifts, ordained mankind to rule,
He, like a Titian, formed his brilliant school. . . .
Our boasted Goldsmith felt the sovereign sway;
From him derived the sweet yet nervous lay. . . .
With Johnson's fame melodious Burney glows,
While the grand strain in smoother cadence flows. . . .
Amid these names can Boswell be forgot,
Scarce by North Britons now esteemed a Scot?
Who to the Sage devoted from his youth,
Imbibed from him the sacred love of truth,
The keen research and exercise of mind,
And that best art, the art to know mankind.

Poor verses, we may grant, but rather good criticism. Consider, in particular, Johnson's influence upon

Goldsmith. Who can doubt that the style of Doctor
Minor, superior as it is to that of Doctor Major,
would yet have been a very different thing if Goldsmith had never read the *Rambler?* Both Boswell
and Dr. Warton noted the influence of Johnson upon
Goldsmith's conversation, particularly in his attempt
to employ difficult words, but they might have discovered even subtler evidences of it in his writings.
The particular power of Johnson that Goldsmith
longed for was the older man's ability to sum up
a whole department of things in one telling sentence.
It was a power that Goldsmith never attained, but
his attempts were numerous. Hear, for example,
the voice of Johnson speaking through these words
of Goldsmith at the opening of the latter's *Life of
Nash:* " History owes its excellence more to the
writer's manner than to the materials of which it
is composed," or this from the *Life of Voltaire,*
" That life which has been wholly employed in the
study is properly seen only in the author's writings;
there is no variety to entertain, nor adventure to interest us in the calm succession of such anecdotes."
It is only an echo, to be sure, but we know whence
issued the original sound.

   That the influence of Johnson's style was the most
potent brought to bear upon English style in the
second half of the 18th century cannot, I think,
be disputed. Boswell's discussion of it, and his accompanying list of examples of direct imitation are
too convincing to be neglected. There is something
of its fine dignity in the best of Burke and of Gibbon;

and it is probable that the serious student of style
still finds his best examples of the more elaborate
manner in the pages of Johnson.   The very enemies
of the man recognized the force of the authority
he exerted, so that Churchill, in his caricature of him
as Pomposo, dubs him the

> Vain idol of a scribbling crowd,
> Whose very name inspires an awe,
> Whose every word is sense and law.

Influence of a very different kind, which nevertheless reveals the kinetic force which I have been
describing, is shown by his relation with the art of
his time.   This is the more significant because Johnson was by nature unfitted to appreciate the delicate
distinctions of color and form.   It is doubtful if he
ever saw the outlines of paintings clearly.   And yet
he is certainly to be thanked for having inspired some
of the finest pictures in the history of English art.
That Reynolds should have painted Johnson once
is of course no sufficient ground for critical deduc-
tion of any kind; but that he should have returned
to the subject again and again, painting him at least
a dozen times, if we count copies—this is a fact
of which we are not likely to exaggerate the significance.   Most people know the famous portrait
in the National Gallery, the one which Reynolds
painted for Johnson's gay young friend Beauclerk,
and on the frame of which the owner wrote an inscription proclaiming that beneath this rude exterior
there dwelt a giant mind.   To me the most notice-

able thing about the portrait has always been that
in it, almost alone among his portraits, Reynolds
makes no attempt to conceal the crudeness of the
exterior that he is representing. Here surely is the
craglike quality of Johnson. If we had only this
one portrait of Reynolds, it would naturally be assumed that he had the virile realism of a Velasquez.
But I know of no other in which he attains the
utter clarity of the Spaniard, the power of naked
fact. What was the force that woke the gentle
Reynolds to this unaccustomed power? Was the
influence different in kind from that which worked
upon the style of Goldsmith and upon the mind of
Boswell? This conclusion is not so slightly based
as it may seem at first. It is certainly obvious that
a painter bestows prolonged and affectionate attention only upon that which has fascinated his intellect
and his sympathy. No artist of the abilities of a
Reynolds will consent to paint an unsympathetic subject a dozen times. But Reynolds loved the task because he loved the inspiration which he drew from
the mere presence of the man. And so he painted
him as he appeared after the completion of the
Dictionary, seated at his desk in an arm-chair in
complacent meditation on the completed work. He
painted him again for his step-daughter, Miss Lucy
Porter, and this time in a form more or less idealized,
in conventional Roman costume, without his wig. It
is Reynolds's most touching portrait of him, for
in it he has allowed the suffering and the sympathy
of Johnson which he had witnessed so often to pre-

dominate over the ruder strength of countenance.
Yet again he painted him as he appeared when reading a book, "tearing the heart out" of it in his
impatience to be at the core of the author's meaning.
He painted him as he must have appeared when a
young man, resting his chin upon his hand, and holding a copy of *Irene;* and as if this were not enough,
went farther, and painted a wholly imaginary and
wholly delightful portrait of him in his infancy, representing a Herculean babe, with head sunk in pre-
cocious contemplation of the insoluble problem of
human existence, a veritable Infant Samuel.   Such
is the nature of Johnson's impress upon the painter.

But the impress of which it is most necessary to
speak is that upon James Boswell, for this is the
very greatest instance of Johnson's dynamic energy.
It is strange that it should be necessary to point this
out; but critics will do all they can to explain away
the miracle which Johnson wrought in creating out
of Boswell a greater author than himself.   The wonder of the result has actually obscured appreciation
of the man who produced it.   Boswell himself realized it fully.   Here is an unpublished passage from
one of his own letters (March 3, 1772) to Johnson:

> I fairly own that after an absence from you
> for any length of time, I feel that I require
> a renewal of that spirit which your presence
> always gives me, and which makes me a better
> and a happier man than I had imagined I could
> be, before I was introduced to your acquaintance.

The greatness of Boswell's record, when all is said, is simply Samuel Johnson, who is not merely the subject, but in the last analysis the author too. We have heard overmuch of Boswell's hero-worship and of the service which he did that hero in preserving his memory; but it is time that we remind ourselves of what the hero did for the disciple. Genius begot genius. The greatest contribution of Samuel Johnson to English literature was James Boswell.

I have a suspicion that in saying this I am perhaps in danger of ending, as I began, with a commonplace. But in an age which has somewhat overindulged itself in the subtleties of criticism, it is sometimes well to remind ourselves of the simple old truths. We have heard too much of the inessential Johnson, of spilled pudding-sauce, irrelevant ejaculations of the Lord's Prayer, slipper-snatchings, and other stories interesting to schoolboys, but of doubtful authenticity and of small significance. It is time to dwell again upon Johnson's kindness, his courage, his respect for rank and achievement in an age whose general tendency was downwards, his Catholic faith in an era of timid skepticism and cheap tolerance, and above all, to reckon with his dynamic influence upon his friends.

LIST OF ILLUSTRATIONS

ABBREVIATIONS FOR BOOKS COMMONLY REFERRED TO
IN THE NOTES.

Life, Boswell's Life of Johnson, Hill's Edition, Oxford, 1887. Six volumes.

Letters, Letters of Dr. Samuel Johnson, Hill's edition, Oxford, 1892. Two volumes.

Miscellanies, Johnsonian Miscellanies, Hill's edition, Oxford, 1897. Two volumes.

Diary, The Diary and Letters of Mme. D'Arblay, edited by Austin Dobson, London, 1904. Six volumes.

Early Diary, The Early Diary of Frances Burney, 1768-1778, edited by Annie Raine Ellis, London, 1889. Two volumes.

Memoirs, Memoirs of Doctor Burney, by his daughter, Mme. D'Arblay, London, 1832. Three volumes.

Works, The Works of Samuel Johnson, London, 1787. Eleven volumes.

N. E. D., A New English Dictionary on Historical Principles, Oxford.

D. N. B., Dictionary of National Biography.

DR. JOHNSON AND FANNY BURNEY

EXTRACT FROM THE EARLY DIARY

28th March.[1]

MY DEAR DADDY,[2]

My dear father seemed well pleased at my returning to my time; and that is no small consolation and pleasure to me. So now, to our Thursday morning party.

Mrs. and Miss Thrale, Miss Owen, and Mr. Seward came long before *Lexiphanes*.[3] Mrs. Thrale is a very pretty woman still; she is extremely lively and chatty; has no supercilious or pedantic airs, and is really gay and agreeable. Her daughter[4] is about

---

[1] A letter of Miss Burney's to Mr. Samuel Crisp, from the *Early Diary*, 2.153 ff. The events described took place at Dr. Burney's residence.

[2] The letter is addressed to Mr. Samuel Crisp, Miss Burney's closest friend and mentor in her earlier days. He was many years older than her father, and she affectionately termed him "Daddy." At this time he was living in retirement at a spot called Chessington, a few miles south of the Thames in Surrey, now within the Metropolitan Police District.

[3] Lexiphanes, a title applied to Johnson in a pamphlet of the same name by "horrible Campbell," and designed to ridicule Johnson's style and works. It appeared in 1767.

[4] Hester Maria, Mrs. Thrale's eldest child, born 1764. Johnson commonly called her "Queeny," "whose name being Esther, she might be assimilated to a Queen." (*Life*, 3.422 n.) This estimate of Miss Thrale is later revised; see p. 25. Susan Burney had originally the same impression, p. 242.

twelve years old, (stiff and proud), I believe, (or
else shy and reserved: I don't yet know which).
Miss Owen, who is a relation, is good-humoured
and *sensible enough;* she is a sort of butt, and, as
such, a general favourite; for those sort of characters
are prodigiously useful in drawing out the wit and
pleasantry of others. Mr. Seward [1] is a very polite,
agreeable young man.

My sister Burney [2] was invited to meet and play to
them. The conversation was supported with a good
deal of vivacity (N.B. my father being at home)
for about half an hour, and then Hetty and *Susette* [2]
for the first time *in public,* played a duet; and in the
midst of this performance Dr. Johnson was announced. He is, indeed, very ill-favoured; is tall and
stout; but stoops terribly; he is almost bent double.
His mouth is almost [continually opening and shut-
ting], [3] as if he was chewing. He has a strange
method of frequently twirling his fingers, and twist-
ing his hands. His body is in continual agitation,
see-sawing up and down; his feet are never a moment
quiet; and, in short, his whole person is in *perpetual
motion.* His dress, too, considering the times, and
that he had meant to put on his *best becomes,* being

---

[1] " Seward, William, was author of *Anecdotes of Distinguished
Persons,* in five volumes, and *Biographiana,* a sequel to the same
in two volumes." (BARRETT.)   Boswell, to whom he furnished
" several communications concerning Johnson," praises him for his
sociability.

[2] Her sisters, Esther ("my sister Burney"), and Susan. It was
only " Susette " who was playing " for the first time in public."

[3] There is a break in the MS. at this point. The words in
brackets are supplied from the parallel (and debased) account in
the *Memoirs,* 2. 91.

engaged to dine in a large company, was as much
out of the common road as his figure; he had a large
wig, snuff-colour coat, and gold buttons, but no
ruffles to his [shirt], doughty fists,[1] and black worsted
stockings.   He is shockingly near-sighted, and did
not, till she held out her hand to him, even know
Mrs. Thrale.[2]   He *poked his nose* over the keys of
the harpsichord, till the duet was finished, and then
my father introduced Hetty to him as an old acquaintance, and he cordially kissed her!   When she
was a little girl, he had made her a present of *The
Idler*.

His attention, however, was not to be diverted five
minutes from the books, as we were in the library;
he pored over them, shelf by shelf, almost touching
the backs of them with his eye-lashes, as he read
their titles.   At last, having fixed upon one, he began, without further ceremony, to read to himself,
all the time standing at a distance from the company.
We were all very much provoked, as we perfectly
languished to hear him talk; but it seems he is the
most silent creature, when not particularly drawn
out,[3] in the world.

My sister then played another duet with my father;
but Dr. Johnson was so deep in the *Encyclopédie*

---

[1] Another passage in which Mme. d'Arblay has tampered with
what Miss Burney wrote.   Mrs. Ellis conjectures that the passage
originally read "dirty fists."

[2] Cf. Appendix, p. 241.

[3] "Mr. Thomas Tyers said he was like the ghosts, who never
speak till they are spoken to; and he [Johnson] liked the expression so well that he often repeated it." (Piozzi's 'Anecdotes,'
Miscellanies, I. 290.)

that, as he is very deaf, I question if he even knew what was going forward.[1] When this was over, Mrs. Thrale, in a laughing manner, said, " Pray, Dr. Burney, can you tell me what that song was and whose, which Savoi sung last night at Bach's [2] Concert, and which you did not hear? " My father confessed himself by no means so good a diviner, not having had time to consult the stars, though in the house of Sir Isaac Newton.[3] However, wishing to draw Dr. Johnson into some conversation, he told him the question. The Doctor, seeing his drift, good-naturedly put away his book, and said very drolly, " And pray, Sir, *who is Bach?* is he a piper? " Many exclamations of surprise, you will believe, followed this question. " Why you have read his name often in the papers," said Mrs. Thrale; and then she gave him some account of his Concert, and the number of fine performances she had heard at it.

" Pray," said he, gravely, " Madam, what is the expense? "

" Oh! " answered she, " much trouble and solicitation, to get a Subscriber's Ticket;—or else, half a Guinea."

---

[1] Probably an extreme statement. Other authentic accounts of Johnson do not lead us to suppose that he was so deaf as this. Dr. Burney himself records (*Life,* 2.409), " he was observed to listen very attentively while Miss Thrale played on the harpsichord, and with eagerness he called to her, ' Why don't you dash away like Burney? ' " (Cf. Hawkins's *Life,* p. 319.)

[2] Johann Christian Bach, 1735-1782, son of the great composer. He lived in London from 1759 until his death.

[3] Dr. Burney's house, No. 1 (now 35), St. Martin's Street, was at one time the residence of Sir Isaac Newton.

"Trouble and solicitation," said he, "I will have nothing to do with; but I would be willing to give eighteen pence." [1]

Ha! ha!

Chocolate being then brought, we adjourned to the drawing-room. And here, Dr. Johnson being taken from the books, entered freely and most cleverly into conversation; though it is remarkable he never speaks at all, but when spoken to; nor does he ever *start*,[2] though he so admirably *supports,* any subject.

The whole party was engaged to dine at Mrs.

---

[1] Cf. p. 245. Music interested Johnson chiefly because of the difficulty of its performance. He praised the *virtuoso,* but owned to Boswell that he was "very insensible of the power of music." (*Life,* 3. 197.) Mme. D'Arblay writes in the *Memoirs,* "It was not till after he had become intimately acquainted with Dr. Burney and his various merits, that he ceased to join in a jargon so unworthy of his liberal judgment, as that of excluding musicians and their art from celebrity. The first symptom that he showed of a tendency to conversion upon this subject, was upon hearing the following paragraph read, accidentally, aloud by Mrs. Thrale, from the preface to the *History of Music,* while yet in manuscript. 'The love of lengthened tones and modulated sounds, seems a passion implanted in human nature throughout the globe; as we hear of no people, however wild and savage in other particulars, who have not music of some kind or other, with which they seem greatly delighted.' 'Sir!' cried Dr. Johnson, after a little pause, 'this assertion I believe may be right.' And then, see-sawing a minute or two in his chair, added: 'All animated nature loves music— except myself!' Some time later, when Dr. Burney perceived that he was generally gaining ground in the house, he said to Mrs. Thrale, who had been civilly listening to some favourite air that he had been playing: 'I have yet hopes, Madam, with the assistance of my pupil, to see yours become a musical family. Nay, I even hope, Sir!' turning to Dr. Johnson, 'I shall some time or other make you also, sensible to the power of my art.' 'Sir,' answered the Doctor, smiling, 'I shall be very glad to have a new sense put into me!'"

[2] See p. 3, and note 3.

Montagu's.[1] Dr. Johnson said he had received the most flattering note he had ever read, or that any body else had ever read, by way of invitation. "Well! so have I too," cried Mrs. Thrale; "so if a note from Mrs. Montagu is to be boasted of, I beg mine may not be forgot."

"*Your* note," cried Dr. Johnson, "can bear no comparison with *mine;* I am *at the head of the Philosophers,* she says."

"And I," cried Mrs. Thrale, "*have all the Muses in my train!*"

"A fair battle," said my father. "Come, compliment for compliment, and see who will hold out longest."

"Oh! I am afraid for Mrs. Thrale," cried Mr. Seward; "for I know Mrs. Montague exerts all her forces, when she attacks Dr. Johnson."

"Oh, yes!" said Mrs. Thrale, "she has often, I know, flattered *him,* till he has been ready to faint."

"Well, ladies," said my father, "you must get him between you to-day, and see which can lay on the paint thickest, Mrs. Thrale or Mrs. Montagu."

"I had rather," cried the Doctor, drily, "go to Bach's Concert!"

After this, they talked of Mr. Garrick and his late

---

[1] For descriptions of the personality, manner, and learning of Mrs. Montagu, the famous Bluestocking, see below, pp. 68 ff. and especially pp. 74-75, where a conversation between her and Johnson is reported. Early in the decade of the 80's a "coolness" sprang up between them, and Johnson humorously complains of being "dropped" by the lady (*Life,* 4. 73); their reconciliation is described below, p. 180. No account of the *femmes savantes* of the eighteenth century is superior to Miss Burney's; but compare Hannah More's *Bas Bleu,* and the letters of Horace Walpole, *passim.*

exhibition before the King, to whom and to the
Queen and Royal Family he read *Lethe* [1] *in character,
c'est à dire,* in different voices, and theatrically. Mr.
Seward gave us an account of a Fable, which Mr.
Garrick had written, by way of prologue or introduction, upon the occasion. In this he says, that a
blackbird, grown old and feeble, droops his wings,
etc. etc., and gives up singing; but being called upon
by the eagle, his voice recovers its powers, his spirits
revive, he sets age at defiance, and sings better than
ever. The application is obvious.

"There is not," said Dr. Johnson, "much of the
spirit of *fabulosity* in this Fable; for the *call* of an
eagle never yet had much tendency to restore the
voice of a *blackbird!* 'Tis true that the fabulists
frequently make the *wolves* converse with the *lambs;*
but, when the conversation is over, the *lambs* are sure
to be eaten! And so the *eagle* may entertain the
blackbird; but the entertainment always ends in a
feast for the *eagle.*"

"They say," cried Mrs. Thrale, "that Garrick
was extremely hurt at the coolness of the King's applause, and did not find his reception such as he
expected."

---

[1] An old farce of Garrick's, produced as early as 1740, in which
he had commonly acted the part of Lord Chalkstone. "The tiresome and unnatural profundity of respectful solemnity" observed
at court during the recitation of farces is amusingly illustrated in
a later volume of the *Diary* (4. 359 ff.), when it was Miss Burney's
fate to read Colman's *Polly Honeycomb* to the queen. She adds,
"Easily can I now conceive the disappointment and mortification
of poor Mr. Garrick when he read *Lethe* to a royal audience."
    Garrick had retired from the stage in January of the previous
year (1776).

"He has been so long accustomed," said Mr. Seward, "to the thundering approbation of the Theatre, that a mere 'Very well,' must necessarily and naturally disappoint him."

"Sir," said Dr. Johnson, "he should not, in a Royal apartment, expect the hallowing and clamour of the One Shilling Gallery. The King, I doubt not, gave him as much applause as was rationally his due; and, indeed, great and uncommon as is the merit of Mr. Garrick, no man will be bold enough to assert he has not had his just proportion both of fame and of profit. He has long reigned the unequalled favourite of the public; and therefore nobody will mourn his hard fate, if the King and the Royal Family were not transported into rapture, upon hearing him read *Lethe*. Yet Mr. Garrick will complain to his friends, and his friends will lament the King's want of feeling and taste;—and then Mr. Garrick will kindly *excuse* the King. He will say that His Majesty might be thinking of something else; that the affairs of America might occur to him; or some subject of more importance than *Lethe;* but, though he will say this himself, he will not forgive his friends, if they do not contradict him!"

But now that I have written this satire, it is but just both to Mr. Garrick and to Dr. Johnson, to tell you what he said of him afterwards, when he discriminated his character with equal candour and humour.[1]

---

[1] "Sir Joshua Reynolds observed, with great truth, that Johnson considered Garrick to be as it were his property. He would allow no man either to blame or to praise Garrick in his presence, without contradicting him." (*Life*, 3. 312.) See below, pp. 20-21.

"Garrick," said he, "is accused of vanity; but few men would have borne such unremitting prosperity with greater, if with equal moderation. He is accused, too, of avarice; but, were he not, he would be accused of just the contrary; for he now lives rather as *a prince* than an actor; but the frugality[1] he practised, when he first appeared in the world, and which, even then was perhaps beyond his necessity, has marked his character ever since; and now, though his table, the equipage, and manner of living, are all the most expensive, and equal to those of a nobleman, yet the original stain still blots his name! Though, had he not fixed upon himself the charge of avarice, he would long since have been reproached with luxury and with living beyond his station in magnificence and splendour."

Another time he said of him, "Garrick never enters a room, but he regards himself as the object of general attention, from whom the entertainment of the company is expected; and true it is, that he seldom disappoints them; for he has infinite humour, a very just proportion of wit, and more convivial pleasantry, than almost any other man. But then *off*, as well as *on* the Stage,[2] he is always an Actor; for he thinks it so incumbent upon him to be sportive, that his gaiety becomes mechanical from being habitual, and he can exert his spirits at all times alike, without consulting his real disposition to hilarity."

---

[1] For Garrick's frugality, cf. *Life*, 1. 392; 3. 264.
[2] "On the stage he was natural, simple, affecting;
    'Twas only that, when he was off, he was acting."
                    Goldsmith, *Retaliation* (1774).

EXTRACTS FROM THE DIARY AND LETTERS

July 20. . . . I have also had a letter from
Susanne. She informs me that my father, when he
took the books back to Streatham,[1] actually acquainted
Mrs. Thrale with my secret.[2] He took an opportunity, when they were alone together, of saying that
upon her recommendation, he had himself, as well as
my mother, been reading *Evelina.*

" Well ! " cried she, " and is it not a very pretty
book ? and a very clever book ? and a very comical
book ? "

" Why," answered he, " 'tis well enough ; but I
have something to tell you about it."

" Well ? what ? " cried she ; " has Mrs. Cholmondeley [3] found out the author ? "

" No," returned he, " not that I know of ; but I
believe I have, though but very lately."

" Well, pray let's hear ! " cried she eagerly, " I
want to know him of all things."

How my father must laugh at the *him!* He then,
however, undeceived her in regard to that particular, by telling her it was *" our Fanny!"* for she
knows all about all our family, as my father talks

---

[1] Streatham is some six miles south of London. The house, a
beautiful Georgian structure, was demolished in 1863. Johnson,
who had met the Thrales in 1765, was living there as early as July,
1766. (*Letters,* 1.43.) See below, p. 241.

[2] That she was the author of *Evelina.* For Susan Burney's account of Mrs. Thrale's interest in the anonymous author, see
Appendix, pp. 239-40.

[3] Mrs. Cholmondeley, the famous wit and *femme savante,* whose
name appears often in the pages of the *Diary.* She was " the first
person who publicly praised and commended *Evelina* among the
wits." (Below, p. 239.)

to her of his domestic concerns without any
reserve.

A hundred handsome things, of course, followed;
and she afterwards read some of the comic parts to
Dr. Johnson, Mr. Thrale, and whoever came near
her. How I should have quivered had I been there!
but they tell me that Dr. Johnson laughed as heartily
as my father himself did.

August 3.—I have an immensity to write. Susan
has copied me a letter which Mrs. Thrale has written
to my father, upon the occasion of returning my
mother two novels by Madame Riccoboni. It is so
honourable to me, and so sweet in her, that I must
copy it for my faithful journal.

" Wednesday, 22 (July), 1778,
" Streatham.

" Dear Sir—I forgot to give you the novels home
in your carriage which I now send by Mr. Abingdon's.
Evelina certainly excels *them* far enough, both in
probability of story, elegance of sentiment, and general power over the mind, whether exerted in humour
or pathos. Add to this, that Riccoboni is a veteran
author, and all she ever can be; but I cannot tell what
might not be expected from *Evelina,* was she to try
her genius at Comedy. So far had I written of my
letter, when Mr. Johnson returned home, full of the
praises of the *Book* I had lent him, and protesting
there were passages in it which might do *honour* to
Richardson. We talk of it for ever, and he feels

ardent after the *dénouement;* he could not get rid of
the Rogue, he said! I lent him the second volume,
and he is now busy with the other two [sic]. You
must be more a philosopher, and less a father, than
I wish you, not to be pleased with this letter;—and
the giving such pleasure yields to nothing but receiving it. Long my Dear Sir, may you live to enjoy the
just praises of your children, and long may they live
to deserve and delight such a parent! These are
things that you would say in verse; but Poetry im-
plies Fiction, and all this is naked truth.

" Give my letter to my little friend, and a warm
invitation to come and eat fruit, while the season
lasts. My Compliments to Mrs. Burney, and kindest wishes to all your flock, etc."

How sweet, how amiable in this charming woman
is her desire of making my dear father satisfied with
his scribbler's attempt! I do, indeed, feel the most
grateful love for her.

But Dr. Johnson's approbation!—it almost crazed
me with agreeable surprise—it gave me such a flight
of spirits, that I danced a jig to Mr. Crisp, without
any preparation, music, or explanation—to his no
small amazement and diversion. I left him, however,
to make his own comments upon my friskiness, without affording him the smallest assistance.

Susan also writes me word, that when my father
went last to Streatham,[1] Dr. Johnson was not there,
but Mrs. Thrale told him, that when he gave her the

[1] Cf. below, p. 239.

first volume of *Evelina,* which she had lent him, he
said, " Why, madam, why, what a charming book
you lent me! " and eagerly inquired for the rest.
He was particularly pleased with the Snow-hill scenes,
and said that Mr. Smith's vulgar gentility was admirably portrayed; and when Sir Clement joins them,[1]
he said there was a shade of character prodigiously
well marked. Well may it be said, that the greatest
minds are ever the most candid to the inferior
set! I think I should love Dr. Johnson for such
lenity to a poor mere worm in literature, even
if I were not myself the identical grub he has
obliged.

Susan has sent me a little note which has really
been less pleasant to me, because it has alarmed me
for my future concealment. It is from Mrs. Williams,[2] an exceedingly pretty poetess, who has the
misfortune to be blind, but who has, to make some
amends, the honour of residing in the house of Dr.
Johnson; for though he lives almost wholly at
Streatham, he always keeps his apartments in town,
and this lady acts as mistress of his house.

" July 25,
" Mrs. Williams sends compliments to Dr. Burney,
and begs he will intercede with Miss Burney to
do her the favour to lend her the reading of
Evelina."

[1] See *Evelina,* letter 46.
[2] Miss Anna Williams, Johnson's well-known housekeeper. Her
verses were published in 1766, with the title, *Miscellanies.* Some
of the poems were contributed by the lady's friends, and the revising
hand of Johnson is seen throughout. (*Life,* 2. 25-26.)

I was quite confounded at this request, which proves that Mrs. Thrale has told Dr. Johnson of my secret, and that he has told Mrs. Williams, and that she has told the person whoever it be, whom she got to write the note.

I instantly scrawled a hasty letter to town to entreat my father would be so good as to write to her, to acquaint her with my earnest and unaffected desire to remain unknown.

And yet, though I am frightened at this affair, I am by no means insensible to the honour which I receive from the certainty that Dr. Johnson must have spoken very well of the book, to have induced Mrs. Williams to send to our house for it.   She has known my father indeed for some years, but not with any intimacy; and I never saw her, though the perusal of her poems has often made me wish to be acquainted with her.

I now come to last Saturday evening, when my beloved father came to Chessington,[1] in full health, charming spirits, and all kindness, openness, and entertainment.

I inquired what he had done about Mrs. Williams. He told me he went to her himself at my desire, for if he had written she could not herself have read the note.   She apologised very much for the liberty she had taken, and spoke highly of the book, though she had only heard the first volume, as she was dependent upon a lady's good nature and time for hearing any part of it, but she went so far as to say that " his

[1] See above, p. 1, note 2, and below, p. 218, note

daughter was certainly the first writer, in that way, now living."

In his way hither, he had stopped at Streatham, and he settled with Mrs. Thrale that he would call on her again in his way to town, and carry me with him! and Mrs. Thrale said, " We all long to know her."

I have been in a kind of twitter ever since, for there seems something very formidable in the idea of appearing as an authoress! I ever dreaded it, as it is a title which must raise more expectations than I have any chance of answering. Yet I am highly flattered by her invitation, and highly delighted in the prospect of being introduced to the Streatham society.

London, August.—I have now to write an account of the most consequential day I have spent since my birth; namely, my Streatham visit.

Our journey to Streatham was the least pleasant part of the day, for the roads were dreadfully dusty, and I was really in the fidgets from thinking what my reception might be, and from fearing they would expect a less awkward and backward kind of person than I was sure they would find.

Mr. Thrale's house is white, and very pleasantly situated, in a fine paddock. Mrs. Thrale was strolling about, and came to us as we got out of the chaise.

" Ah," cried she, " I hear Dr. Burney's voice! And you have brought your daughter?—well, now you are good! "

She then received me, taking both my hands, and

with mixed politeness and cordiality welcoming me to Streatham. She led me into the house, and addressed herself almost wholly for a few minutes to my father, as if to give me an assurance she did not mean to regard me as a show, or to distress or frighten me by drawing me out. Afterwards she took me upstairs, and showed me the house, and said she had very much wished to see me at Streatham, and should always think herself much obliged to Dr. Burney for his goodness in bringing me, which she looked upon as a very great favour.

But though we were some time together, and though she was so very civil, she did not *hint* at my book, and I love her very much more than ever for her delicacy in avoiding a subject which she could not but see would have greatly embarrassed me.

When we returned to the music-room we found Miss Thrale was with my father. Miss Thrale is a very fine girl, about fourteen years of age, but cold and reserved, though full of knowledge and intelligence.[1]

Soon after, Mrs. Thrale took me to the library; she talked a little while upon common topics, and then, at last, she mentioned *Evelina*.

" Yesterday at supper," said she, " we talked it all over, and discussed all your characters; but Dr. Johnson's favourite is Mr. Smith. He declares the fine gentleman *manqué* was never better drawn; and he

[1] See above, p. 1. Passages in the *Early Diary* seem to have been employed by Miss Burney (or by the first editor of her *Diary*, Mrs. Barrett) in the later and more famous Journal. The careful reader will notice many repetitions from this earlier volume both in the *Diary* and the *Memoirs*.

Streatham, 1787

acted him [1] all the evening, saying he was ' all for the
ladies ! ' He repeated whole scenes by heart.[2] I
declare I was astonished at him. Oh you can't
imagine how much he is pleased with the book; he
' could not get rid of the rogue,' [3] he told me. ' But
was it not droll,' he said, ' that I should recommend
it to Dr. Burney? and tease him, so innocently, to
read it?' "

I now prevailed upon Mrs. Thrale to let me amuse
myself, and she went to dress. I then prowled about
to choose some book, and I saw, upon the reading-
table, *Evelina*.—I had just fixed upon the new translation of Cicero's *Lælius* when the library door was
opened, and Mr. Seward entered. I instantly put
away my book, because I dreaded being thought
studious and affected. He offered his service to find
anything for me, and then, in the same breath, ran on
to speak of the book with which I had myself " favoured the world ! "

The exact words he began with I cannot recollect, for I was actually confounded by the attack;
and his abrupt manner of letting me know he was
au fait equally astonished and provoked me. How
different from the delicacy of Mr. and Mrs. Thrale !

When we were summoned to dinner, Mrs. Thrale
made my father and me sit on each side of her. I

---

[1] Another instance of his " acting " is given later, p. 30. He
once indulged in an imitation of a kangaroo. (*Letters*, 1. 241,
note.) He, however, disliked too much of it in others. (Hawkins's
Life, p. 386.) Cf. p. 208.

[2] This remark is to be taken literally. Johnson's verbal memory
was truly extraordinary. (See *Life*, 1. 39 and 1. 148.)

[3] Cf. above, p. 13.

said that I hoped I did not take Dr. Johnson's place;
for he had not yet appeared.

"No," answered Mrs. Thrale, "he will sit by you,
which I am sure will give him great pleasure."

Soon after we were seated, this great man entered.
I have so true a veneration for him, that the very
sight of him inspires me with delight and reverence,
notwithstanding the cruel infirmities to which he is
subject; for he has almost perpetual convulsive move-
ments, either of his hands, lips, feet, or knees, and
sometimes of all together.

Mrs. Thrale introduced me to him, and he took
his place. We had a noble dinner, and a most elegant dessert. Dr. Johnson, in the middle of dinner,
asked Mrs. Thrale what was in some little pies that
were near him.

"Mutton," answered she, "so I don't ask you to
eat any, because I know you despise it."

"No, madam, no," cried he; "I despise nothing
that is good of its sort; I am too proud now to eat of
it. Sitting by Miss Burney makes me very proud to-
day!"

"Miss Burney," said Mrs. Thrale, laughing, "you
must take great care of your heart if Dr. Johnson
attacks it; for I assure you he is not often success-
less."

"What's that you say, madam?" cried he; "are
you making mischief between the young lady and me
already?"

A little while after he drank Miss Thrale's health
and mine and then added:

" 'Tis a terrible thing that we cannot wish young ladies well, without wishing them to become old women! "

" But some people," said Mr. Seward, " are old and young at the same time, for they wear so well that they never look old."

" No, sir, no," cried the Doctor, laughing; " that never yet was; you might as well say that they are at the same time tall and short.   I remember an epitaph to that purpose, which is in ———."

(I have quite forgot what,—and also the name it was made upon, but the rest I recollect exactly:)

"———lies buried here;
So early wise, so lasting fair,
That none, unless her years you told,
Thought her a child, or thought her old."

Mrs. Thrale then repeated some lines in French, and Dr. Johnson some more in Latin.   An epilogue of Mr. Garrick's to *Bonduca* [1] was then mentioned, and everybody agreed it was the worst he has ever made.

" And yet," said Mr. Seward, " it has been very much admired; but it is in praise of English valour, and so I suppose the subject made it popular."

" I don't know, sir," said Dr. Johnson, " anything about the subject, for I could not read on till I came to it; I got through half a dozen lines, but I could

---

[1] Garrick's Prologue (not Epilogue) to Fletcher's *Bonduca* is printed in the *Gentleman's Magazine* for September, 1778; the same number contains a laudatory notice of *Evelina*.

observe no other subject than eternal dulness. I don't know what is the matter with David; I am afraid he is grown superannuated, for his prologues and epilogues used to be incomparable." [1]

" Nothing is so fatiguing," said Mrs. Thrale, " as the life of a wit: he and Wilkes are the two oldest men of their ages I know; for they have both worn themselves out, by being eternally on the rack to give entertainment to others."

" David, madam," said the Doctor, " looks much older than he is; for his face has had double the business of any other man's; it is never at rest; when he speaks one minute, he has quite a different countenance to what he assumes the next; I don't believe he ever kept the same look for half an hour together, in the whole course of his life; and such an eternal, restless, fatiguing play of the muscles, must certainly wear out a man's face before its real time."

" Oh yes," cried Mrs. Thrale, " we must certainly make some allowance for such wear and tear of a man's face." [2]

The next name that was started, was that of Sir John Hawkins:[3] and Mrs. Thrale said, " Why now, Dr. Johnson, he is another of those whom you suffer nobody to abuse but yourself; Garrick is one, too;

---

[1] "David Garrick has written more good prologues than Dryden has done. It is wonderful that he has been able to write such a variety of them." (*Life*, 2. 325.)

[2] Mrs. Thrale is probably quoting a well-known remark of Johnson's. "Dr. Burney having remarked that Mr. Garrick was beginning to look old, he said, ‘Why, Sir, you are not to wonder at that; no man's face has had more wear and tear.'" (*Life*, 2. 410.)

[3] Johnson's literary executor and biographer.

for if any other person speaks against him, you brow-
beat him in a minute!"[1]

"Why, madam," answered he, "they don't know
when to abuse him, and when to praise him; I will
allow no man to speak ill of David that he does not
deserve; and as to Sir John, why really I believe him
to be an honest man at the bottom: but to be sure he
is penurious, and he is mean, and it must be owned he
has a degree of brutality, and a tendency to savage-
ness, that cannot easily be defended."

We all laughed, as he meant we should, at this
curious manner of speaking in his favour, and he then
related an anecdote that he said he knew to be true
in regard to his meanness.   He said that Sir John
and he once belonged to the same club,[2] but that as
he eat no supper after the first night of his admission,
he desired to be excused paying his share.

"And was he excused?"

"Oh yes; for no man is angry at another for being
inferior to himself; we all scorned him, and admitted
his plea.   For my part I was such a fool as to pay
my share for wine, though I never tasted any.[3]   But
Sir John was a most *unclubable*[4] man!"

How delighted was I to hear this master of lan-

---

[1] A common observation (cf. above, p. 8, note 1), possibly first
made by Garrick himself (*Life*, 3. 70) ; Boswell remarked, "'You
attack Garrick yourself, but will suffer nobody else to do it.' Johnson (smiling), 'Why, Sir, that is true'" (*ib.* 1. 393, note).
[2] The famous Literary Club.   For the gossip connected with
Hawkins's resignation, see *Life,* 1. 460.
[3] He practically refrained from drinking during the last twenty
years of his life.
[4] A word coined by Johnson, not found in his Dictionary.   Boswell
is called clubable. (*Life,* 1. 254, note.)

guages so unaffectedly and socially and good-naturedly make words, for the promotion of sport and good-humour.

"And this," continued he, "reminds me of a gentleman and lady with whom I travelled once; I suppose I must call them gentleman and lady, according to form, because they travelled in their own coach and four horses. But at the first inn where we stopped, the lady called for—a pint of ale! and when it came, quarrelled with the waiter for not giving full measure.—Now, Madame Duval [1] could not have done a grosser thing!"

Oh, how everybody laughed! and to be sure I did not glow at all, nor munch fast, nor look on my plate, nor lose any part of my usual composure! But how grateful do I feel to this dear Dr. Johnson, for never naming me and the book as belonging one to the other, and yet making an allusion that showed his thoughts led to it, and, at the same time, that seemed to justify the character as being natural! But, indeed, the delicacy I met with from him, and from all the Thrales, was yet more flattering to me than the praise with which I have heard they have honoured my book.

After dinner, when Mrs. Thrale and I left the gentlemen, we had a conversation that to me could not but be delightful, as she was all good-humour, spirits, sense and *agreeability*. Surely, I may make words, when at a loss, if Dr. Johnson does.[2]

---

[1] A prominent character in *Evelina*.
[2] The word had, however, been used by Chaucer. (*N. E. D.*)

However I shall not attempt to write any more particulars of this day—than which I have never known a happier, because the chief subject that was started and kept up, was an invitation for me to Streatham, and a desire that I might accompany my father thither next week, and stay with them some time.

We left Streatham at about eight o'clock, and Mr. Seward, who handed me into the chaise, added his interest to the rest, that my father would not fail to bring me again next week to stay with them some time. In short I was loaded with civilities from them all. And my ride home was equally happy with the rest of the day, for my kind and most beloved father was so happy in *my* happiness, and congratulated me so sweetly that he could, like myself, think on no other subject: and he told me that, after passing through such a house as that, I could have nothing to fear—meaning for my book, my honoured book.

Yet my honours stopped not here; for Hetty, who with her *sposo* [1] was here to receive us, told me she had lately met Mrs. Reynolds,[2] sister of Sir Joshua; and that she talked very much and very highly of a new novel called *Evelina;* though without a shadow of suspicion as to the scribbler; and not contented with her own praise, she said that Sir Joshua, who began it one day when he was too much engaged to go on with it, was so much caught, that

---

[1] Hetty's husband was her cousin, Charles Rousseau Burney.

[2] Miss Frances Reynolds, herself an artist, though of no great ability.

he could think of nothing else, and was quite absent all the day, not knowing a word that was said to him: and, when he took it up again, found himself so much interested in it, that he sat up all night to finish it!

Sir Joshua, it seems, vows he would give fifty pounds to know the author! I have also heard, by the means of Charles,[1] that other persons have declared they *will* find him out!

This intelligence determined me upon going myself to Mr. Lowndes,[2] and discovering what sort of answers he made to such curious inquirers as I found were likely to address him. But as I did not dare trust myself to speak, for I felt that I should not be able to act my part well, I asked my mother to accompany me.

Streatham, Sunday, Aug. 23.—I know not how to express the fulness of my contentment at this sweet place. All my best expectations are exceeded, and you know they were not very moderate. If, when my dear father comes, Susan and Mr. Crisp were to come too, I believe it would require at least a day's pondering to enable me to form another wish.

Our journey was charming. The kind Mrs. Thrale would give courage to the most timid. She did not ask me questions, or catechise me upon what I knew, or use any means to draw me out, but made it her

[1] Her cousin and brother-in-law, mentioned p. 23, note 1.
[2] Her publisher.

business to draw herself out—that is, to start subjects, to support them herself, and to take all the weight of the conversation, as if it behoved her to find me entertainment. But I am so much in love with her, that I shall be obliged to run away from the subject, or shall write of nothing else.

When we arrived here, Mrs. Thrale showed me my room, which is an exceedingly pleasant one, and then conducted me to the library, there to divert myself while she dressed.

Miss Thrale soon joined me: and I begin to like her. Mr. Thrale was neither well nor in spirits all day. Indeed, he seems not to be a happy man, though he has every means of happiness in his power. But I think I have rarely seen a very rich man with a light heart and light spirits.

Dr. Johnson was in the utmost good humour.

There was no other company at the house all day.

After dinner, I had a delightful stroll with Mrs. Thrale, and she gave me a list of all her "good neighbours" in the town of Streatham, and said she was determined to take me to see Mr. T——, the clergyman, who was a character I could not but be diverted with, for he had so furious and so absurd a rage for building, that in his garden he had as many temples, and summer houses, and statues as in the gardens of Stow, though he had so little room for them that they all seemed tumbling one upon another.

In short, she was all unaffected drollery and sweet good humour.

At tea we all met again, and Dr. Johnson was gaily sociable. He gave a very droll account of the children of Mr. Langton,[1]

"Who," he said, "might be very good children if they were let alone; but the father is never easy when he is not making them do something which they cannot do; they must repeat a fable, or a speech, or the Hebrew alphabet; and they might as well count twenty, for what they know of the matter: however, the father says half, for he prompts every other word. But he could not have chosen a man who would have been less entertained by such means."

"I believe not!" cried Mrs. Thrale; "nothing is more ridiculous than parents cramming their children's nonsense down other people's throats. I keep mine as much out of the way as I can."

"Yours, madam," answered he, "are in nobody's way; no children can be better managed or less troublesome; but your fault is a too great perverseness in not allowing anybody to give them anything. Why should they not have a cherry or a gooseberry as well as bigger children?"

"Because they are sure to return such gifts by wiping their hands upon the giver's gown or coat, and nothing makes children more offensive. People only make the offer to please the parents, and they wish the poor children at Jericho when they accept it."

"But, madam, it is a great deal more offensive to refuse them. Let those who make the offer look to

---

[1] "He has his children too much about him." (*Life,* 3.128.) Cf. below, p. 172.

their own gowns and coats, for when you interfere, they only wish *you* at Jericho."

" It is difficult," said Mrs. Thrale, " to please everybody."

Indeed, the freedom with which Dr. Johnson condemns whatever he disapproves, is astonishing; and the strength of words he uses would, to most people, be intolerable; but, Mrs. Thrale seems to have a sweetness of disposition that equals all her other excellences, and far from making a point of vindicating herself, she generally receives his admonitions with the most respectful silence.

But I fear to say all I think at present of Mrs. Thrale, lest some flaws should appear by and by, that may make me think differently. And yet, why should I not indulge the *now*, as well as the *then*, since it will be with so much more pleasure? In short, I do think her delightful; she has talents to create admiration, good humour to excite love, understanding to give entertainment, and a heart which, like my dear father's, seems already fitted for another world. My own knowledge of her, indeed, is very little for such a character; but all I have heard, and all I see, so well agree, that I won't prepare myself for a future disappointment.

But to return. Mrs. Thrale then asked whether Mr. Langton took any better care of his affairs than formerly? [1]

---

[1] " He [Langton] has the crime of prodigality and the wretchedness of parsimony." (*Life,* 3. 317.) " He is ruining himself without pleasure. . . . It is a sad thing to pass through the quagmire of parsimony to the gulph of ruin. To pass over the flowery path of extravagance is very well " (*ib.* 3. 348).

"No, madam," cried the doctor, "and never will;
he complains of the ill effects of habit, and rests
contentedly upon a confessed indolence. He told
his father himself that he had ' no turn to economy ';
but a thief might as well plead that he had ' no turn
to honesty.' "

Was not that excellent?

At night, Mrs. Thrale asked if I would have anything? I answered, " No "; but Dr. Johnson said,

"Yes: she is used, madam, to suppers; she would
like an egg or two, and a few slices of ham, or a
rasher—a rasher, I believe, would please her better."

How ridiculous! However, nothing could per-
suade Mrs. Thrale not to have the cloth laid: and
Dr. Johnson was so facetious, that he challenged
Mr. Thrale to get drunk!

"I wish," said he, "my master [1] would say to
me, Johnson, if you will oblige me, you will call
for a bottle of Toulon, and then we will set to it,
glass for glass, till it is done; and after that, I will
say, Thrale, if you will oblige me, you will call for
another bottle of Toulon, and then we will set to it,
glass for glass, till that is done: and by the time we
should have drunk the two bottles, we should be so
happy, and such good friends, that we should fly

---

[1] Mrs. Thrale's manner of referring to her husband, caught up
by Johnson, and later (*Diary*, 1.450) even used by Miss Burney.
In general, as noted above (p. 21), he abstained from wine; but
he was occasionally prevailed upon to take a glass of claret (the
"drinks for boys") upon some great occasion (e.g., p. 18, above).
His vivacity of spirits at this time, therefore, is perhaps worthy
of comparison with his joy at the elevation of Reynolds to
knighthood, to celebrate which he drank claret.

into each other's arms, and both together call for the
third!"

I ate nothing, that they might not again use such
a ceremony with me. Indeed, their late dinners forbid suppers, especially as Dr. Johnson made me eat
cake at tea, for he held it till I took it, with an odd
or absent complaisance.

He was extremely comical after supper, and would
not suffer Mrs. Thrale and me to go to bed for near
an hour after we made the motion.[1]

The Cumberland[2] family was discussed. Mrs.
Thrale said that Mr. Cumberland was a very amiable
man in his own house; but as a father mighty simple;
which accounts for the ridiculous conduct and manners of his daughters, concerning whom we had much
talk, and were all of a mind; for it seems they used
the same rude stare to Mrs. Thrale that so much dis-
gusted us at Mrs. Ord's:[3] she says that she really

---

[1] Johnson's love of late hours was notorious. "Whoever thinks
of going to bed before twelve o'clock," he is said to have remarked,
"is a scoundrel." ('Apophthegms,' etc., *Works*, 11.211.) Hawkins tells (Hawkins's *Life*, p. 286) of an all night session of
Johnson and some of his friends: "About five, Johnson's face
shone with meridian splendour, though his drink had been only
lemonade; but the far greater part of us had deserted the colours
of Bacchus, and were with difficulty rallied to partake of a second refreshment of coffee, which was scarcely ended when the
day began to dawn."

[2] Richard Cumberland, the dramatist, was well acquainted with
Johnson, though never one of his more intimate or popular friends.
He was satirized by Foote in *Piety in Pattens* (1777) and as
Sir Fretful Plagiary in Sheridan's *Critic* (1779).

[3] For Miss Burney's account of Mrs. Ord, see the *Early Diary*
2.138 ff. The meeting with the Cumberlands is not mentioned
earlier by Miss Burney; but compare a later reference to them
(*Diary*, 1.287), "The eldest of the girls . . . quite turned round
her whole person every time we passed each other, to keep me in
sight, and stare at me as long as possible."

concluded something was wrong, and that, in getting out of the coach, she had given her cap some unlucky cuff,—by their merciless staring.

I told her that I had not any doubt, when I had met with the same attention from them, but that they were calculating the exact cost of all my dress. Mrs. Thrale then told me that, about two years ago they were actually hissed out of the playhouse, on account of the extreme height of their feathers!

Dr. Johnson instantly composed an extempore dialogue between himself and Mr. Cumberland upon this subject, in which he was to act the part of a provoking condoler:

"Mr. Cumberland (I should say), how monstrously ill-bred is a playhouse mob! How I pitied poor Miss Cumberland's about that affair!"

"What affair?" cries he, for he has tried to forget it.

"Why," says I, "that unlucky accident they met with some time ago."

"Accident? what accident, sir?"

"Why, you know, when they were hissed out of the playhouse—you remember the time—oh, the English mob is most insufferable! they are boors, and have no manner of taste!"

Mrs. Thrale accompanied me to my room, and stayed chatting with me for more than an hour. . . .

Now for this morning's breakfast.

Dr. Johnson, as usual, came last into the library; he was in high spirits, and full of mirth and sport. I had the honour of sitting next to him; and now,

all at once, he flung aside his reserve, thinking, perhaps, that it was time I should fling aside mine.

Mrs. Thrale told him that she intended taking
me to Mr. T——'s.[1]

"So you ought, madam," cried he; " 'tis your
business to be Cicerone to her."

Then suddenly he snatched my hand, and kissing it,
" Ah!" he added, " they will little think what a
tartar you carry to them!"

"No, that they won't!" cried Mrs. Thrale;
" Miss Burney looks so meek and so quiet, nobody
would suspect what a comical girl she is; but I believe she has a great deal of malice at heart."

" Oh, she's a toad!" cried the doctor, laughing—
" a sly young rogue! with her Smiths and her
Branghtons!"

"Why, Dr. Johnson," said Mrs. Thrale, " I hope
you are very well this morning! if one may judge by
your spirits and good humour, the fever you threatened us with is gone off."

He had complained that he was going to be ill last
night.

" Why no, madam, no," answered he, " I am not
yet well; I could not sleep at all; there I lay restless and uneasy, and thinking all the time of Miss
Burney. Perhaps I have offended her, thought I;
perhaps she is angry; I have seen her but once, and I
talked to her of a rasher!—Were you angry?"

I think I need not tell you my answer.

" I have been endeavouring to find some excuse,"

continued he, "and, as I could not sleep, I got up, and looked for some authority for the word;[1] and I find, madam, it is used by Dryden: in one of his prologues, he says—'And snatch a homely rasher from the coals.' So you must not mind me, madam; I say strange things, but I mean no harm."

I was almost afraid he thought I was really idiot enough to have taken him seriously; but, a few minutes after, he put his hand on my arm, and shaking his head, exclaimed,

"Oh, you are a sly little rogue!—what a Holborn beau have you drawn!"

"Ay, Miss Burney," said Mrs. Thrale, "the Holborn beau is Dr. Johnson's favourite; and we have all your characters by heart, from Mr. Smith up to Lady Louisa."

"Oh, Mr. Smith, Mr. Smith is the man!" cried he, laughing violently. "Harry Fielding never drew so good a character!—such a fine varnish of low politeness!—such a struggle to appear a gentleman! Madam, there is no character better drawn anywhere—in any book or by any author."[2]

I almost poked myself under the table. Never did I feel so delicious a confusion since I was born! But he added a great deal more, only I cannot recol-

---

[1] Had he consulted his own *Dictionary*, he would have found other examples of its use, notably from *The Merchant of Venice* and from Dryden's *Cock and the Fox*. The present quotation is from the prologue to *All for Love*, lines 33-34. One somewhat similar to it is also cited in the *Dictionary*, but is attributed to King.

[2] Johnson used to rebuke Mrs. Thrale for her exaggerated praise: "I know nobody who blasts by praise as you do." (*Life*, 4. 82.) Cf. below, pp. 54, 80, note 1.

lect his exact words, and I do not choose to give him mine.

" Come, come," cried Mrs. Thrale, " we'll torment her no more about her book, for I see it really plagues her. I own I thought for awhile it was only affectation, for I'm sure if the book were mine I should wish to hear of nothing else. But we shall teach her in time how proud she ought to be of such a performance."

" Ah, madam," cried the Doctor, " be in no haste to teach her that; she'll speak no more to us when she knows her own weight."

" Oh, but, sir," cried she, " if Mr. Thrale has his way, she will become our relation, and then it will be hard if she won't acknowledge us."

You may think I stared, but she went on,

" Mr. Thrale says nothing would make him half so happy as giving Miss Burney to Sir J—— L——." [1]

Mercy! what an exclamation did I give. I wonder you did not hear me to St. Martin's Street. However, she continued,

" Mr. Thrale says, Miss Burney seems more formed to draw a husband to herself, by her humour when gay, and her good sense when serious, than almost anybody he ever saw."

" He does me much honour," cried I: though I

---

[1] Sir John Lade, a " rich extravagant young gentleman," nephew of Mr. Thrale. He was seven years younger than Miss Burney. In 1780 Johnson wrote some excellent satiric verses on his attainment of " long-expected one-and-twenty." (*Life,* 4. 413.) See also below, p. 189, note 4.

cannot say I much enjoyed such a proof of his good
opinion as giving me to Sir J—— L——; but Mr.
Thrale is both his uncle and his guardian, and thinks,
perhaps, he would do a mutual good office in securing
me so much money, and his nephew a decent companion. Oh, if he knew how little I require with
regard to money—how much to even bear with a
companion! But he was not brought up with such
folks as my father, my Daddy Crisp, and my Susan,
and does not know what indifference to all things, but
good society such people as those inspire.

" My master says a very good speech," cried the
Doctor, " if Miss Burney's husband should have anything in common with herself; but I know not how
we can level her with Sir J—— L——, unless she
would be content to put her virtues and talents in a
scale against his thousands; and poor Sir J—— must
give cheating weight even then! However, if we
bestow such a prize upon him he shall settle his whole
fortune on her."

Ah! thought I, I am more mercenary than you
fancy me, for not even that would bribe me high
enough.

Before Dr. Johnson had finished his *éloge,* I was
actually on the ground, for there was no standing
it,—or sitting it, rather; and Mrs..Thrale seemed
delighted for me.

" I assure you," she said, " nobody can do your
book more justice than Dr. Johnson does; and yet,
do you remember, sir, how unwilling you were to
read it? He took it up, just looked at the first let-

ter, and then put it away, and said, ' I don't think I
have any taste for it! '—but when he was going to
town, I put the first volume into the coach with him;
and then, when he came home, the very first words
he said to me were ' Why, madam, this *Evelina* is a
charming creature!—and then he teased me to know
who she married, and what became of her,—and I
gave him the rest. For my part, I used to read it in
bed, and could not part with it: I laughed at the second, and I cried at the third; but what a trick was that
of Dr. Burney's, never to let me know whose it was
till I had read it! Suppose it had been something I
had not liked! Oh, it was a vile trick! "

" No, madam, not at all! " cried the Doctor, " for,
in that case, you would never have known;—all
would have been safe, for he would neither have
told you who wrote it, nor Miss Burney what you
said of it."

Some time after the Doctor began laughing to
himself, and then, suddenly turning to me, he called
out, " Only think, Polly! Miss has danced with a
lord! " [1]

" Ah, poor Evelina! " cried Mrs. Thrale, " I see
her now in Kensington Gardens. What she must
have suffered! Poor girl! what fidgets she must
have been in! And I know Mr. Smith, too, very
well;—I always have him before me at the Hampstead Ball, dressed in a white coat, and a tambour
waistcoat, worked in green silk. Poor Mr. Seward!
Mr. Johnson made him so mad t'other day! ' Why,

[1] The utterance of Miss Branghton in Letter 55 of *Evelina*.

Seward,' said he, ' how smart you are dressed! why,
you only want a tambour waistcoat to look like Mr.
Smith.' But I am very fond of Lady Louisa; I
think her as well drawn as any character in the book;
so fine, so affected, so languishing; and, at the same
time so insolent! "

She then ran on with several of her speeches.

Some time after, she gave Dr. Johnson a letter
from Dr. Jebb,[1] concerning one of the gardeners
who is very ill. When he had read it, he grumbled
violently to himself, and put it away with marks of
displeasure.

" What's the matter, sir! " said Mrs. Thrale; " do
you find any fault with the letter? "

" No, madam, the letter's well enough, if the man
knew how to write his own name; but it moves my
indignation to see a gentleman take pains to appear a
tradesman. Mr. Branghton would have written his
name with just such beastly flourishes."

" Ay, well," said Mrs. Thrale, " he is a very agreeable man, and an excellent physician, and a great
favourite of mine, and so he is of Miss Burney's."

" Why, I have no objection to the man, madam,
if he would write his name as he ought to do."

" Well, it does not signify," cried Mrs. Thrale;
" but the commercial fashion of writing gains ground
every day, for all Miss Burney abuses it, with her
Smiths and her Branghtons. Does not the great
Mr. Pennant[2] write like a clerk, without any pro-

---

[1] Sir Richard Jebb, one of Johnson's physicians.
[2] Thomas Pennant (1726-1798) a Welsh antiquary, author of a
Tour in Scotland, praised by Johnson.

nouns? and does not everybody flourish their names till nobody can read them? "

After this they talked over a large party of company who are invited to a formal and grand dinner for next Monday, and among others Admiral Montagu [1] was mentioned. The Doctor, turning to me with a laugh, said,

" You must mark the old sailor, Miss Burney; he'll be a character."

" Ah! " cried Mrs. Thrale, who was going out of the room, " how I wish you would hatch up a comedy between you! do, fall to work! "

A pretty proposal! to be sure Dr. Johnson would be very proud of such a fellow-labourer!

As soon as we were alone together, he said,

" These are as good people as you can be with; you can go to no better house; they are all good nature; nothing makes them angry."

As I have always heard from my father that every individual at Streatham spends the morning alone, I took the first opportunity of absconding to my room, and amused myself in writing till I tired. About noon, when I went into the library, book hunting, Mrs. Thrale came to me.

We had a very nice confab about various books, and exchanged opinions and imitations of Baretti; [2] she told me many excellent tales of him, and I, in return, related my stories.

[1] John Montagu (1719-1785), at this time vice-admiral, and commander-in-chief at Newfoundland during the American Revolution.
[2] For Joseph Baretti, the Piedmontese friend of Johnson, see *Life,* I. 302, *et passim.* Accounts of him are also found in later passages of the *Diary,* I. 186; I. 264-65.

She gave me a long and very entertaining account of Dr. Goldsmith, who was intimately known here; but in speaking of *The Goodnatured Man,* when I extolled my favourite Croaker, I found that admirable character was a downright theft from Dr. Johnson. Look at the *Rambler,*[1] and you will find Suspirius is the man, and that not merely the idea, but the particulars of the character, are all stolen thence! [2]

While we were yet reading this *Rambler,* Dr. Johnson came in: we told him what we were about.

" Ah, madam! " cried he, " Goldsmith was not scrupulous; but he would have been a great man had he known the real value of his own internal resources."

" Miss Burney," said Mrs. Thrale, " is fond of his *Vicar of Wakefield:* and so am I;—don't you like it, sir? "

" No, madam, it is very faulty; there is nothing of real life in it, and very little of nature. It is a mere fanciful performance." [3]

---

[1] No. 59.

[2] A common charge against Goldsmith, not to be taken too seriously. (Cf. *Life,* 1.213 and 2.48.) Taking the charge at its face value (which some later editors are disinclined to do), Goldsmith's use of another author's idea yet represented a practice common to most great dramatists and one most improperly described as "theft." The development and illustration of Croaker's "humor," which is sufficiently indicated by his name, are all Goldsmith's.

[3] Johnson, from the first, considered the *Vicar* a slight performance, always, for example, ranking it below *The Traveller.* The estimate of the book here given is illustrative of a certain critical rashness all too common in Johnson's utterances. Goldsmith's own estimate of the faults and virtues of the book as given in his short " Advertisement " (or Preface) to the work is still the best.

He then seated himself upon a sofa, and calling to me, said, " Come,—Evelina,—come and sit by me."

I obeyed; and he took me almost in his arms,— that is, one of his arms, for one would go three times at least, round me,—and, half-laughing, half-serious, he charged me to " be a good girl! "

" But, my dear," continued he with a very droll look, " what makes you so fond of the Scotch? I don't like you for that; I hate these Scotch, and so must you. I wish Branghton had sent the dog to jail! That Scotch dog Macartney." [1]

" Why, sir," said Mrs. Thrale, " don't you remember he says he would, but that he should get nothing by it? "

" Why, ay, true," cried the doctor, see-sawing very solemnly, " that, indeed, is some palliation for his forbearance. But I must not have you so fond of the Scotch, my little Burney; make your hero what you will but a Scotchman. Besides, you write Scotch— you say ' the one,' [2]—my dear, that's not English. Never use that phrase again."

" Perhaps," said Mrs. Thrale, " it may be used in Macartney's letter, and then it will be a propriety."

" No, madam, no! " cried he; " you can't make a beauty of it; it is in the third volume; put it in Macartney's letter, and welcome!—that, or anything that is nonsense."

" Why, surely," I cried, " the poor man is used ill enough by the Branghtons."

[1] See *Evelina,* Letter 42.
[2] In phrases like " on the one side of the street."

"But Branghton," said he, "only hates him because of his wretchedness,—poor fellow!—But, my
dear love, how should he ever have eaten a good
dinner before he came to England?"

And then he laughed violently at young Branghton's idea.

"Well," said Mrs. Thrale, "I always liked
Macartney; he is a very pretty character, and I took
to him, as the folks say."

"Why, madam," answered he. "I like Macartney myself. Yes, poor fellow, I liked the man, but
I love not the nation."

And then he proceeded, in a dry manner, to make
at once sarcastic reflections on the Scotch and flattering speeches to me, for Macartney's firing at the
national insults of young Branghton: his stubborn
resolution in not owning, even to his bosom friend,
his wretchedness of poverty; and his fighting at last
for the honour of his nation, when he resisted all
other provocations; he said, were all extremely well
marked.

We stayed with him till just dinner time, and
then we were obliged to run away and dress; but Dr.
Johnson called out to me as I went—

"Miss Burney, I must settle that affair of the
Scotch with you at our leisure."

At dinner we had the company, or rather the presence, for he did not speak two words, of Mr. E——,[1]
the clergyman, I believe, of Streatham. And after-

---

[1] Perhaps the Rev. Mr. Evans, mentioned later (*Diary*, 1. 318),
the "dear little Evans" of Johnson's *Letters*.

wards, Mrs. Thrale took the trouble to go with me
to the T——'s.

Dr. Johnson, who has a love of social converse
that nobody, without living under the same roof with
him, would suspect, quite begged us not to go till
he went to town; but as we were hatted and ready,
Mrs. Thrale only told him she rejoiced to find him
so jealous of our companies, and then away we
whisked,—she, Miss Thrale, and my ladyship.

I could write some tolerable good sport concerning this visit, but that I wish to devote all the time
I can snatch for writing, to recording what passes
here; themes of mere ridicule offer everywhere.

We got home late, and had the company of Mr.
E——, and of Mr. Rose Fuller,[1] a young man who
lives at Streatham, and is nephew of the famous
Rose Fuller; and whether Dr. Johnson did not like
them, or whether he was displeased that we went
out, or whether he was not well, I know not; but he
never opened his mouth, except in answer to a question, till he bid us good-night.

Saturday Morning.—Dr. Johnson was again all
himself; and so civil to me!—even admiring how I
dressed myself.   Indeed, it is well I have so much of
his favour; for it seems he always speaks his mind
concerning the dress of ladies, and all ladies who
are here obey his injunctions implicitly, and alter
whatever he disapproves.   This is a part of his character that much surprises me; but notwithstanding

[1] Sufficient account of him is given here and below, pp. 51, 81.

he is sometimes so absent, and always so near sighted, he scrutinises into every part of almost everybody's appearance. They tell me of a Miss Brown,[1] who often visits here, and who has a slovenly way of dressing. "And when she comes down in the morning," says Mrs. Thrale, "her hair will be all loose, and her cap half off; and then Dr. Johnson, who sees something is wrong, and does not know where the fault is, concludes it is in the cap, and says, ' My dear, what do you wear such a vile cap for?' 'I'll change it, sir,' cries the poor girl, 'if you don't like it.' 'Ay, do,' he says; and away runs poor Miss Brown; but when she gets on another, it's the same thing, for the cap has nothing to do with the fault. And then she wonders Dr. Johnson should not like the cap, for she thinks it very pretty. And so on with her gown, which he also makes her change; but if the poor girl were to change through all her wardrobe, unless she could put her things on better, he would still find fault."

When Dr. Johnson was gone, she told me of my mother's [2] being obliged to change her dress.

"Now," said she, " Mrs. Burney had on a very pretty linen jacket and coat, and was going to church, but Dr. Johnson, who, I suppose, did not like her in a jacket, saw something was the matter, and so found fault with the linen; and he looked and peered,

---

[1] "A gay, careless, lively good-humoured girl. . . . She con-fessed to me that both she and Miss S. S. [Sophie Streatfield] were in fevers in his [Johnson's] presence, from apprehension." (*Diary,* I. 103, 209.)
[2] Her stepmother.

and said, ' Why, madam, this won't do ! you must not
go to church so ! ' So away went poor Mrs. Burney
and changed her gown ! And when she had done so,
he did not like it, but he did not know why; so he
told her she should not wear a black hat and cloak
in summer. Oh, how he did bother poor Mrs. Burney ! and himself too, for if the things had been put
on to his mind, he would have taken no notice of
them."

"Why," said Mr. Thrale, very drily, "I don't
think Mrs. Burney a very good dresser."

"Last time she came," said Mrs. Thrale, "she
was in a white cloak, and she told Dr. Johnson she
had got her old white cloak scoured on purpose to
oblige him ! ' Scoured ! ' said he, ' ay,—have you,
madam ? '—so he see-sawed, for he could not for
shame find fault, but he did not seem to like the
scouring."

So I think myself amazingly fortunate to be approved by him; for, if he disliked, alack-a-day, how
could I change ! But he has paid me some very fine
compliments upon this subject.

I was very sorry when the doctor went to town,
though Mrs. Thrale made him promise to return to
Monday's dinner; and he has very affectionately
invited me to visit him in the winter, when he is at
home: and he talked to me a great deal of Mrs.
Williams, and gave me a list of her works, and said
I must visit them;—which I am sure I shall be very
proud of doing.

And now let me try to recollect an account he

gave us of certain celebrated ladies of his acquaintance: an account which, had you heard from himself, would have made you die with laughing, his manner is so peculiar, and enforces his humour so originally.

It was begun by Mrs. Thrale's apologising to him for troubling him with some question she thought trifling— Oh, I remember! We had been talking of colours, and of the fantastic names given to them, and why the palest lilac should be called a *soupir étouffé;* and when Dr. Johnson came in she applied to him.

" Why, madam," said he with wonderful readiness, " it is called a stifled sigh because it is checked in its progress, and only half a colour."

I could not help expressing my amazement at his universal readiness upon all subjects, and Mrs. Thrale said to him,

" Sir, Miss Burney wonders at your patience with such stuff; but I tell her you are used to me, for I believe I torment you with more foolish questions than anybody else dares to."

" No, madam," said he, " you don't torment me; —you tease me, indeed, sometimes."

" Ay, so I do, Dr. Johnson, and I wonder you bear with my nonsense."

" No, madam, you never talk nonsense; you have as much sense, and more wit, than any woman I know! "

" Oh," cried Mrs. Thrale, blushing, " it is my turn to go under the table this morning, Miss Burney! "

" And yet," continued the doctor, with the most

comical look, " I have known all the wits, from Mrs.
Montagu down to Bet Flint! " [1]

" Bet Flint! " cried Mrs. Thrale; " pray, who is
she? "

" Oh, a fine character, madam! She was habitu-
ally a slut and a drunkard, and occasionally a thief
and a harlot."

" And, for Heaven's sake, how came you to know
her? "

" Why, madam, she figured in the literary world,
too! Bet Flint wrote her own life, and called herself
Cassandra, and it was in verse;—it began:

" ' When Nature first ordained my birth,
  A diminutive I was born on earth:
  And then I came from a dark abode
  Into a gay and gaudy world.'

" So Bet brought me her verses to correct; but I
gave her half a crown, and she liked it as well. Bet
had a fine spirit;—she advertised for a husband, but
she had no success, for she told me no man aspired to
her! Then she hired very handsome lodgings and
a footboy; and she got a harpsichord, but Bet could
not play; however she put herself in fine attitudes,
and drummed."

Then he gave an account of another of these
geniuses, who called herself by some fine name, I
have forgotten what.

---

[1] Boswell (*Life*, 4. 103) gives a shorter version of the same story.
Miss Burney apparently (*ib.*, note 2) repeated the verses to him,
though he does not quote them exactly as they are here; it is
of course likely that Miss Burney (or her first editor) slightly
modified the stanza.

"She had not quite the same stock of virtue," continued he, "nor the same stock of honesty as Bet Flint; but I suppose she envied her accomplishments, for she was so little moved by the power of harmony, that while Bet thought she was drumming divinely, the other jade had her indicted for a nuisance!"

"And pray what became of her, sir?"

"Why, madam, she stole a quilt from the man of the house, and he had her taken up, but Bet Flint had a spirit not to be subdued; so when she found herself obliged to go to jail, she ordered a sedan-chair and bid her footboy walk before her. However, the boy proved refractory, for he was ashamed, though his mistress was not."

"And did she ever get out of jail again, sir?"

"Yes, madam, when she came to her trial the judge acquitted her.[1] 'So now,' she said to me, 'the quilt is my own, and now I'll make a petticoat of it.' Oh, I loved Bet Flint!"

Oh, how we all laughed! Then he gave an account of another lady, who called herself Laurinda, and who wrote verses and stole furniture; but he had not the same affection for her, he said, though she too "was a lady who had high notions of honour."

Then followed the history of another, who called herself Hortensia, and who walked up and down the park repeating a book of Virgil.

"But," said he, "though I know her story, I never had the good fortune to see her."

---

[1] The reason for the acquittal is given by Hill. (*Life*, 4. 103, note.)

After this he gave us an account of the famous
Mrs. Pinkethman.[1] "And she," he said, "told me
she owed all her misfortunes to her wit; for she was
so unhappy as to marry a man who thought himself
also a wit, though I believe she gave him not implicit
credit for it, but it occasioned much contradiction
and ill-will."

"Bless me, sir!" cried Mrs. Thrale, "how can
all these vagabonds contrive to get at *you*, of all
people?"[2]

"Oh, the dear creatures!" cried he, laughing
heartily, "I can't but be glad to see them!"

"Why, I wonder, sir, you never went to see Mrs.
Rudd[3] among the rest?"

"Why, madam, I believe I should," said he, "if it
was not for the newspapers; but I am prevented many
frolics that I should like very well, since I am become such a theme for the papers."

Now would you ever have imagined this? Bet
Flint, it seems, once took Kitty Fisher[4] to see him,

---

[1] The "fame" of this lady, like that of Hortensia and Laurinda,
has unfortunately passed away. Dobson is inclined to identify
Mrs. Pinketham with Mrs. Pilkington (1700-1750).

[2] Doubtless he had met them during his wanderings about London in the decade of the 40's.

[3] Mrs. Margaret Caroline Rudd was tried for forgery in 1775, and
acquitted. Boswell, whose interest in criminals amounted almost to
a passion, became intimately acquainted with her. See Fitz-
gerald's *Boswell's Life,* and the *Life of Johnson,* 3. 79 ff., 330,
where Johnson gives a reason similar to the one that follows
here for not becoming acquainted with her, and adds, "I envy
[Boswell] his acquaintance with Mrs. Rudd." (Cf. below, p. 195.)

[4] A famous beauty of the time, of no very savory reputation.
She is the subject of at least six portraits by Sir Joshua. "She
was known as a daring horsewoman, and also credited with the
possession of beauty and wit." (*D. N. B.*) She died in 1767.

but to his no little regret he was not at home. " And
Mrs. Williams," he added, " did not love Bet Flint,
but Bet Flint made herself very easy about that."

How Mr. Crisp would have enjoyed this account!
He gave it all with so droll a solemnity, and it was
all so unexpected, that Mrs. Thrale and I were both
almost equally diverted.

Streatham, August 26.—My opportunities for
writing grow less and less, and my materials more
and more.   After breakfast, I have scarcely a moment that I can spare all day.

Mrs. Thrale I like more and more.   Of all the
people I have ever seen since I came into the " gay
and gaudy world," I never before saw the person
who so strongly resembles our dear father.   I find
the likeness perpetually; she has the same natural
liveliness, the same general benevolence, the
same rare union of gaiety and of feeling in her
disposition.

And so kind is she to me!   She told me at first that
I should have all my mornings to myself, and therefore I have actually studied to avoid her, lest I should
be in her way; but since the first morning she seeks
me, sits with me, saunters with me in the park, or
compares notes over books in the library; and her
conversation is delightful; it is so entertaining, so
gay, so enlivening, when she is in spirits, and so intelligent and instructive when she is otherwise, that
I almost as much wish to record all she says as all
Dr. Johnson says.

Proceed—no! Go back, my muse, to Thursday.
Dr. Johnson came home to dinner.

In the evening he was as lively and full of wit and
sport as I have ever seen him; and Mrs. Thrale and
I had him quite to ourselves; for Mr. Thrale came
in from giving an election dinner [1] (to which he sent
two bucks and six pine apples) so tired, that he
neither opened his eyes nor mouth, but fell fast asleep.
Indeed, after tea he generally does.

Dr. Johnson was very communicative concerning
his present work of the *Lives of the Poets;*[2] Dryden
is now in the press, and he told us he had been just
writing a dissertation upon *Hudibras.*

He gave us an account of Mrs. Lennox.[3] Her
Female Quixote is very justly admired here. But
Mrs. Thrale says that though her books are generally approved, nobody likes her. I find she, among
others, waited on Dr. Johnson upon her commencing
writer, and he told us that, at her request, he carried her to Richardson.

" Poor Charlotte Lennox! " continued he; " when
we came to the house, she desired me to leave her,
' for,' says she ' I am under great restraint in your
presence, but if you leave me alone with Richardson
I'll give you a very good account of him '; however,

---

[1] He was at this time Member of Parliament for Streatham,
in which capacity he was in the habit of giving treats to his
constituents.

[2] The work had been contracted for May 29, 1777; the volumes
here mentioned as in press appeared in March of the following
year.

[3] 1720-1804. Johnson issued *Proposals* for publishing her works
in 1775.

I fear poor Charlotte was disappointed, for she gave me no account at all!"

He then told us of two little productions of our Mr. Harris,[1] which we read; they are very short and very clever: one is called *Fashion,* the other *Much Ado,* and they are both of them full of a sportive humour, that I had not suspected to belong to Mr. Harris, the learned grammarian.

Some time after, turning suddenly to me, he said, " Miss Burney, what sort of reading do you delight in? History?—travels?—poetry?—or romances?"

" Oh, sir!" cried I, " I dread being catechised by you. I dare not make any answer, for I fear whatever I should say would be wrong!"

" Whatever you should say—how's that?"

" Why, not whatever I should—but whatever I could say."

He laughed, and to my great relief spared me any further questions upon the subject. Indeed, I was very happy I had the presence of mind to evade him as I did, for I am sure the examination which would have followed, had I made any direct answer, would have turned out sorely to my discredit.

" Do you remember, sir," said Mrs. Thrale, " how you tormented poor Miss Brown [2] about reading?"

[1] James Harris (1709-1780), grammarian, called by Johnson a "prig and a bad prig." (*Life,* 3.245; cf. note.) In the year in which Miss Burney is writing he published *Philological Inquiries.* He was also interested in music, and wrote words for Italian and German airs. Probably the two compositions mentioned in the text belong to this class. He was popular with Miss Burney, and figures prominently in the *Early Diary* (1.207; 2.57, *et passim*).

[2] See above, p. 42.

" She might soon be tormented, madam," answered he, " for I am not yet quite clear she knows what a book is."

" Oh, for shame! " cried Mrs. Thrale, " she reads not only English, but French and Italian. She was in Italy a great while."

" Pho! " exclaimed he; " Italian, indeed! Do you think she knows as much Italian as Rose Fuller does English? "

" Well, well," said Mrs. Thrale, " Rose Fuller is a very good young man, for all he has not much command of language, and though he is silly enough, yet I like him very well, for there is no manner of harm in him."

Then she told me that he once said, " Dr. Johnson's conversation is so instructive that I'll ask him a question. ' Pray, sir, what is Palmyra? I have heard of it often, but never knew what it was.' ' Palmyra, sir? ' said the doctor; ' why, it is a hill in Ireland, situated in a bog, and has palm-trees at the top, when it is called palm-mire." [1]

Whether or not he swallowed this account, I know not yet.

" But Miss Brown," continued she, " is by no means such a simpleton as Dr. Johnson supposes her

---

[1] " Mrs. Thrale (then Mrs. Piozzi), in relating this story after Johnson's death, in her *Anecdotes* of him, adds—' Seeing, however, that the lad ' (whom she does not name, but calls a ' young fellow '), ' thought him serious, and thanked him for his information, he undeceived him very gently indeed; told him the history, geography, and chronology of Tadmor in the Wilderness, with every incident that literature could furnish, I think, or eloquence express, from the building of Solomon's palace to the voyage of Dawkins and Wood." (BARRETT.)

to be; she is not very deep, indeed, but she is a sweet, and a very ingenuous girl, and nobody admired Miss Streatfield more. But she made a more foolish speech to Dr. Johnson than she would have done to anybody else, because she was so frightened and embarrassed that she knew not what she said. He asked her some questions about reading, and she did, to be sure, make a very silly answer; but she was so perplexed and bewildered, that she hardly knew where she was, and so she said the beginning of a book was as good as the end, or the end as good as the beginning, or some such stuff; and Dr. Johnson told her of it so often, saying, 'Well, my dear, which part of a book do you like best now?' that poor Fanny Brown burst into tears!"

"I am sure I should have compassion for her," cried I; "for nobody would be more likely to have blundered out such, or any such speech, from fright and terror."

"You?" cried Dr. Johnson. "No; you are another thing; she who could draw Smiths and Branghtons, is quite another thing."

Mrs. Thrale then told some other stories of his degrading opinion of us poor fair sex; I mean in general, for in particular he does them noble justice. Among others, was a Mrs. Somebody who spent a day here once, and of whom he asked, "Can she read?"

"Yes, to be sure," answered Mrs. Thrale; "we have been reading together this afternoon."

"And what book did you get for her?"

" Why, what happened to lie in the way, Hogarth's
Analysis of Beauty." [1]

" Hogarth's *Analysis of Beauty!* What made you
choose that? "

" Why, sir, what would you have had me take? "

" What she could have understood—*Cow-hide,* or
Cinderella! "

" Oh, Dr. Johnson! " cried I; " 'tis not for nothing you are feared! "

" Oh, you rogue! " cried he, laughing, " and they
would fear *you* if they knew you! "

" That they would," said Mrs. Thrale; " but she's
so shy they don't suspect her. Miss P—— gave her
an account of all her dress, to entertain her, t'other
night! To be sure she was very lucky to fix on Miss
Burney for such conversation! But I have been telling her she must write a comedy; [2] I am sure nobody
could do it better. Is it not true, Dr. Johnson? "

I would fain have stopt her, but she was not to be
stopped, and ran on saying such fine things! though we
had almost a struggle together; and she said at last:

" Well, authors may say what they will of modesty;
but I believe Miss Burney is really modest about her
book, [3] for her colour comes and goes every time it
is mentioned."

---

[1] An ill-considered work, published in 1753, which was far from
treating its subject with any success and which only yielded its
opinionated author severe, though merited, censure.

[2] Cf. above, p. 37, and below, pp. 61-62; 106 ff. Unfortunately
Miss Burney took this advice. Her comedy, *The Witlings,* which
she composed soon after this, was suppressed, largely as a result of Mr. Crisp's advice. (See Dobson's *Fanny Burney,* 101-105.)

[3] Probably the weary reader is no longer able to agree with Mrs.
Thrale.

I then escaped to look for a book which we had been talking of, and Dr. Johnson, when I returned to my seat, said he wished Richardson had been alive.

" And then," he added, " she should have been introduced to him—though I don't know neither—Richardson would have been afraid of her." [1]

" Oh yes! that's a likely matter," quoth I.

" It's very true," continued he; " Richardson would have been really afraid of her; there is merit in *Evelina* which he could not have borne. No; it would not have done! unless, indeed, she would have flattered him prodigiously. Harry Fielding, too, would have been afraid of her; there is nothing so delicately finished in all Harry Fielding's works, as in *Evelina!* " [2] Then shaking his head at me, he exclaimed, " Oh, you little character-monger, you! "

Mrs. Thrale then returned to her charge, and again urged me about a comedy; and again I tried to silence her, and we had a fine fight together; till she called upon Dr. Johnson to back her.

" Why, madam," said he, laughing, " she *is* writing one. What a rout is here, indeed! she is writing one upstairs all the time. Who ever knew when she began *Evelina?* She is working at some drama, depend upon it."

---

[1] Richardson's jealousy of his rivals was notorious.

[2] Cf. above, p. 32. Later (*Diary,* 1. 95), he is reported to have said of it, "there were things and characters in it more than worthy of Fielding," and when objection was made to this statement, added, "Harry Fielding knew nothing but the shell of life." Time has hardly corroborated these *dicta*.

. "True, true, O king!" thought I.

"Well, that will be a sly trick!" cried Mrs. Thrale; "however, you know best, I believe, about that, as well as about every other thing."

Friday was a very full day. In the morning we began talking of *Irene*, and Mrs. Thrale made Dr. Johnson read some passages which I had been remarking as uncommonly applicable, and told us he had not ever read so much of it before since it was first printed.[1]

"Why, there is no making you read a play," said Mrs. Thrale, "either of your own, or any other person. What trouble had I to make you hear Murphy's *Know your own Mind!*[2] 'Read rapidly, read rapidly,' you cried, and then took out your watch to see how long I was about it![3] Well, we won't serve Miss Burney so, sir; when we have her comedy we will do it all justice." . . .

The day was passed most agreeably. In the evening we had, as usual, a literary conversation. I say we, only because Mrs. Thrale will make me take

---

[1] At another time when one was reading his tragedy of *Irene* to a company at a house in the country, he left the room, and somebody having asked him the reason of this, he replied, 'Sir, I thought it had been better.'" (*Life,* 4. 5.)

[2] A comedy which appeared in the year in which Miss Burney is writing. Arthur Murphy was one of Johnson's friends and biographers; his *Essay on the Life and Genius of Samuel Johnson* appeared in 1792, a year later than Boswell's *Life.* There is an account of him in the *Memoirs,* 2. 174.

[3] Murphy himself says (*Essay,* Hill's ed., p. 363) that it is doubtful whether Johnson ever read any book save the Bible entirely through, and that he was disinclined to believe that others read books through. (Cf. *Life,* 2. 226.)

some share, by perpetually applying to me; and, indeed, there can be no better house for rubbing up the memory, as I hardly ever read, saw, or heard of any book that by some means or other has not been mentioned here.

Mr. Lort [1] produced several curious MSS. of the famous Bristol Chatterton; [2] among others, his will, and divers verses written against Dr. Johnson [3] as a placeman and pensioner; all which he read aloud, with a steady voice and unmoved countenance.

I was astonished at him; Mrs. Thrale not much pleased; Mr. Thrale silent and attentive; and Mr. Seward was slily laughing. Dr. Johnson himself, listened profoundly and laughed openly. Indeed, I believe he wishes his abusers no other than a good dinner, like Pope.

Just as we had got our biscuits and toast-and-water, which make the Streatham supper, and which, indeed, is all there is any chance of eating after our late and great dinners, Mr. Lort suddenly said,

" Pray, ma'am, have you heard anything of a novel that runs about a good deal, called *Evelina?* "

What a ferment did this question, before such a set, put me in!

[1] He is described by Miss Burney (*Diary*, 1.91), as "one of the most learned men alive, and . . . a collector of curiosities in literature and natural history." His manners, she adds, were somewhat blunt and odd.

[2] Although Chatterton had died in 1770, there was still some controversy regarding the genuineness of the Rowley MSS. (Cf. *Diary*, 1.356.) For Johnson's interest in the marvellous boy, see *Life*, 3.51-52.

[3] "Rigid Johnson" is mentioned in *Fables for the Court*, lines 28 ff., and several times in *Kew Gardens*, lines 280 ff., 360 ff, 463 ff., etc.

I did not know whether he spoke to me, or Mrs.
Thrale; and Mrs. Thrale was in the same doubt,
and as she owned, felt herself in a little palpitation
for me, not knowing what might come next. Between us both, therefore, he had no answer,

' It has been recommended to me," continued he;
" but I have no great desire to see it, because it has
such a foolish name. Yet I have heard a great deal
of it, too."

He then repeated *Evelina*—in a very languishing
and ridiculous tone.

My heart beat so quick against my stays that I
almost panted with extreme agitation, from the dread
either of hearing some horrible criticism, or of being
betrayed; and I munched my biscuit as if I had not
eaten for a fortnight.

I believe the whole party were in some little consternation; Dr. Johnson began see-sawing; Mr.
Thrale awoke; Mr. E——— [1] who I fear has picked
up some notion of the affair from being so much in
the house, grinned amazingly; and Mr. Seward, bit-
ing his nails and flinging himself back in his chair, I
am sure had wickedness enough to enjoy the whole
scene.

Mrs. Thrale was really a little fluttered, but without looking at me, said,

" And pray what, Mr. Lort, what have you heard
of it? "

Now, had Mrs. Thrale not been flurried, this was
the last question she should have ventured to ask

---

[1] See above, p. 40, note.

before me. Only suppose what I must feel when I
heard it.

"Why, they say," answered he, "that it's an account of a young lady's first entrance into company,
and of the scrapes she gets into; and they say there's
a great deal of character in it, but I have not cared
to look in it, because the name is so foolish—
Evelina!"

"Why foolish, sir?" cried Dr. Johnson.
"Where's the folly o it?"

"Why, I won't say much for the name myself,"
said Mrs. Thrale, "to those who don't know the
reason of it, which I found out, but which nobody
else seems to know."

She then explained the name from Evelyn, according to my own meaning.

"Well," said Dr. Johnson, "if that was the reason, it is a very good one."

"Why, have you had the book here?" cried Mr.
Lort, staring.

"Ay, indeed, have we," said Mrs. Thrale; "I
read it when I was last confined, and I laughed over
it, and I cried over it!"

"Oh, ho!" said Mr. Lort, "this is another thing!
If you have had it here, I will certainly read it."

"Had it? ay," returned she; "and Dr. Johnson,
who would not look at it at first, was so caught by
it when I put it in the coach with him that he has
sung its praises ever since,—and he says Richardson
would have been proud to have written it."

"Oh, ho! this is a good hearing!" cried Mr. Lort;

"if Dr. Johnson can read it, I shall get it with all speed."

"You need not go far for it," said Mrs. Thrale, "for it's now upon yonder table."

I could sit still no longer; there was something so awkward, so uncommon, so strange in my then situation, that I wished myself a hundred miles off; and, indeed, I had almost choked myself with the biscuit, for I could not for my life swallow it; and so I got up, and, as Mr. Lort went to the table to look at *Evelina,* I left the room, and was forced to call for water to wash down the biscuit, which literally stuck in my throat. . . .

Dr. Johnson was later than usual this morning, and did not come down till our breakfast was over, and Mrs. Thrale had risen to give some orders, I believe: I, too, rose, and took a book at another end of the room. Some time after, before he had yet appeared, Mr. Thrale called out to me,

"So, Miss Burney, you have a mind to feel your legs before the doctor comes?"

"Why so?" cried Mr. Lort.

"Why, because when he comes she will be confined."

"Ay?—how is that?"

"Why, he never lets her leave him, but keeps her prisoner till he goes to his own room."

"Oh, ho!" cried Mr. Lort, "she is in great favour with him."

"Yes," said Mr. Seward, "and I think he shows his taste."

" I did not know," said Mr. Lort, " but he might keep her to help him in his *Lives of the Poets,* if she's so clever."

" And yet," said Mrs. Thrale, " Miss Burney never flatters him, though she is such a favourite with him;—but the tables are turned, for he sits and flatters her all day long."

" I don't flatter him," said I, " because nothing I could say would flatter him."

Mrs. Thrale then told a story of Hannah More, which I think exceeds, in its severity, all the severe things I have yet heard of Dr. Johnson's saying.

When she was introduced to him, not long ago, she began singing his praise in the warmest manner, and talking of the pleasure and the instruction she had received from his writings, with the highest encomiums. For some time he heard her with that quietness which a long use of praise has given him: she then redoubled her strokes, and, as Mr. Seward [1] calls it, peppered still more highly: till, at length, he turned suddenly to her, with a stern and angry countenance, and said, " Madam, before you flatter a man so grossly to his face, you should consider whether or not your flattery is worth his having." [2]

Mr. Seward then told another instance of his determination not to mince the matter, when he thought reproof at all deserved. During a visit of Miss

---

[1] Rather Goldsmith; see the description of Garrick in *Retaliation.*
[2] Cf. the more accurate account given in the *Life* (4. 341), in which Johnson appears to less disadvantage. For the whole matter of Miss More's flattery of Johnson and of Johnson's flattery of Miss More, see both the *Life* and the *Miscellanies, passim.*

Brown's to Streatham, he was inquiring of her several things that she could not answer; and as he held her so cheap in regard to books,[1] he began to question her concerning domestic affairs—puddings, pies, plain work, and so forth. Miss Brown, not at all more able to give a good account of herself in these articles than in the others, began all her answers with, " Why, sir, one need not be obliged to do so,—or so," whatever was the thing in question. When he had finished his interrogatories, and she had finished her " need nots " he ended the discourse with saying, " As to your needs, my dear, they are so very many, that you would be frightened yourself if you knew half of them."

After breakfast on Friday,[2] or yesterday, a curious trait occurred of Dr. Johnson's jocosity. It was while the talk ran so copiously upon their urgency that I should produce a comedy. While Mrs. Thrale was in the midst of her flattering persuasions, the doctor, see-sawing in his chair, began laughing to himself so heartily as to almost shake his seat as well as his sides. We stopped our confabulation, in which he had ceased to join, hoping he would reveal the subject of his mirth; but he enjoyed it inwardly, without heeding our curiosity,—till at last he said he had been struck with a notion that " Miss Burney would begin her dramatic career by writing a piece called *Streatham*."

[1] See above, pp. 50-51.
[2] This entry has no other date than 1778; it immediately follows the preceding.

He paused, and laughed yet more cordially, and then suddenly commanded a pomposity to his countenance and his voice, and added, " Yes ! *Streatham— a Farce."*

How little did I expect from this Lexiphanes,[1] this great and dreaded lord of English literature, a turn for burlesque humour !

Streatham, September.—Our journey hither proved, as it promised, most sociably cheerful, and Mrs. Thrale opened still further upon the subject she began in St. Martin's Street, of Dr. Johnson's kindness towards me. To be sure she saw it was not totally disagreeable to me; though I was really astounded when she hinted at my becoming a rival to Miss Streatfield [2] in the doctor's good graces.

" I had a long letter," she said, " from Sophy Streatfield t'other day, and she sent Dr. Johnson her elegant edition of the *Classics;* but when he had read the letter he said, ' She is a sweet creature, and I love her much; but my little Burney writes a better letter.' Now," continued she, " that is just what I wished him to say of you both."

Before dinner, to my great joy, Dr. Johnson returned home from Warley Common.[3] I followed

---

[1] See above, p. 1, note 3.

[2] A young and beautiful Bluestocking, "half adored by Mr. and Mrs. Thrale." (*Diary*, 1.19.) Her learning, however, is not to be taken too seriously, for Johnson once said of her that, "taking away her Greek, she was as ignorant as a butterfly." (*Diary*, 1.231.)

[3] A full account of Johnson's visit to Warley Camp, where his friend, Bennet Langton, Captain in the Lincolnshire militia, was stationed, may be found in the *Life*, 3.361 ff.

Thursday Morn.
St. Martin's Street.

I found all at Home well, & 4 to 1 in good humour,—& when the Odds are so much in our favour, who has a right to Grumble?—Charles is expected To Day or to-morrow: my Sister is better, & has taken another Body— a poor Cousin!—into the Country instead of Susan,—who, as well as myself, has nothing now to do but wait upon our High land Laddie. The Defence, the Ship of which James was sent in search, has got, as we find by the Papers, safe Home: but whether he is still cruizing for it in ignorance, or only work-ing his crazy Vessel slowly after her, we know not. You will have, I hope, a pleasant Day with Lady ___, who, as She knows me—Not,—I the less regret missing. I am very glad of the mistake about Susan's Letter, as it hastened such sweet Words from my dearest Tyo to her

Letter of Miss Burney's to Mrs. Thrale

Mrs. Thrale into the library to see him, and he is so near-sighted that he took me for Miss Streatfield:[1] but he did not welcome me less kindly when he found his mistake, which Mrs. Thrale made known by saying, " No, 'tis Miss Streatfield's rival, Miss Burney."

At tea-time the subject turned upon the domestic economy of Dr. Johnson's own household. Mrs. Thrale has often acquainted me that his house is quite filled and overrun with all sorts of strange creatures, whom he admits for mere charity, and because nobody else will admit them—for his charity is unbounded— or, rather, bounded only by his circumstances.

The account he gave of the adventures and absurdities of the set was highly diverting, but too diffused for writing, though one or two speeches I must give. I think I shall occasionally theatricalise my dialogues.

Mrs. Thrale.—Pray, sir, how does Mrs. Williams like all this tribe?

Dr. Johnson.—Madam, she does not like them at all; but their fondness for her is not greater. She and De Mullin[2] quarrel incessantly; but as they can both be occasionally of service to each other, and as neither of them have any other place to go to, their animosity does not force them to separate.

---

[1] Similar instances are recorded above, p. 3, and below, p. 241.

[2] The name is more properly spelled Desmoulins. Beside their lodging, Johnson gave her and her daughter a half guinea a week. For account of the various inmates of Johnson's house, see *Life*, 3, Appendix D.

Mrs. T.—And pray, sir, what is Mr. Macbean?[1]

Dr. J.—Madam, he is a Scotchman; he is a man of great learning, and for his learning I respect him, and I wish to serve him. He knows many languages, and knows them well; but he knows nothing of life. I advised him to write a geographical dictionary; but I have lost all hopes of his ever doing anything properly, since I found he gave as much labour to Capua as to Rome.

Mr. T.—And pray who is clerk of your kitchen, sir?

Dr. J.—Why, sir, I am afraid there is none; a general anarchy prevails in my kitchen, as I am told by Mr. Levat, who says it is not now what it used to be!

Mrs. T.—Mr. Levat, I suppose, sir, has the office of keeping the hospital in health? for he is an apothecary.

Dr. J.—Levat, madam, is a brutal fellow, but I have a good regard for him; for his brutality is in his manners, not his mind.

Mr. T.—But how do you get your dinners drest?

Dr. J.—Why, De Mullin has the chief management of the kitchen; but our roasting is not magnificent, for we have no jack.

Mr. T.—No jack? Why, how do they manage without?

---

[1] He had been one of Johnson's amanuenses when he was at work on the *Dictionary*. "Johnson wrote for him a Preface to *A System of Ancient Geography;* and, by the favour of Lord Thurlow, got him admitted a poor brother of the Charterhouse." (*Life,* 1.187.)

Dr. J.—Small joints, I believe, they manage with a string, and larger are done at the tavern. I have some thoughts (with a profound gravity) of buying a jack, because I think a jack is some credit to a house.

Mr. T.—Well, but you'll have a spit, too?

Dr. J.—No, sir, no; that would be superfluous; for we shall never use it; and if a jack is seen, a spit will be presumed!

Mrs. T.—But pray, sir, who is the Poll you talk of?[1] She that you used to abet in her quarrels with Mrs. Williams, and call out, " At her again, Poll! Never flinch, Poll "?

Dr. J.—Why, I took to Poll very well at first, but she won't do upon a nearer examination.

Mrs. T.—How came she among you, sir?

Dr. J.—Why, I don't rightly remember, but we could spare her very well from us. Poll is a stupid slut; I had some hopes of her at first; but, when I talked to her tightly and closely, I could make nothing of her; she was wiggle-waggle, and I could never persuade her to be categorical. I wish Miss Burney would come among us; if she would only give us a week, we should furnish her with ample materials for a new scene in her next work.[2]

[1] This question has, so far as I am aware, never been answered. Johnson seems to avoid answering it here. Apart from the information here given, we know only that she was a Miss Carmichael. I have sometimes wondered whether she might not be the prostitute whom Johnson rescued. (*Life*, 4. 321.) In support of this rather vague assumption, we may note that Boswell derived his information regarding this woman from Mrs. Desmoulins, who obviously knew the " Poll " here referred to.

[2] Her comedy, *The Witlings;* see above, p. 53, note 2.

A little while after he asked Mrs. Thrale, who had read *Evelina* in his absence?

" Who? " cried she,—" why, Burke!—Burke sat up all night to finish it; [1] and Sir Joshua Reynolds is mad about it, and said he would give fifty pounds to know the author.[2] But our fun was with his nieces—we made them believe I wrote the book,[3] and the girls gave me the credit of it at once."

" I am very sorry for it, madam," cried he, quite angrily,—" you were much to blame; deceits of that kind ought never to be practised; they have a worse tendency than you are aware of."[4]

Mr. T.—Why, don't frighten yourself, sir; Miss Burney will have all the credit she has a right to, for I told them whose it was before they went.

Dr. J.—But you were very wrong for misleading them for a moment; such jests are extremely blameable; they are foolish in the very act, and they are wrong, because they always leave a doubt upon the mind. What first passed will be always recollected by those girls, and they will never feel clearly convinced which wrote the book, Mrs. Thrale or Miss Burney.

Mrs. T.—Well, well, I am ready to take my Bible

---

[1] See *Diary*, 1.107.
[2] See *Diary*, 1.104.
[3] See *Diary*, 1.104 ff.
[4] Johnson's hatred of deceit almost amounted to a ruling passion. " He inculcated upon all his friends the importance of perpetual vigilance against the slightest degrees of falsehood." (*Life*, 3.229-230.) A conversation with Mrs. Thrale and Boswell on the same subject is recorded on p. 228 of the same volume.

oath it was not me; and if that won't do, Miss Burney must take hers too.

I was then looking over the *Life of Cowley*, which he had himself given me to read, at the same time that he gave to Mrs. Thrale that of Waller. They are now printed, though they will not be published for some time.[1] But he bade me put it away.

" Do," cried he, " put away that now, and prattle with us; I can't make this little Burney prattle, and I am sure she prattles well; but I shall teach her another lesson than to sit thus silent before I have done with her."

" To talk," cried I, " is the only lesson I shall be backward to learn from you, sir."

" You shall give me," cried he, " a discourse upon the passions: come, begin! Tell us the necessity of regulating them, watching over and curbing them! Did you ever read Norris's *Theory of Love?*"[2]

" No, sir," said I, laughing, yet staring a little.

Dr. J.—Well, it is worth your reading. He will make you see that inordinate love is the root of all evil: inordinate love of wealth brings on avarice; of wine, brings on intemperance; of power, brings on cruelty; and so on. He deduces from inordinate love all human frailty.

Mrs. T.—To-morrow, sir, Mrs. Montagu dines here, and then you will have talk enough.

Dr. Johnson began to see-saw, with a countenance strongly expressive of inward fun, and after enjoying

---

[1] They were published late in March of the following year.
[2] A work published in 1688 by the Rev. John Norris (1657-1711).

it some time in silence, he suddenly and with great animation turned to me and cried,

"Down with her, Burney!—down with her!—spare her not! attack her, fight her, and down with her at once! You are a rising wit, and she is at the top; and when I was beginning the world, and was nothing and nobody, the joy of my life was to fire at all the established wits;[1] and then everybody loved to halloo me on. But there is no game now; everybody would be glad to see me conquered; but then, when I was new, to vanquish the great ones was all the delight of my poor little dear soul! So at her, Burney,—at her, and down with her!"

Oh, how we were all amused! By the way I must tell you that Mrs. Montagu is in very great estimation here, even with Dr. Johnson himself, when others do not praise her improperly. Mrs. Thrale ranks her as the first of women in the literary way. I should have told you that Miss Gregory, daughter of the Gregory [2] who wrote the *Letters,* or *Legacy of Advice,* lives with Mrs. Montagu, and was invited to accompany her.

"Mark now," said Dr. Johnson, "if I contradict her to-morrow. I am determined, let her say what she will, that I will not contradict her."

Mrs. T.—Why, to be sure, sir, you did put her a little out of countenance last time she came. Yet

---

[1] A famous instance of this is his interruption of a conversation between Richardson and Hogarth (*Life,* I. 147), at a time when he himself was almost unknown.
[2] John Gregory (1724-1773), professor of medicine at Edinburgh University.

you were neither rough, nor cruel, nor ill-natured; but still, when a lady changes colour, we imagine her feelings are not quite composed.

Dr. J.—Why, madam, I won't answer that I shan't contradict her again, if she provokes me as she did then; but a less provocation I will withstand. I believe I am not high in her good graces already; and I begin (added he, laughing heartily) to tremble for my admission into her new house.[1] I doubt I shall never see the inside of it.

(Mrs. Montagu is building a most superb house.)

Mrs. T.—Oh, I warrant you, she fears you, indeed; but that, you know, is nothing uncommon; and dearly I love to hear your disquisitions; for certainly she is the first woman for literary knowledge in England, and if in England, I hope I may say in the world.

Dr. J.—I believe you may, madam. She diffuses more knowledge in her conversation than any woman I know, or, indeed, almost any man.

Mrs. T.—I declare I know no man equal to her, take away yourself and Burke, for that art. And you who love magnificence, won't quarrel with her, as everybody else does, for her love of finery.

Dr. J.—No, I shall not quarrel with her upon that topic. (Then, looking earnestly at me), "Nay," he added, "it's very handsome!"

"What, sir?" cried I, amazed.

"Why, your cap:—I have looked at it some time, and I like it much. It has not that vile bandeau across it, which I have so often cursed."

[1] See pp. 74-75.

Did you ever hear anything so strange? nothing escapes him. My Daddy Crisp is not more minute in his attentions: nay, I think he is even less so.

Mrs. T.—Well, sir, that bandeau you quarrelled with was worn by every woman at court the last birthday, and I observed that all the men found fault with it.

Dr. J.—The truth is, women, take them in general, have no idea of grace. Fashion is all they think of. I don't mean Mrs. Thrale and Miss Burney, when I talk of women!—They are goddesses! and therefore I accept them.

Mrs. T.—Lady Ladd [1] never wore the bandeau, and said she never would, because it is unbecoming.

Dr. J.—(laughing) Did not she? Then is Lady Ladd a charming woman, and I have yet hopes of entering into engagements with her!

Mrs. T.—Well, as to that I can't say; but to be sure, the only similitude I have yet discovered in you, is in size; there you agree mighty well.

Dr. J. Why, if anybody could have worn the bandeau, it must have been Lady Ladd; for there is enough of her to carry it off; but you are too little for anything ridiculous; that which seems nothing upon a Patagonian, will become very conspicuous upon a Lilliputian, and of you there is so little in all, that one single absurdity would swallow up half of you.

Some time after, when we had all been a few minutes wholly silent, he turned to me and said,

[1] Another spelling of Lade. She was Mr. Thrale's sister.

" Come, Burney, shall you and I study our parts against Mrs. Montagu comes? "

" Miss Burney," cried Mr. Thrale, " you must get up your courage for this encounter! I think you should begin with Miss Gregory; and down with her first."

Dr. J.—No, no, always fly at the eagle! down with Mrs. Montagu herself! I hope she will come full of *Evelina!*

Wednesday.—At breakfast, Dr. Johnson asked me, if I had been reading his *Life of Cowley?*

" Oh yes," said I.

" And what do you think of it? "

" I am delighted with it," cried I; " and if I was somebody, I should not have read it without telling you sooner what I think of it, and unasked."

Again, when I took up Cowley's *Life,* he made me put it away to talk. I could not help remarking how very like Dr. Johnson is to his writing; and how much the same thing it was to hear or to read him; [1] but that nobody could tell that without coming to Streatham, for his language was generally imagined to be laboured and studied, instead of the mere common flow of his thoughts.

---

[1] His style in his last work was, in general, much simpler than in his earlier writings. It is also true that in general his conversational style was much easier when talking with Miss Burney and Mrs. Thrale than when "talking for victory." Mrs. Thrale said of his style that it was " so natural to him, and so much like his natural mode of conversing, that I was myself but little astonished when he told me, that he had scarcely read over one of those inimitable essays [*The Rambler*] before they went to the press." ('Anecdotes,' *Miscellanies,* 1. 348.)

"Very true," said Mrs. Thrale, "he writes and talks with the same ease, and in the same manner; but, sir (to him), if this rogue is like her book, how will she trim all of us by and by! Now, she dainties us up with all the meekness in the world; but when we are away, I suppose she pays us off finely."

"My paying off," cried I, "is like the Latin of Hudibras,

"' . . . who never scanted,
His learning unto such as wanted;'

for I can figure like anything when I am with those who can't figure at all."

Mrs. T.—Oh, if you have any *mag*[1] in you, we'll draw it out!

Dr. J.—A rogue! she told me that if she was somebody instead of nobody, she would praise my book!

F. B.—Why, sir, I am sure you would scoff my praise.

Dr. J.—If you think that, you think very ill of me; but you don't think it.

Mrs. T.—We have told her what you said to Miss More, and I believe that makes her afraid.[2]

Dr. Johnson.—Well, and if she was to serve me as Miss More did, I should say the same thing of her. But I think she will not. Hannah More has very good intellects, too; but she has by no means the elegance of Miss Burney.

---

[1] "Chatter." (*N.E.D.*) The first recorded use of the word.
[2] See above, p. 60.

" Well," cried I, " there are folks that are to be spoilt, and folks that are not to be spoilt, as well in the world as in the nursery; but what will become of me, I know not."

Mrs. T.—Well, if you are spoilt, we can only say, nothing in the world is so pleasant as being spoilt.

Dr. J.—No, no; Burney will not be spoilt; she knows too well what praise she has a claim to, and what not, to be in any danger of spoiling.

F. B.—I do, indeed, believe I shall never be spoilt at Streatham, for it is the last place where I can feel of any consequence.

Mrs. T.—Well, sir, she is *our* Miss Burney, however; we were the first to catch her, and now we have got, we will keep her And so she is all our own.

Dr. J.—Yes, I hope she is; I should be very sorry to lose Miss Burney.

F. B.—Oh, dear! how can two such people sit and talk such——

Mrs. T.—Such stuff, you think? but Dr. Johnson's love——

Dr. J.—Love? no, I don't entirely love her yet; I must see more of her first; I have much too high an opinion of her to flatter her. I have, indeed, seen nothing of her but what is fit to be loved, but I must know her more. I admire her, and greatly too.

F. B.—Well, this is a very new style to me! I have long enough had reason to think myself loved, but admiration is perfectly new to me.

Dr. J.—I admire her for her observation, for her good sense, for her humour, for her discernment, for her manner of expressing them, and for all her writing talents.

I quite sigh beneath the weight of such praise from such persons—sigh with mixed gratitude for the present, and fear for the future; for I think I shall never, never be able to support myself long so well with them.

We could not prevail with him to stay till Mrs. Montagu arrived. . . .

When dinner was upon table, I followed the procession, in a tragedy step, as Mr. Thrale will have it, into the dining-parlour. Dr. Johnson was returned.

The conversation was not brilliant, nor do I remember much of it; but Mrs. Montagu behaved to me just as I could have wished, since she spoke to me very little, but spoke that little with the utmost politeness. But Miss Gregory, though herself a very modest girl, quite stared me out of countenance, and never took her eyes off my face.

When Mrs. Montagu's new house was talked of, Dr. Johnson, in a jocose manner, desired to know if he should be invited to see it.

"Ay, sure," cried Mrs. Montague, looking well pleased; "or else I shan't like it: but I invite you all to a house warming; I shall hope for the honour of seeing all this company at my new house next Easter day: I fix the day now that it may be remembered."

Everybody bowed and accepted the invite but me,

and I thought fitting not to hear it; for I have no
notion of snapping at invites from the eminent.
But Dr. Johnson, who sat next to me, was determined
I should be of the party, for he suddenly clapped
his hand on my shoulder, and called out aloud,
    " Little Burney, you and I will go together! "
    " Yes, surely," cried Mrs. Montagu, " I shall
hope for the pleasure of seeing ' Evelina.' "
    " Evelina? " repeated he; " has Mrs. Montagu
then found out Evelina? "
    " Yes," cried she, " and I am proud of it; I am
proud that a work so commended should be a
woman's."
    Oh, how my face burnt!
    " Has Mrs. Montagu," asked Dr. Johnson, " read
Evelina? "
    " No, sir, not yet; but I shall immediately, for
I feel the greatest eagerness to read it."
    " I am very sorry, madam," replied he, " that you
have not read it already, because you cannot speak
of it with a full conviction of its merits: which, I
believe, when you have read it, you will find great
pleasure in acknowledging."
    Some other things were said, but I remember them
not, for I could hardly keep my place: but my sweet,
naughty Mrs. Thrale looked delighted for me.
    I made tea as usual, and Mrs. Montagu and Miss
Gregory seated themselves on each side of me.
    " I can see," said the former, " that Miss Burney
is very like her father, and that is a good thing, for
everybody would wish to be like Dr. Burney. Pray,

when you see him, give my best respects to him; I am
afraid he thinks me a thief with his *Linguet;*[1] but I
assure you I am a very honest woman, and I spent
full three hours in looking for it."

"I am sure," cried Mrs. Thrale, "Dr. Burney
would much rather you should have employed that
time about the other book."

They went away very early, because Mrs. Montagu is a great coward in a carriage. She repeated
her invitation as she left the room. So now that I
am invited to Mrs. Montagu's, I think the measure of
my glory full!

When they were gone, how did Dr. Johnson as-
tonish me by asking if I had observed what an ugly
cap Miss Gregory had on? And then taking both
my hands, and looking at me with an expression of
much kindness, he said,

"Well, Miss Burney, Mrs. Montagu now will
read *Evelina.*"

To read it he seems to think is all that is wanted,
and, far as I am from being of the same opinion, I
dare not to him make disqualifying speeches, because
it might seem impertinent to suppose her more difficult to please than himself.

"You are very kind, sir," cried I, "to speak of
it with so much favour and indulgence at dinner;
yet I hardly knew *how* to sit it then, though I shall
be always proud to remember it hereafter."

---

[1] A French polemical writer (1736-1794). Dr. Burney had lent a
volume of his works to Mrs. Montagu; she had lost it. (*Diary,*
I. 121.)

"Why, it is true," said he, kindly, "that such things are disagreeable to sit, nor do I wonder you were distressed; yet sometimes they are necessary."

Was this not very kind? I am sure he meant that the sanction of his good opinion, so publicly given to Mrs. Montagu, would in a manner stamp the success of my book; and though, had I been allowed to preserve the snugness I had planned, I need not have concerned myself at all about its fate, yet now that I find myself exposed with it, I cannot but wish it insured from disgrace.

"Well, sir," cried I, "I don't think I shall mind Mrs. Montagu herself now; after what you have said, I believe I should not mind even abuse from any one."

"No, no, never mind them!" cried he; "resolve not to mind them: they can do you no serious hurt."

Mrs. Thrale then told me such civil things. Mrs. Montagu, it seems, during my retreat, inquired very particularly what kind of book it was?

"And I told her," continued Mrs. Thrale, "that it was a picture of life, manners, and characters. 'But won't she go on?' says she; 'surely she won't stop here?'

"'Why,' said I, 'I want her to go on a new path —I want her to write a comedy.'

"'But,' said Mrs. Montagu, 'one thing must be considered; Fielding, who was so admirable in novel-writing, never succeeded when he wrote for the stage.'"

"Very well said," cried Dr. Johnson; "that was

an answer which showed she considered her subject."

Monday, September 21.—I am more comfortable
here than ever; Dr. Johnson honours me with increasing kindness; Mr. Thrale is much more easy and sociable than when I was here before; I am quite jocose,
whenever I please, with Miss Thrale; and the charming head and life of the house, her mother, stands the
test of the closest examination, as well and as much to
her honour as she does a mere cursory view. She is,
indeed, all that is excellent and desirable in woman.

I have had a thousand delightful conversations
with Dr. Johnson, who, whether he loves me or not,
I am sure seems to have some opinion of my discretion, for he speaks of all this house to me with unbounded confidence, neither diminishing faults, nor
exaggerating praise. Whenever he is below stairs he
keeps me a prisoner, for he does not like I should
quit the room a moment; if I rise he constantly calls
out, " Don't you go, little Burney! "

Last night, when we were talking of compliments
and gross speeches, Mrs. Thrale most justly said
that nobody could make either like Dr. Johnson.
" Your compliments, sir, are made seldom, but when
they are made they have an elegance unequalled;
but then when you are angry, who dares make
speeches so bitter and so cruel? "

Dr. J.—Madam, I am always sorry when I make
bitter speeches, and I never do it but when I am
insufferably vexed.

Mrs. T.—Yes, sir; but you suffer things to vex you, that nobody else would vex at. I am sure I have had my share of scolding from you!

Dr. J.—It is true, you have; but you have borne it like an angel, and you have been the better for it.

Mrs. T.—That I believe, sir: for I have received more instruction from you than from any man, or any book; and the vanity that you should think me worth instruction, always overcame the vanity of being found fault with. And you had the scolding and I the improvement.

F. B.—And I am sure both make for the honour of both.

Dr. J.—I think so too. But Mrs. Thrale is a sweet creature, and never angry; she has a temper the most delightful of any woman I ever knew.

Mrs. T.—This I can tell you, sir, and without any flattery—I not only bear your reproofs when present, but in almost everything I do in your absence, I ask myself whether you would like it, and what you would say to it. Yet I believe there is nobody you dispute with oftener than me.

F. B.—But you two are so well established with one another, that you can bear a rebuff that would kill a stranger.

Dr. J.—Yes; but we disputed the same before we were so well established with one another.

Mrs. T.—Oh, sometimes I think I shall die no other death than hearing the bitter things he says to others. What he says to myself I can bear, because

I know how sincerely he is my friend, and that he means to mend me; but to others it is cruel.

Dr. J.—Why, madam, you often provoke me to say severe things, by unreasonable commendation.[1] If you would not call for my praise, I would not give you my censure; but it constantly moves my indignation to be applied to, to speak well of a thing which I think contemptible.

F. B.—Well, this I know, whoever I may hear complain of Dr. Johnson's severity, I shall always vouch for his kindness, as far as regards myself, and his indulgence.

Mrs. T.—Ay, but I hope he will trim you yet, too!

Dr. J.—I hope not: I should be very sorry to say anything that should vex my dear little Burney.

F. B.—If you did, sir, it would vex me more than you can imagine. I should sink in a minute.

Mrs. T.—I remember, sir, when we were travelling in Wales,[2] how you called me to account for my civility to the people; "Madam," you said, "let me have no more of this idle commendation of nothing. Why is it, that whatever you see, and whoever you

---

[1] "Mrs. Thrale gave high praise to Mr. Dudley Long (now North). JOHNSON. 'Nay, my dear lady, don't talk so. Mr. Long's character is very *short*. It is nothing. He fills a chair. He is a man of genteel appearance, and that is all. I know nobody who blasts by praise as you do: for wherever there is exaggerated praise, everybody is set against a character. They are provoked to attack it. Now there is Pepys; you praised that man with such disproportion, that I was incited to lessen him, perhaps more than he deserves. His blood is upon your head.'" (*Life*, 4. 81-82.)
[2] In 1774.

see, you are to be so indiscriminately lavish of
praise?" "Why, I'll tell you, sir," said I, "when I
am with you, and Mr. Thrale, and Queeny, I am
obliged to be civil for four!"

There was a cutter for you! But this I must say,
for the honour of both—Mrs. Thrale speaks to Dr.
Johnson with as much sincerity (though with greater
softness), as he does to her.

Streatham, September 26.—I have, from want of
time, neglected my journal so long, that I cannot
now pretend to go on methodically, and be particular
as to dates.

Messrs. Stephen and Rose Fuller [1] stayed very
late on Monday; the former talking very rationally
upon various subjects, and the latter boring us with
his systems and "those sort of things." Yet he is
something of a favourite, "in that sort of way," at
this house, because of his invincible good humour,
and Mrs. Thrale says she would not change him as a
neighbour for a much wiser man. Dr. Johnson says
he would make a very good Mr. Smith: [2] "Let him
but," he adds, "pass a month or two in Holborn,
and I would desire no better."

The other evening the conversation fell upon Rom-
ney, the painter, who has lately got into great business, and who was first recommended and patronized
by Mr. Cumberland.

[1] For Rose Fuller, see above, p. 41. Stephen Fuller was his
uncle.
[2] A character in *Evelina,* a notable bore and intruder.

" See, madam," said Dr. Johnson, laughing, " what it is to have the favour of a literary man! I think I have had no hero a great while; Dr. Goldsmith was my last; but I have had none since his time till my little Burney came! "

" Ay, sir," said Mrs. Thrale, " Miss Burney is the heroine now; is it not really true, sir? "

" To be sure it is, my dear! " answered he, with a gravity that made not only me, but Mr. Thrale laugh heartily.

Another time, Mr. Thrale said he had seen Dr. Jebb,[1] " and he told me he was afraid Miss Burney would have gone into a consumption," said he; " but I informed him how well you are, and he committed you to my care; so I shall insist now upon being sole judge of what wine you drink."

(N.B. He had often disputed this point.)

Dr. J.—Why, did Dr. Jebb forbid her wine?

F. B.—Yes, sir.

Dr. J.—Well, he was in the right; he knows how apt wits are to transgress that way. He was certainly right!

In this sort of ridiculous manner he *wits* me eternally. But the present chief sport with Mrs. Thrale is disposing of me in the holy state of matrimony, and she offers me whoever comes to the house. This was begun by Mrs. Montagu, who, it seems, proposed a match for me in my absence, with Sir Joshua Reynolds!—no less a man, I assure you!

---

[1] Mr. Thrale's physician; see above, p. 36.

When I was dressing for dinner, Mrs. Thrale told me that Mr. Crutchley was expected.

" Who's he? " quoth I.

" A young man of very large fortune, who was a ward of Mr. Thrale.¹ Queeny, what do you say of him for Miss Burney? "

" Him? " cried she; " no, indeed; what has Miss Burney done to have him? "

" Nay, believe me, a man of his fortune may offer himself anywhere. However, I won't recommend him."

" Why then, ma'am," cried I, with dignity, " I reject him! "

This Mr. Crutchley stayed till after breakfast the next morning. I can't tell you anything of him, because I neither like nor dislike him.

Mr. Crutchley was scarce gone, ere Mr. Smith arrived. Mr. Smith is a second cousin of Mr. Thrale, and a modest pretty sort of young man.

He stayed till Friday morning. When he was gone,

" What say you to him, Miss Burney? " cried Mrs. Thrale—" I am sure I offer you variety."

" Why, I like him better than Mr. Crutchley, but I don't think I shall pine for either of them."

" Dr. Johnson," said Mrs. Thrale, " don't you think Jerry Crutchley very much improved? "

Dr. J.—Yes, madam, I think he is.

---

¹ Jeremiah Crutchley was thought by Mrs. Thrale to be her husband's natural son. He was later one of Thrale's executors.

Mrs. T.—Shall he have Miss Burney?

Dr. J.—Why, I think not; at least I must know more of him; I must inquire into his connections, his recreations, his employments, and his character, from his intimates, before I trust Miss Burney with him. And he must come down very handsomely with a settlement. I will not have him left to his generosity; for as he will marry her for her wit, and she him for his fortune, he ought to bid well; and let him come down with what he will, his price will never be equal to her worth.

Mrs. T.—She says she likes Mr. Smith better.

Dr. J.—Yes, but I won't have her like Mr. Smith without the money, better than Mr Crutchley with it. Besides, if she has Crutchley, he will use her well, to vindicate his choice. The world, madam, has a reasonable claim upon all mankind to account for their conduct; therefore, if with his great wealth he marries a woman who has but little, he will be more attentive to display her merit than if she was equally rich,— in order to show that the woman he has chosen deserves from the world all the respect and admiration it can bestow, or that else she would not have been his choice.

Mrs. T.—I believe young Smith is the better man.

F. B.—Well, I won't be rash in thinking of either; I will take some time for consideration before I fix.

Dr. J.—Why, I don't hold it to be delicate to offer marriage to ladies, even in jest, nor do I approve such sort of jocularity; yet for once I must break through the rules of decorum, and propose a match myself

for Miss Burney. I therefore nominate Sir J——
L——.[1]

Mrs. T.—I'll give you my word, sir, you are not
the first to say that, for my master, the other morning,
when we were alone, said, " What would I give that
Sir J—— L—— was married to Miss Burney; it
might restore him to our family." So spoke his
uncle and guardian.

F. B.—He, he! Ha, ha! He, he! Ha, ha!

Dr. J.—That was elegantly said of my master, and
nobly said, and not in the vulgar way we have been
saying it. And where, madam, will you find another
man in trade, who will make such a speech—who will
be capable of making such a speech? Well, I am
glad my master takes so to Miss Burney; I would
have everybody take to Miss Burney, so as they
allow me to take to her most! Yet I don't know
whether Sir J—— L—— should have her, neither.
I should be afraid for her; I don't think I would
hand her to him.

F. B.—Why, now, what a fine match is here broken
off!

Some time after, when we were in the library, he
asked me very gravely if I loved reading?

" Yes," quoth I.

" Why do you doubt it, sir? " cried Mrs. Thrale.

" Because," answered he, " I never see her with
a book in her hand. I have taken notice that she
never has been reading whenever I have come into
the room."

---

[1] Sir John Lade; see above, pp. 33 ff.

" Sir," quoth I courageously, " I am always afraid of being caught reading, lest I should pass for being studious or affected, and therefore instead of making a display of books, I always try to hide them, as is the case at this very time, for I have now your *Life of Waller* under my gloves behind me. However, since I am piqued to it, I'll boldly produce my voucher."

And so saying, I put the book on the table, and opened it with a flourishing air. And then the laugh was on my side, for he could not help making a droll face; and if he had known Kitty Cooke,[1] I would have called out, " There I had you, my lad! "

" And now," quoth Mrs. Thrale, " you must be more careful than ever of not being thought bookish, for now you are known for a wit and a *bel esprit*, you will be watched, and if you are not upon your guard, all the misses will rise up against you."

Dr. J.—Nay, nay, now it is too late. You may read as much as you will now, for you are in for it,— you are dipped over head and ears in the Castalian stream, and so I hope you will be invulnerable.

Another time, when we were talking of the licentiousness of the newspapers, Dr. Johnson said,

" I wonder they have never yet had a touch at little Burney."

" Oh, Heaven forbid! " cried I: " I am sure if they did, I believe I should try the depth of Mr. Thrale's spring-pond."

" No, no, my dear, no," cried he kindly, " you must

---

[1] The niece of the woman with whom Mr. Crisp lodged, noted for her quaint absurdities of speech. (See *Early Diary, passim.*)

resolve not to mind them; you must set yourself against them, and not let any such nonsense affect you."

" There is nobody," said Mrs. Thrale, " tempers the satirist with so much meekness as Miss Burney."

Satirist, indeed! is it not a satire upon words, to call me so?

" I hope to Heaven I shall never be tried," cried I, " for I am sure I should never bear it. Of my book they may say what they will and welcome, but if they touch at me—I shall be——"

" Nay," said Mrs. Thrale, " if you are not afraid for the book, I am sure they can say no harm of the author."

" Never let them know," said Dr. Johnson, " which way you shall most mind them, and then they will stick to the book; but you must never acknowledge how tender you are for the author."

Monday was the day for our great party; and the doctor came home, at Mrs. Thrale's request, to meet them. . . .

Lady Ladd; I ought to have begun with her.[1] I beg her ladyship a thousand pardons—though if she knew my offence, I am sure I should not obtain one. She is own sister to Mr. Thrale. She is a tall and stout woman, has an air mingled with dignity and haughtiness, both of which wear off in conversation. She dresses very youthfully and gaily, and attends to her person with no little complacency. She appears

[1] She has just been enumerating the guests.

to me uncultivated in knowledge, though an adept in
the manners of the world, and all that. She chooses
to be much more lively than her brother; but liveliness sits as awkwardly upon her as her pink ribbons.
In talking her over with Mrs. Thrale, who has a very
proper regard for her, but who, I am sure, cannot be
blind to her faults, she gave me another proof to
those I have already had, of the uncontrolled freedom of speech which Dr. Johnson exercises to everybody, and which everybody receives quietly from him.
Lady Ladd has been very handsome, but is now, I
think, quite ugly—at least she has a sort of face I
like not. Well, she was a little while ago dressed in
so showy a manner as to attract the doctor's notice,
and when he had looked at her some time he broke
out aloud into this quotation:

> "With patches, paint, and jewels on,
> Sure Phillis is not twenty-one!
> But if at night you Phillis see,
> The dame at least is forty-three!"

I don't recollect the verses exactly, but such was their
purport.

"However," said Mrs. Thrale, "Lady Ladd took
it very good-naturedly, and only said,

"'I know enough of that forty-three—I don't desire to hear any more about it!'" . . .

In the evening the company divided pretty much
into parties, and almost everybody walked upon the
gravel-walk before the windows. I was going to have

joined some of them, when Dr. Johnson stopped me, and asked how I did.

"I was afraid, sir," cried I, "you did not intend to know me again, for you have not spoken to me before since your return from town."

"My dear," cried he, taking both my hands, "I was not sure of you, I am so near-sighted,[1] and I apprehended making some mistake."

Then drawing me very unexpectedly towards him, he actually kissed me!

To be sure, I was a little surprised, having no idea of such facetiousness from him. However, I was glad nobody was in the room but Mrs. Thrale, who stood close to us, and Mr. Embry, who was lounging on a sofa at the farthest end of the room, Mrs. Thrale laughed heartily, and said she hoped I was contented with his amends for not knowing me sooner.

A little after she said she would go and walk with the rest if she did not fear for my reputation in being left with the doctor.

"However, as Mr. Embry is yonder, I think he'll take some care of you," she added.

"Ay, madam," said the doctor, "we shall do very well; but I assure you I shan't part with Miss Burney!"

And he held me by both hands; and when Mrs. Thrale went, he drew me a chair himself facing the window, close to his own; and thus *tête-à-tête* we continued almost all the evening. I say *tête-à-tête*, be-

[1] Cf. pp. 3, 63, 156.

cause Mr. Embry kept at an humble distance, and offered us no interruption. And though Mr. Seward soon after came in, he also seated himself in a distant corner, not presuming, he said, to break in upon us! Everybody, he added, gave way to the doctor.

Our conversation chiefly was upon the Hebrides, for he always talks to me of Scotland, out of sport; and he wished I had been of that tour [1]—quite gravely, as I assure you!

Tuesday morning our breakfast was delightful. We had Mr. Seward, Mr. Embry, and Lady Ladd added to our usual party, and Dr. Johnson was quite in a sportive humour. But I can only write some few speeches, wanting time to be prolix, not inclination.

"Sir," said Mrs. Thrale to Dr. Johnson, "why did you not sooner leave your wine yesterday, and come to us? we had a Miss who sung and played like anything!"

"Ay, had you?" said he drolly; "and why did you not call me to the rapturous entertainment?"

"Why, I was afraid you would not have praised her, for I sat thinking all the time myself whether it were better to sing and play as she sang and played, or to do nothing. And at first I thought she had the best of it, for we were but stupid before she began; but afterwards she made it so long, that I thought *nothing* had all the advantage. But, sir, Lady Ladd has had the same misfortune you had, for she has fallen down and hurt herself woefully."

[1] The famous tour with Boswell in 1773.

"How did that happen, madam?"

"Why, sir, the heel of her shoe caught in something."

"Heel?" replied he; "nay, then, if her ladyship, who walks six foot high" (*N.B.* this is a fact), "will wear a high heel, I think she almost deserves a fall."

"Nay, sir, my heel was not so high!" cried Lady Ladd.

"But, madam, why should you wear any? That for which there is no occasion, had always better be dispensed with. However, a fall to your ladyship is nothing," continued he, laughing; "you, who are light and little, can soon recover; but I who am a gross man, might suffer severely; with your ladyship the case is different, for

"'Airy substance soon unites again.'"

Poor Lady Ladd, who is quite a strapper,[1] made no answer, but she was not offended. Mrs. Thrale and I afterwards settled, that not knowing his allusion from the *Rape of the Lock,* she only thought he had made a stupid sort of speech, and did not trouble herself to find a meaning to it.

"However," continued he, "if my fall does confine me, I will make my confinement pleasant, for Miss Burney shall nurse me—positively!" (and he slapped his hand on the table), "and then, she shall sing to me, and soothe my cares."

[1] See above, p. 70, where she and Johnson are said to be of a size.

When public news was started, Mr. Thrale desired the subject might be waived till my father came, and could let us know what part of the late accounts were true.

Mr. Thrale then offered to carry Mr. Seward, who was obliged to go to town, in the coach with him, —and Mr. Embry also left us. But Dr. Johnson sat with Mrs. Thrale and Lady Ladd, and me for an hour or two.

The subject was given by Lady Ladd; it was the respect due from the lower class of the people.

" I know my place," said she, " and I always take it: and I've no notion of not taking it. But Mrs. Thrale lets all sort of people do just as they've a mind by her."

" Ay," said Mrs. Thrale, " why should I torment and worry myself about all the paltry marks of respect that consist in bows and courtesies?—I have no idea of troubling myself about the manners of all the people I mix with."

" No,' said Lady Ladd, " so they will take all sorts of liberties with you. I remember, when you were at my house, how the hair-dresser flung down the comb as soon as you were dressed, and went out of the room without making a bow."

" Well, all the better," said Mrs. Thrale; " for if he had made me one, ten thousand to one if I had seen it. I was in as great haste to have done with him, as he could be to have done with me. I was glad enough to get him out of the room; I did not want him to stand bowing and cringing."

"If any man had behaved so insolently to me," answered she, "I would never again have suffered him in my house."

"Well," said Mrs. Thrale, "your ladyship has a great deal more dignity than I have!—Dr. Johnson, we are talking of the respect due from inferiors;—and Lady Ladd is of the same side you are."

"Why, madam," said he, "subordination is always necessary to the preservation of order and decorum."[1]

"I protest," said Lady Ladd, "I have no notion of submitting to any kind of impertinence: and I never will bear either to have any person nod to me, or enter a room, where I am, without bowing."

"But, madam," said Dr. Johnson, "what if they will nod, and what if they won't bow?—how then?"

"Why, I always tell them of it," said she.

"Oh, commend me to that!" cried Mrs. Thrale; "I'd sooner never see another bow in my life, than turn dancing-master to hair-dressers."

The doctor laughed his approbation, but said that every man had a right to a certain degree of respect, and no man liked to be defrauded of that right.

"Well, sir," said Mrs. Thrale, "I hope you meet with respect enough!"

"Yes, madam," answered he, "I am very well contented."

"Nay, if you an't, I don't know who should be; for I believe there is no man in the world so greatly respected."

[1] Cf. *Life,* 3. 383.

Soon after he went, I went, and shut myself up in a sweet cool summer-house, to read *Irene:*—which, indeed, though not a good play, is a beautiful poem.

As my dear father spent the rest of the day here, I will not further particularize, but leave accounts to his better communication. He probably told you that the P—— family came in to tea; and, as he knows Mrs. P——, pray tell him what Dr. Johnson says of her. When they were gone Mrs. Thrale complained that she was quite worn out with that tiresome silly woman, who had talked of her family and affairs till she was sick to death of hearing her.

"Madam," said he, "why do you blame the woman for the only sensible thing she can do—talking of her family and her affairs? For how should a woman who is as empty as a drum, talk upon any other subject?—If you speak to her of the sun, she does not know it rises in the east;—if you speak to her of the moon, she does not know it changes at the full; if you speak to her of the queen, she does not know she is the king's wife;—how, then, can you blame her for talking of her family and affairs?"

On Friday, I had a visit from Dr. Johnson! he came on purpose to reason with me about this pamphlet, which he had heard from my father had so greatly disturbed me.[1]

Shall I not love him more than ever? However,

---

[1] Soon after her return home, a pamphlet entitled *Warley: a Satire,* appeared, announcing the name of the author of *Evelina.* It was anonymous, but was addressed to Sir Joshua Reynolds. Its appearance well-nigh prostrated Miss Burney.

Miss Young [1] was just arrived, and Mr. Bremner [1] spent the evening here, and therefore he had the delicacy and goodness to forbear coming to the point. Yet he said several things that I understood, though they were unintelligible to all others; and he was more kind, more good-humoured, more flattering to me than ever. Indeed, my uneasiness upon this subject has met with more indulgence from him than from anybody. He repeatedly charged me not to fret; and bid me not repine at my success, but think of Floretta,[2] in the Fairy Tale, who found sweetness and consolation in her wit sufficient to counter-balance her scoffers and libellers! Indeed he was all good humour and kindness, and seemed quite bent on giving me comfort as well as flattery.

I shall now skip to the Thursday following, when I accompanied my father to Streatham. We had a delightful ride, though the day was horrible.

In two minutes we were joined by Mr. Seward, and in four, by Dr. Johnson. Mr. Seward, though a reserved, and cold young man, has a heart open to friendship, and very capable of good-nature and goodwill, though I believe it abounds not with them to all indiscriminately: but he really loves my father, and his reserve once, is always, conquered. He seemed heartily glad to see us both: and the dear

---

[1] Miss Dorothy Young and Mr. Robert Bremner were friends of the family, who make an occasional but no very important appearance in the pages of the *Diary*.

[2] Johnson's own creation, the heroine of a fairy-tale entitled, *The Fountains*, which Johnson contributed to Mrs. Williams's *Miscellanies*. (See *Life*, 2. 232.)

Dr. Johnson was more kind, more pleased, and more delightful than ever. Our several meetings in town seem to have quite established me in his favour, and I flatter myself that if he were now accused of loving me, he would not deny it, nor, as before, insist on waiting longer ere he went so far.[1]

"I hope, Dr. Burney," cried Mr. Seward, "you are now come to stay?"

"No!" cried my father, shaking his head, "that is utterly out of my power at present."

"Well, but this fair lady"— (N.B.—Fair and brown are synonymous terms in conversation, however opposite in looks) "I hope will stay?"

"No, no, no!" was the response, and he came to me and pressed the invitation very warmly; but Dr. Johnson, going to the window, called me from him.

"Well, my dear," cried he, in a low voice, "and how are you now? have you done fretting? have you got over your troubles?"

"Ah, sir," quoth I, "I am sorry they told you of my folly; yet I am very much obliged to you for bearing to hear of it with so much indulgence, for I had feared it would have made you hold me cheap ever after."

"No, my dear, no! What should I hold you cheap for? It did not surprise me at all; I thought it very natural; but you must think no more of it."

F. B.—Why, sir, to say the truth, I don't know, after all, whether I do not owe the affair in part to you!

[1] See above, p. 73.

An unpublished letter of Sir Joshua Reynolds' to Mrs. Thrale,
referring to Miss Burney

Dr. J.—To me? how so?

F. B.—Why, the appellation of " little Burney," I think, must have come from you, for I know of nobody else that calls me so.

This is a fact, Susy, and the " dear little Burney," makes it still more suspicious, for I am sure Sir Joshua Reynolds would never speak of me so facetiously after only one meeting.

Dr. Johnson seemed almost shocked, and warmly denied having been any way accessory.

" Why, sir," cried I, " they say the pamphlet was written by a Mr. Huddisford. Now I never saw, never heard of him before; how, therefore, should he know whether I am little or tall? he could not call me little by inspiration; I might be a Patagonian for anything he could tell."

Dr. J.—Pho! fiddle-faddle; do you suppose your book is so much talked of and not yourself? Do you think your readers will not ask questions, and inform themselves whether you are short or tall, young or old? Why should you put it on me?

After this he made me follow him into the library, that we might continue our confab without interruption; and just as we were seated, entered Mrs. Thrale. I flew to her, and she received me with the sweetest cordiality. They placed me between them, and we had a most delicious trio.

We talked over the visit at Sir Joshua's; and Dr. Johnson told me that Mrs. Cholmondeley was the first person who publicly praised and recommended *Evelina* among the wits. Mrs. Thrale told me that at Tunbridge and Brightelmstone it was the universal topic; and that Mrs. Montagu had pronounced the dedication to be so well written, that she could not but suppose it must be the doctor's.

" She is very kind," quoth I, " because she likes one part better than another, to take it from me!"

" You must not mind that," said Dr. Johnson, " for such things are always said where books are successful. There are three distinct kind of judges upon all new authors or productions; the first are those who know no rules, but pronounce entirely from their natural taste and feelings; the second are those who know and judge by rules; and the third are those who know, but are above the rules. These last are those you should wish to satisfy. Next to them rate the natural judges; but ever despise those opinions that are formed by the rules."

Mrs. Thrale wanted me much to stay all night, but it could not be.

Last week I called on Mrs. Williams, and Dr. Johnson, who had just returned from Streatham, came down stairs to me, and was so kind! I quite doat on him; and I really believe that, take away Mr. Crisp, there is no man out of this house who has so real and affectionate a regard for me; and I am sure, take away the same person, I can with the utmost truth say the same thing in return.

I asked after the Streathamites.

" Why," said he, " we now only want you—we have Miss Streatfield, Miss Brown, Murphy, and

Seward [1]—we only want you! Has Mrs. Thrale
called on you lately? "

" Yes, sir."

" Ah," said he, " you are such a darling! "

Mrs. Williams added a violent compliment to
this, but concluded with saying,

" My only fear is lest she should put me in a
book! "

" Sir Joshua Reynolds," answered Dr. Johnson,
" says, that if he were conscious to himself of any
trick, or any affectation, there is nobody he should
so much fear as this little Burney! "

This speech he told me once before, so that I find
it has struck him much.

Streatham, February.—I have been here so long,
my dearest Susan, without writing a word, that now
I hardly know where or how to begin. But I will
try to draw up a concise account of what has passed
for this last fortnight, and then endeavour to be
more minute.

Mrs. Thrale and Dr. Johnson vied with each other
in the kindness of their reception of me. Mr. Thrale
was, as usual at first, cold and quiet, but soon, as
usual also, warmed into sociality.

The next day Sir Philip Jennings Clerke [2] came.
He is not at all a man of letters, but extremely well-
bred, nay, elegant, in his manners, and sensible and
agreeable in his conversation. He is a professed

[1] See above, pp. 2, 17, 35-36.
[2] For an account of him and of a similar discussion with Johnson,
see *Life*, 4. 80-81.

minority man, and very active and zealous in the opposition. He had, when I came, a bill in agitation concerning contractors—too long a matter to explain upon paper—but which was levelled against bribery and corruption in the ministry, and which he was to make a motion upon in the House of Commons the next week.

Men of such different principles as Dr. Johnson and Sir Philip, you may imagine, cannot have much sympathy or cordiality in their political debates; however, the very superior abilities of the former, and the remarkable good breeding of the latter, have kept both upon good terms; though they have had several arguments, in which each has exerted his utmost force for conquest.

The heads of one of their debates I must try to remember, because I should be sorry to forget. Sir Philip explained his bill; Dr. Johnson at first scoffed it; Mr. Thrale betted a guinea the motion would not pass, and Sir Philip, that he should divide a hundred and fifty upon it.

I am afraid, my dear Susan, you already tremble at this political commencement, but I will soon have done, for I know your taste too well to enlarge upon this theme.

Sir Philip, addressing himself to Mrs. Thrale, hoped she would not suffer the Tories to warp her judgment, and told me he hoped my father had not tainted my principles; and then he further explained his bill, and indeed made it appear so equitable, that Mrs. Thrale gave in to it, and wished her husband to

vote for it. He still hung back; but, to our general
surprise, Dr. Johnson, having made more particular
inquiries into its merits, first softened towards it,
and then declared it a very rational and fair bill, and
joined with Mrs. Thrale in soliciting Mr. Thrale's
vote.

Sir Philip was, and with very good reason, quite
delighted. He opened upon politics more amply,
and freely declared his opinions, which were so
strongly against the Government, and so much border-
ing upon the republican principles, that Dr. Johnson suddenly took fire; he called back his recantation, begged Mr. Thrale not to vote for Sir
Philip's bill, and grew very animated against his
antagonist.

" The bill," said he, " ought to be opposed by all
honest men! in itself, and considered simply, it is
equitable, and I would forward it; but when we find
what a faction it is to support and encourage, it
ought not to be listened to. All men should oppose
it who do not wish well to sedition! "

These, and several other expressions yet more
strong, he made use of; and had Sir Philip had less
unalterable politeness, I believe they would have had
a vehement quarrel. He maintained his ground,
however, with calmness and steadiness, though he had
neither argument nor wit at all equal to such an
opponent.

Dr. Johnson pursued him with unabating vigour
and dexterity, and at length, though he could not
convince, he so entirely baffled him, that Sir Philip

was self-compelled to be quiet—which, with a very good grace, he confessed.

Dr. Johnson, then, recollecting himself, and thinking as he owned afterwards, that the dispute grew too serious, with a skill all his own, suddenly and unexpectedly turned it to burlesque; and taking Sir Philip by the hand at the moment we arose after supper, and were separating for the night,

"Sir Philip," said he, "you are too liberal a man for the party to which you belong; I shall have much pride in the honour of converting you; for I really believe, if you were not spoiled by bad company, the spirit of faction would not have possessed you. Go, then, sir, to the House, but make not your motion! Give up your Bill, and surprise the world by turning to the side of truth and reason. Rise, sir, when they least expect you, and address your fellow-patriots to this purpose:—Gentlemen, I have, for many a weary day, been deceived and seduced by you. I have now opened my eyes; I see that you are all scoundrels—the subversion of all government is your aim. Gentlemen, I will no longer herd among rascals in whose infamy my name and character must be included. I therefore renounce you all, gentlemen, as you deserve to be renounced."

Then, shaking his hand heartily, he added,

"Go, sir, go to bed; meditate upon this recantation, and rise in the morning a more honest man than you laid down" [sic].

Now I must try to be rather more minute. On

Thursday, while my dear father was here, who should be announced but Mr. Murphy;[1] the man of all other strangers to me whom I most longed to see.

He is tall and well made, has a very gentleman-like appearance, and a quietness of manner upon his first address that, to me, is very pleasing. His face looks sensible, and his deportment is perfectly easy and polite.

When he had been welcomed by Mrs. Thrale, and had gone through the reception-salutations of Dr. Johnson and my father, Mrs. Thrale, advancing to me, said,

"But here is a lady I must introduce to you, Mr. Murphy; here is another F. B."

"Indeed!" cried he, taking my hand; "is this a sister of Miss Brown's?"

"No, no; this is Miss Burney."

"What!" cried he, staring, "is this—is this—this is not the lady that—that——"

"Yes, but it is," answered she, laughing.

"No, you don't say so? You don't mean the lady that——"

"Yes, yes, I do; no less a lady, I assure you."

He then said he was very glad of the honour of seeing me; and I sneaked away.

When we came up stairs, Mrs. Thrale charged me to make myself agreeable to Mr. Murphy.

"He may be of use to you, in what I am most eager for—your writing a play: he knows stage business so well; and if you will but take a fancy to one

[1] See above, p. 55, note 2.

another, he may be more able to serve you than all of us put together. My ambition is that Johnson should write your prologue, and Murphy your epilogue; then I shall be quite happy."

At tea-time, when I went into the library, I found Dr. Johnson reading, and Mrs. Thrale in close conference with Mr. Murphy.

" It is well, Miss Burney," said the latter, " that you have come, for we were abusing you most vilely; we were in the very act of pulling you to pieces."

" Don't you think her very like her father? " said Mrs. Thrale.

" Yes; but what a sad man is Dr. Burney for running away so! how long had he been here? "

Mrs. Thrale.—Oh, but an hour or two. I often say Dr. Burney is the most of a male coquet of any man I know; for he only gives one enough of his company to excite a desire for more.

Mr. Murphy.—Dr. Burney is, indeed, a most extraordinary man; I think I don't know such another; he is at home upon all subjects, and upon all so agreeable! he is a wonderful man! "

And now let me stop this conversation, to go back to a similar one with Dr. Johnson, who, a few days since, when Mrs. Thrale was singing our father's praise, used this expression:

" I love Burney: my heart goes out to meet him! "

" He is not ungrateful, sir," cried I; " for most heartily does he love you."

" Does he, madam? I am surprised at that."

"Why, sir? why should you have doubted it?"

"Because, madam, Dr. Burney is a man for all the world to love: it is but natural to love him."

I could almost have cried with delight at this cordial unlaboured *éloge*. Another time, he said:

"I much question if there is, in the world, such another man as Dr. Burney."

But to return to the tea-table.

"If I," said Mr. Murphy, looking very archly, "had written a certain book—a book I won't name, but a book I have lately read—I would next write a comedy."

"Good," cried Mrs. Thrale, colouring with pleasure; "do you think so too?"

"Yes, indeed; I thought so while I was reading it; it struck me repeatedly."

"Don't look at me, Miss Burney," cried Mrs. Thrale, "for this is no doing of mine. Well, I do wonder what Miss Burney will do twenty years hence, when she can blush no more; for now she can never bear the name of her book."

Mr. Murphy.—Nay, I name no book; at least no author: how can I, for I don't know the author; there is no name given to it: I only say, whoever wrote that book ought to write a comedy. Dr. Johnson might write it for aught I know.

F. B.—Oh yes!

Mr. Murphy.—Nay, I have often told him he does not know his own strength, or he would write a comedy; and so I think.

Dr. Johnson (laughing).—Suppose Burney and I begin together.

Mr. Murphy.—Ah, I wish you would! I wish you would Beaumont and Fletcher us!

F. B.—My father asked me, this morning, how my head stood. If he should have asked me this evening, I don't know what answer I must have made.

Mr. Murphy.—I have no wish to turn anybody's head: I speak what I really think;—comedy is the forte of that book. I laughed over it most violently: and if the author—I won't say who (all the time looking away from me)—will write a comedy, I will most readily, and with great pleasure, give any advice or assistance in my power.

" Well, now you are a sweet man! " cried Mrs. Thrale, who looked ready to kiss him. " Did not I tell you, Miss Burney, that Mr. Murphy was the man? "

Mr. Murphy.—All I can do, I shall be very happy to do; and at least, I will undertake to say I can tell what the sovereigns of the upper gallery will bear; for they are the most formidable part of an audience. I have had so much experience in this sort of work, that I believe I can always tell what will be hissed at least. And if Miss Burney will write, and will show me——

Dr. Johnson.—Come, come, have done with this now; why should you overpower her? Let's have no more of it. I don't mean to dissent from what you say; I think well of it, and approve of it; but you have said enough of it.

Mr. Murphy, who equally loves and reverences Dr. Johnson, instantly changed the subject.

The rest of the evening was delightful. Mr. Murphy told abundance of most excellent stories; Dr. Johnson was in exceeding good humour; and Mrs. Thrale all cheerfulness and sweetness.

For my part, in spite of her injunctions, I could not speak; I was in a kind of consternation. Mr. Murphy's speeches flattering as they were, made me tremble; for I cannot get out of my head the idea of disgracing so many people.[1]

After supper, Dr. Johnson turned the discourse upon silent folks—whether by way of reflection and reproof, or by accident, I know not; but I do know he is provoked with me for not talking more; and I was afraid he was seriously provoked; but, a little while ago, I went into the music-room, where he was *tête-à-tête* with Mrs. Thrale, and calling me to him, he took my hand, and made me sit next him, in a manner that seemed truly affectionate.

" Sir," cried I, " I was much afraid I was going out of your favour! "

" Why so? what should make you think so? "

" Why, I don't know—my silence, I believe. I began to fear you would give me up."

" No, my darling!—my dear little Burney, no. When I give you up——"

" What then, sir? " cried Mrs. Thrale.

" Why, I don't know; for whoever could give her

---

[1] Could a better explanation be given for her failure with *The Witlings?*

up would deserve worse than I can say; I know not what would be bad enough."

Yesterday, at night, I told Dr. Johnson the inquiry,[1] and added that I attributed it to my being at Streatham, and supposed the folks took it for granted nobody would be admitted there without knowing Latin, at least.

"No, my dear, no," answered he; "the man thought it because you have written a book—he concluded that a book could not be written by one who knew no Latin. And it is strange that it should—but, perhaps you do know it—for your shyness, and slyness, and pretending to know nothing, never took me in, whatever you may do with others. I always knew you for a toadling."

At our usual time of absconding, he would not let us go,[2] and was in high good humour; and when, at last, Mrs. Thrale absolutely refused to stay any longer, he took me by the hand and said,

"Don't you mind her, my little Burney; do you stay whether she will or not."

So away went Mrs. Thrale, and left us to a *tête-à-tête*.

Now I had been considering that perhaps I ought to speak to him of my new castle, lest hereafter he should suspect that I preferred the counsel of Mr. Murphy. I therefore determined to take this oppor-

[1] A gentleman had asked her whether she knew Latin. (*Diary,* 1. 207.)
[2] Cf. p. 29.

tunity, and after some general nothings, I asked if he would permit me to take a liberty with him?

He assented with the most encouraging smile. And then I said,

"I believe, sir, you heard part of what passed between Mr. Murphy and me the other evening, concerning—a—a comedy. Now, if I should make such an attempt, would you be so good as to allow me, any time before Michaelmas, to put it in the coach, for you to look over as you go to town?"

"To be sure, my dear!—What, have you begun a comedy, then?"

I told him how the affair stood. He then gave me advice which just accorded with my own wishes, viz., not to make known that I had any such intention; to keep my own counsel; not to whisper even the name of it; to raise no expectations, which were always prejudicial, and finally to have it performed while the town knew nothing of whose it was.

I readily reassured him of my hearty concurrence in his opinion; but he somewhat distressed me when I told him that Mr. Murphy must be in my confidence, as he had offered his services, by desiring he might be the last to see it.

What I shall do, I know not, for he has, himself, begged to be the first. Mrs. Thrale, however, shall guide me between them. He spoke highly of Mr. Murphy, too, for he really loves him. He said he would not have it in the coach, but that I should read it to him; however, I could sooner drown or hang!

When I would have offered some apology for the

attempt, he stopped me, and desired I would never make any.

" For," said he, " if it succeeds, it makes its own apology, if not——"

" If not," quoth I, " I cannot do worse than Dr. Goldsmith, when his play failed,—go home and cry! " [1]

He laughed, but told me repeatedly (I mean twice, which, for him, is very remarkable) that I might depend upon all the service in his power; and, he added, it would be well to make Murphy the last judge, " for he knows the stage," he said, " and I am quite ignorant of it."

Afterwards, grasping my hand with the most affectionate warmth, he said,

" I wish you success! I wish you well! my dear little Burney! "

When, at length, I told him I could stay no longer, and bid him good night, he said, " There is none like you, my dear little Burney! there is none like you!—good-night, my darling! " . . .

I forgot to mention that, when I told Dr. Johnson Mr. Murphy's kind offer of examining my plan, and the several rules he gave me, and owned that I had already gone too far to avail myself of his obliging intention, he said, " Never mind, my dear,—ah! you'll do without,—you want no rules! "

And now I cannot resist telling you of a dispute which Dr. Johnson had with Mrs. Thrale, the next

---

[1] See Mme. Piozzi's ' Anecdotes,' *Miscellanies,* 1. 311.

morning,[1] concerning me, which that sweet woman
had the honesty and good sense to tell me. Dr.
Johnson was talking to her and Sir Philip Jennings [2]
of the amazing progress made of late years in literature by the women. He said he was himself astonished at it, and told them he well remembered when
a woman who could spell a common letter was regarded as all accomplished; but now they vied with
the men in everything.

"I think, sir," said my friend Sir Philip, "the
young lady we have here is a very extraordinary
proof of what you say."

"So extraordinary, sir," answered he, "that I
know none like her,—nor do I believe there is, or
there ever was, a man who could write such a book so
young."

They both stared—no wonder, I am sure!—and Sir
Philip said,

"What do you think of Pope, sir? could not Pope
have written such a one?"

"Nay, nay," cried Mrs. Thrale, "there is no
need to talk of Pope; a book may be a clever book,
and an extraordinary book, and yet not want a Pope
for its author. I suppose he was no older than
Miss Burney when he wrote *Windsor Forest*;[3]
and I suppose *Windsor Forest* is equal to
Evelina!"

[1] June 24.
[2] Sir Philip Clerke; see above, p. 99.
[3] Pope began the composition of *Windsor Forest* at sixteen, and
completed it at twenty-five; Miss Burney wrote *Evelina* at twenty-
five.

"*Windsor Forest,*" repeated Dr. Johnson, "though so delightful a poem, by no means required the knowledge of life and manners, nor the accuracy of observation, nor the skill of penetration, necessary for composing such a work as *Evelina;* he who could ever write *Windsor Forest,* might as well write it young or old. Poetical abilities require not age to mature them; but *Evelina* seems a work that should result from long experience, and deep and intimate knowledge of the world; yet it has been written without either. Miss Burney is a real wonder. What she is, she is intuitively. Dr. Burney told me she had had the fewest advantages of any of his daughters, from some peculiar circumstances.[1] And such has been her timidity, that he himself had not any suspicion of her powers."

"Her modesty," said Mrs. Thrale (as she told me), "is really beyond bounds. It quite provokes me. And, in fact, I can never make out how the mind that could write that book could be ignorant of its value."

[1] These "peculiar circumstances" appear to have been simply Fanny's extreme shyness and her father's extreme carelessness. "At the age of eight she had not learned to read, and her sailor brother used often to divert himself by giving her a book upside down in order to see what she would make of it. Mrs. Burney's friends used to call her the ' little dunce.' " (Dobson's *Fanny Burney,* 11.) Dr. Burney placed two of his daughters at school in Paris during Fanny's girlhood, but Fanny is said to have been left at home for fear that she might turn Roman Catholic in Paris. When she was fifteen, her father again considered the plan of sending her away to school, but " the project, first postponed, was afterwards abandoned in consequence of Mr. Burney's second marriage." (Dobson, p. 7.) Fanny's education, therefore, was almost entirely derived from undirected private reading and from observation of such members of the " great world " as she chanced to meet.

"That, madam, is another wonder," answered my dear, dear Dr. Johnson, "for modesty with her is neither pretence nor decorum; 'tis an ingredient of her nature; for she who could part with such a work for twenty pounds, could know so little of its worth, or of her own, as to leave no possible doubt of her humility."

My kind Mrs. Thrale told me this with a pleasure that made me embrace her with gratitude; but the astonishment of Sir Philip Clerke at such an *éloge* from Dr. Johnson was quite, she says, comical.

Streatham, July 5.—I have hardly had any power to write, my dear Susy, since I left you, for my cold has increased so much that I have hardly been able to do anything.

Mr. Thrale, I think, is better, and he was cheerful all the ride. Mrs. Thrale made as much of me as if the two days had been two months.

I was heartily glad to see Dr. Johnson, and I believe he was not sorry to see me: he had inquired very much after me, and very particularly of Mrs. Thrale whether she loved me as well as she used to do.

He is better in health than I have ever seen him before; his journey [1] has been very serviceable to him, and he has taken a very good resolution to reform his diet; [2]—so has my daddy Crisp. I wish I could

---

[1] To Ashbourne and Lichfield. (See *Life,* 3. 395, note.)

[2] On August 3, he wrote to Dr. Taylor, "Since my return hither I have applied myself very diligently to the care of my health. My nights grew better at your house, and have never since been bad; . . . of the last fifty days I have . . . lived with much less animal food than has been my custom of late." (*Letters,* 2. 101.)

pit them one against the other, and see the effect of their emulation.

I wished twenty times to have transmitted to paper the conversation of the evening, for Dr. Johnson was as brilliant as I have ever known him—and that's saying something;—but I was not very well, and could only attend to him for present entertainment.

July 10.—Since I wrote last, I have been far from well—but I am now my own man again—*à peu-près*.

Very concise, indeed, must my journal grow, for I have now hardly a moment in my power to give it; however, I will keep up its chain, and mark, from time to time, the general course of things.

Sir Philip Jennings [1] has spent three days here, at the close of which he took leave of us for the summer, and set out for his seat in Hampshire. We were all sorry to lose him; he is a most comfortable man in society, for he is always the same—easy, good-humoured, agreeable, and well-bred. He has made himself a favourite to the whole house, Dr. Johnson included, who almost always prefers the company of an intelligent man of the world to that of a scholar.

July 20.—What a vile journalist do I grow!—it is, however, all I can do to keep it at all going; for, to let you a little into the nature of things, you must know that my studies occupy almost every moment that I spend by myself. Dr. Johnson gives us a Latin lesson every morning. I pique myself somewhat upon

---

[1] See above, pp. 99, 111.

being ready for him; so that really, when the copying my play, and the continual returning occurrences of every fresh day are considered, you will not wonder that I should find so little opportunity for scrawling letters.

What progress we may make in this most learned scheme I know not; but, as I have always told you, I am sure I fag more for fear of disgrace than for hope of profit. To devote so much time to acquire something I shall always dread to have known, is really unpleasant enough, considering how many things there are I might employ myself in that would have no such drawback. However, on the other side, I am both pleased and flattered that Dr. Johnson should think me worth inviting to be his pupil, and I shall always recollect with pride and with pleasure the instructions he has the goodness to give me; so, since I cannot without dishonour alter matters, 'tis as well to turn Frenchwoman, and take them in the *tant mieux* fashion.

Dr. Johnson has made resolutions exactly similar to yours,[1] and in general adheres to them with strictness, but the old Adam, as you say, stands in his way, as well as in his neighbours'. I wish I could pit you against each other for the sake of both. Yet he professes an aversion to you, because he says he is sure you are very much in his way with me! however, I believe you would neither of you retain much aversion if you had a fair meeting.

[1] This is an extract from a letter to Mr. Crisp dated July 30. The resolution was to reform his diet.

Do you know I have been writing to Dr. Johnson! I tremble to mention it; but he sent a message in a letter to Mrs. Thrale, to wonder why his pupils did not write to him,[1] and to hope they did not forget him: Miss Thrale, therefore, wrote a letter immediately, and I added only this little postscript:

" P.S.—Dr. Johnson's other pupil a little longs to add a few lines to this letter,—but knows too well that all she has to say might be comprised in signing herself his obliged and most obedient servant, F. B.: so that's better than a long rigmarole about nothing."

Thursday morning, April 13th.—I am now come to the present time, and will try, however brief, to be tolerably punctual.

Dr. Johnson has sent a bitter reproach to Mrs. Thrale of my not writing to him,[2] for he has not yet received a scrawl I have sent him. He says Dr. Barnard, the provost of Eton, has been singing the praises of my book, and that old Dr. Lawrence has read it through three times within this last month!

---

[1] In a letter to Mrs. Thrale dated October 28, Johnson says, " The two younglings, what hinders them from writing to me. I hope they do not forget me." (*Letters*, 2. 116.)

[2] In a letter to Mrs. Thrale dated April 11, Johnson says, " Queeney has been a good girl, and wrote me a letter; if Burney told you she would write, she told you a fib. She writes nothing to me. She can write home fast enough. I have a good mind not to let her know that Dr. Bernard, to whom I had recommended her novel, speaks of it with great recommendation; and that the copy which she lent me, has been read by Dr. Lawrence three times over. And yet what a gypsey it is. She no more minds me than if I were a Brangton. Pray speak to Queeney to write again." (*Letters*, 2.136-137.) Dr. Lawrence was Johnson's physician.

I am afraid he will pass for being superannuated for his pains!

"But don't tell Burney this," adds Dr. Johnson, "because she will not write to me, and values me no more than if I were a Branghton!"

Bath, May 28. . . . I found my dear Mrs. Thrale so involved in business, electioneering,[1] canvassing, and letter-writing, that after our first *embrassades,* we hardly exchanged a word till we got into the chaise next morning.

Dr. Johnson, however, who was with her, received me even joyfully; and, making me sit by him, began a gay and spirited conversation, which he kept up till we parted, though in the midst of all this bustle.

The next morning we rose at four o'clock, and when we came downstairs, to our great surprise, found Dr. Johnson waiting to receive and breakfast with us; though the night before he had taken leave of us, and given me the most cordial and warm assurances of the love he has for me, which I do indeed believe to be as sincere as I can wish; and I failed not to tell him the affectionate respect with which I return it; though, as well as I remember, we never came to this open declaration before.

We therefore drank our coffee with him, and then he handed us both into the chaise. He meant to have followed us to Bath, but Mrs. Thrale discour-

---

[1] Mr. Thrale was then engaged in canvassing for his re-election as M.P. for Southwark; in which work he was assisted not only by his wife, but by Johnson himself.

aged him, from a firm persuasion that he would be soon very horribly wearied of a Bath life:[1] an opinion in which I heartily join.

I have not seen Dr. Johnson since the day you left me,[2] when he came hither, and met Mrs. Ord, Mr. Hoole, Mrs. Reynolds, Baretti, the Paradises, Pepys, Castles, Dr. Dunbar,[3] and some others; and then he was in high spirits and good humour, talked all the talk, affronted nobody, and delighted everybody. I never saw him more sweet, nor better attended to by his audience. I have not been able to wait upon him since, nor, indeed, upon anybody, for we have not spent one evening alone since my return.

Since I wrote last I have drunk tea with Dr. Johnson.[4] My father took me to Bolt Court, and we found him, most fortunately, with only one brass-headed cane gentleman. Since that, I have had the pleasure to meet him again at Mrs. Reynolds's, when he offered to take me with him to Grub Street,[5] to see the ruins of the house demolished there in the late riots,[6] by a mob that, as he observed, could be no friend to the Muses! He inquired if I had ever yet

---

[1] He therefore went up to his lodgings in Bolt-Court, Fleet Street.
[2] Miss Burney writes from London to Mrs. Thrale, July 8.
[3] All these people, except the Castles, appear *passim* in the *Life*. Johnson mentions the same list in a letter to Mrs. Thrale, dated July 4, and adds, "And Pepys and I had all the talk." (*Letters*, 2. 183.) Cf. below, pp. 124 ff.
[4] From another letter to Mrs. Thrale.
[5] Now Milton Street.
[6] For Johnson's own description of the Gordon Riots, see *Life*, 3. 428 ff.

visited Grub Street? but was obliged to restrain his anger when I answered "No," because he acknowledged that he had never paid his respects to it himself. "However," says he, "you and I, Burney, will go together; we have a very good right to go, so we'll visit the mansions of our progenitors, and take up our own freedom together."

Well—*mal à propos* to all this [1]—Dr. Johnson, who expects nothing but what is good, and swallows nothing but what he likes, has delighted me with another volume of his *Lives*,[2]—that which contains Blackmore, Congreve, etc., which he tells me you have had! Oh what a writer he is! what instruction, spirit, intelligence, and vigour in almost every paragraph! Addison I think equal to any in the former batch; but he is rather too hard upon Prior, and makes Gay, I think, too insignificant. Some of the little poems of Prior seem to me as charming as any little poems can be; and Gay's pastorals I had hoped to have seen praised more liberally.[3]

Dr. Johnson, you know, came with my dear father the Thursday after our return.[4]

You cannot, I think, have been surprised that I

---

[1] From a letter to Mrs. Thrale, August 16.
[2] Bound proof-sheets, no doubt, for the books had not yet been published.
[3] "A Pastoral of an hundred lines may be endured; but who will hear of sheep and goats and myrtle bowers and purling rivulets, through five acts? Such scenes please barbarians in the dawn of literature, and children in the dawn of life." (*Life of Gay*.)
[4] From the Journal, December 6.

gave up my plan of going to town immediately: indeed I had no heart to leave either Mr. Thrale in a state so precarious,[1] or his dear wife in an agitation of mind hardly short of a fever.

Things now went on tolerably smooth, and Miss Thrale and I renewed our Latin exercises with Dr. Johnson, and with great *éclat* of praise. At another time I could have written much of him and of Mr. Seward, for many very good conversations past; but now I have almost forgot all about them.

Dr. Johnson is very gay and sociable [2] and comfortable, and quite as kind to me as ever; and says the Bodleian librarian has but done his duty,[3] and that when he goes to Oxford, he will write my name in the books, my age when I writ them, and sign the whole with his own; " and then," he says, " the world may know that we

' So mixed our studies, and so joined our fame '

For we shall go down hand in hand to posterity! ".

Mrs. Thrale, in cutting some fruit, had cut her finger, and asked me for some black sticking plaster, and as I gave it her out of my pocket-book, she was struck with the beautiful glossiness of the paper of

---

[1] Mr. Thrale, far from well when the journey had commenced, was taken seriously ill during its progress.

[2] From a letter to Dr. Burney, December 11.

[3] The Bodleian librarian had placed *Evelina* in his noble library, to the author's astonished delight.—*Note by F. B.*

a letter which peeped out of it, and rather *waggishly* asked me who wrote to me with so much elegant attention?

" Mrs. Gast," answered I.

" Oh," cried she, " do pray then let me see her hand."

I showed it her, and she admired it very justly, and said,

" Do show it to Mr. Crutchley; 'tis a mighty genteel hand indeed."

I complied, but took it from him as soon as he had looked at it. Indeed, he is the last man in the world to have even desired to read any letter not to himself.

Dr. Johnson now, who, too deaf to hear what was saying, wondered what we were thus handling about, asked an explanation.

" Why, we are all," said Mrs. Thrale, " admiring the hand of Fanny's Mr. Crisp's sister."

" And mayn't I admire it too? " cried he.

" Oh yes," said she; " show it him, Burney."

I put it in his hand, and he instantly opened and began reading it. Now though there was nothing in it but what must reflect honour upon Mrs. Gast, she had charged me not to show it; and, also, it was so *very* flattering to me, that I was quite consternated at this proceeding, and called out,

" Sir, it was only to show you the handwriting, and you have seen enough for that."

" I shall know best myself," answered he, laughing, " when I have seen enough."

And he read on. The truth is I am sure he took

it for granted they had all read it, for he had not heard a word that had passed.

I then gave Mrs. Thrale a reproachful glance for what she had done, and she jumped up, and calling out,

" So I have done mischief, I see! " and ran out of the room, followed by Queeny. I stayed hovering over the doctor to recover my property . . .

Here Dr. Johnson returned me my letter, with very warm praise of its contents. Mrs. Gast would not only have forgiven me, but have been much delighted had she heard his approbation of all she had written to me.

Streatham, June.—I found Dr. Johnson in admirable good humour, and our journey hither was extremely pleasant. I thanked him for the last batch of his poets,[1] and we talked them over almost all the way.

Sweet Mrs. Thrale received me with her wonted warmth of affection, but shocked me by her own ill looks,[2] and the increasing alteration in her person, which perpetual anxiety and worry have made. . . .

We had a good cheerful day, and in the evening Sir Richard Jebb came; and nothing can I recollect, but that Dr. Johnson *forced* me to sit on a very small sofa with him, which was hardly large enough for himself; and which would have made a subject for a

---

[1] See p. 119.
[2] Mr. Thrale had died in April. (See *Diary*, 1. 468 ff.)

print by Harry Bunbury [1] that would have diverted all London: *ergo,* it rejoiceth me that he was not present.

Wednesday.—We had a terrible noisy day. Mr. and Mrs. Cator came to dinner, and brought with them Miss Collison, a niece. Mrs. Nesbitt was also here, and Mr. Pepys.

The long war which has been proclaimed among the wits concerning Lord Lyttelton's *Life,* [2] by Dr. Johnson, and which a whole tribe of *blues,* with Mrs. Montagu, at their head, have vowed to execrate and revenge, now broke out with all the fury of the first actual hostilities, stimulated by long-concerted schemes and much spiteful information. Mr. Pepys, Dr. Johnson well knew, was one of Mrs. Montagu's steadiest abettors; and, therefore, as he had some time determined to defend himself with the first of

---

[1] The artist and caricaturist. Miss Burney later became well acquainted with him, though she had not yet met him. (*Diary,* 3. 303 ff., 323 ff.)

[2] The life of Lord Lyttelton (1709-1773) is the last of the series of Johnson's *Lives of the Poets.* It was unwillingly undertaken by Johnson, who would have preferred to have it done by one of his Lordship's friends; but it is not therefore either prejudiced or unusually severe. To a modern reader the author will perhaps seem to err on the side of indulgence. Of Lyttelton's works he says: "Lord Lyttelton's Poems are the works of a man of literature and judgment, devoting part of his time to versification. They have nothing to be despised, and little to be admired. Of his *Progress of Love,* it is sufficient blame to say that it is pastoral. His blank verse in *Blenheim* has neither much force nor much elegance. His little performances . . . are sometimes spritely, and sometimes insipid."

Boswell says of this that it "produced a declaration of war from Mrs. Montagu . . . between whom and his Lordship a commerce of reciprocal compliments had been carried on." (*Life,* 4. 64.)

them he met, this day he fell the sacrifice to his wrath.

In a long *tête-à-tête* which I accidentally had with Mr. Pepys before the company was assembled, he told me his apprehensions of an attack, and entreated me earnestly to endeavour to prevent it; modestly avowing he was no antagonist for Dr. Johnson; and yet declaring his personal friendship for Lord Lyttelton made him so much hurt by the *Life,* that he feared he could not discuss the matter without a quarrel, which, especially in the house of Mrs. Thrale, he wished to avoid.

It was, however, utterly impossible for me to serve him. I could have stopped Mrs. Thrale, with ease, and Mr. Seward with a hint, had either of them begun the subject; but, unfortunately, in the middle of dinner it was begun by Dr. Johnson himself, to oppose whom, especially as he spoke with great anger, would have been madness and folly.

Never before have I seen Dr. Johnson speak with so much passion.

" Mr. Pepys," he cried, in a voice the most enraged, " I understand you are offended by my *Life of Lord Lyttelton.* What is it you have to say against it? Come forth, man! Here am I, ready to answer any charge you can bring! "

" No, sir," cried Mr. Pepys, " not at present; I must beg leave to decline the subject. I told Miss Burney before dinner that I hoped it would not be started."

I was quite frightened to hear my own name men-

A caricature of Johnson, published soon after the *Lives of the Poets*

tioned in a debate which began so seriously; but Dr.
Johnson made not to this any answer; he repeated
his attack and his challenge, and a violent disputation
ensued, in which this great but *mortal* man did, to
own the truth, appear unreasonably furious and
grossly severe. I never saw him so before, and I
heartily hope I never shall again. He has been long
provoked, and justly enough, at the *sneaking* com-
plaints and murmurs of the Lytteltonians; and, therefore, his long-excited wrath, which hitherto had met
no object, now burst forth with a vehemence and bitterness almost incredible.

Mr. Pepys meantime never appeared to so much
advantage; he preserved his temper, uttered all that
belonged merely to himself with modesty, and all that
more immediately related to Lord Lyttelton with
spirit. Indeed, Dr. Johnson, in the very midst of the
dispute, had the candour and liberality to make him
a personal compliment by saying,

" Sir, all that you say, while you are vindicating
one who cannot thank you, makes me only think better
of you than I ever did before. Yet still I think you
do *me* wrong," etc., etc.

Some time after, in the heat of the argument, he
called out,

" The more my Lord Lyttelton is inquired after,
the worse he will appear; Mr. Seward has just heard
two stories of him, which corroborate all I have
related."

He then desired Mr. Seward to repeat them. Poor
Mr. Seward looked almost as frightened as myself

at the very mention of his name; but he quietly and immediately told the stories, which consisted of fresh instances, from good authorities, of Lord Lyttelton's illiberal behaviour to Shenstone; [1] and then he flung himself back in his chair and spoke no more during the whole debate, which I am sure he was ready to vote a bore.

One happy circumstance, however, attended the quarrel, which was the presence of Mr. Cator, who would by no means be prevented talking himself, either by reverence for Dr. Johnson, or ignorance of the subject in question; on the contrary, he gave his opinion, quite uncalled, upon everything that was said by either party, and that with an importance and pomposity, yet with an emptiness and verbosity, that rendered the whole dispute, when in his hands, nothing more than ridiculous, and compelled even the disputants themselves, all inflamed as they were, to laugh. To give a specimen—one speech will do for a thousand.

"As to this here question of Lord Lyttelton, I can't speak to it to the purpose, as I have not read his *Life,* for I have only read the *Life of Pope;* I have got the books though, for I sent for them last week, and they came to me on Wednesday, and then I began them; but I have not yet read *Lord Lyttelton. Pope* I have begun, and that is what I am now reading. But what I have to say about Lord Lyttelton is this here: Mr. Seward says that Lord Lyttelton's steward

---

[1] The instances given by Johnson are not in the *Life of Lyttelton* but in the *Life of Shenstone.* (Hill's edition, 3. 351.)

dunned Mr. Shenstone for his rent, by which I understand he was a tenant of Lord Lyttelton's. Well, if
he was a tenant of Lord Lyttelton's, why should not
he pay his rent?"

Who could contradict this?

When dinner was quite over, and we left the men
to their wine, we hoped they would finish the affair;
but Dr. Johnson was determined to talk it through,
and make a battle of it, though Mr. Pepys tried to
be off continually. When they were all summoned to
tea, they entered still warm and violent. Mr. Cator
had the book in his hand, and was reading the *Life
of Lyttelton,* that he might better, he said, understand the cause, though not a creature cared if he
had never heard of it.

Mr. Pepys came up to me and said,

"Just what I had so much wished to avoid! I
have been crushed in the very onset."

I could make him no answer for Dr. Johnson immediately called him off, and harangued and attacked
him with a vehemence and continuity that quite concerned both Mrs. Thrale and myself, and that made
Mr. Pepys, at last, resolutely silent, however called
upon.

This now grew more unpleasant than ever; till Mr.
Cator, having some time studied his book, exclaimed,

"What I am now going to say, as I have not yet
read the *Life of Lord Lyttelton* quite through, must
be considered as being only said aside, because what I
am going to say——"

"I wish, sir," cried Mrs. Thrale, "it had been all

set aside; here is too much about it, indeed, and I
should be very glad to hear no more of it."

This speech, which she made with great spirit and
dignity, had an admirable effect. Everybody was
silenced. Mr. Cator, thus interrupted in the midst of
his proposition, looked quite amazed; Mr. Pepys was
much gratified by the interference; and Dr. Johnson,
after a pause, said,

"Well, madam, you *shall* hear no more about it;
yet I will defend myself in every part and in every
atom!"

And from this time the subject was wholly dropped.
This dear violent Doctor was conscious he had been
wrong, and therefore he most candidly bore the reproof.

Mr. Cator, after some evident chagrin at having
his speech thus rejected, comforted himself by coming up to Mr. Seward, who was seated next me, to
talk to him of the changes of the climates from hot
to *could* in the countries he had visited; and he prated
so much, yet said so little, and pronounced his words
so vulgarly, that I found it impossible to keep my
countenance, and was once, when most unfortunately
he addressed himself to me, surprised by him on the
full grin. To soften it off as well as I could, I pretended unusual complacency, and instead of recover-
ing my gravity, I continued a most ineffable smile
for the whole time he talked, which was indeed no
difficult task. Poor Mr. Seward was as much off
his guard as myself, having his mouth distended to its
fullest extent every other minute.

When the leave-taking time arrived, Dr. Johnson
called to Mr. Pepys to shake hands, an invitation
which was most coldly and forcibly accepted. Mr.
Cator made a point of Mrs. Thrale's dining at his
house soon, and she could not be wholly excused, as
she had many transactions with him; but she fixed the
day for three weeks hence. They have invited me so
often, that I have now promised not to fail making
one.

Thursday morning.—Dr. Johnson went to town
for some days, but not before Mrs. Thrale read him
a very serious lecture upon giving way to such violence; which he bore with a patience and quietness
that even more than made his peace with me; for such
a man's confessing himself wrong is almost more
amiable that another being steadily right.

Wednesday, June 26.—Dr. Johnson, who had been
in town some days, returned, and Mr. Crutchley came
also, as well as my father. I did not see the two
latter till summoned to dinner; and then Dr. Johnson seizing my hand, while with one of his own he
gave me a no very gentle tap on the shoulder, half
drolly and half reproachfully called out,

" Ah, you little baggage, you! and have you known
how long I have been here, and never to come to
me ? "

And the truth is, in whatever sportive mode he ex-
presses it, he really likes not I should be absent from
him half a minute whenever he is here, and not in his
own apartment. . . .

Dr. Johnson, as usual when here, kept me in chat with him in the library after all the rest had dispersed; but when Mr. Crutchley returned again, he went upstairs.

Friday.[1]—The moment breakfast was over, Mr. Crutchley arose, and was taking leave; but Mrs. Thrale told him, with an arch laugh, he had better stay, for he would no get mended by going. He protested, however, that he must certainly go home.

"And why?" cried she; "what do you go for?"

"Nay," cried he, hesitating, "I don't know, I am sure!"

"Never mind him, madam," cried Dr. Johnson; "a man who knows not why he goes, knows not why he stays; therefore never heed him."

"Does anybody expect you?" said Mrs. Thrale. "Do you want to see anybody?"

"Not a soul!"

"Then why can't you stay?"

"No; I can't stay now; I'll meet you on Tuesday."

"If you know so little why you should either go or stay," said Dr Johnson, "never think about it, sir; toss up—that's the shortest way. Heads or tails!—let that decide."

"No, no, sir," answered he; "this is but talk, for I cannot reduce it to that mere difference in my own mind."

"What! must you go, then?" said Mrs. Thrale.

[1] June 28.

"I must go," returned he, "upon a system of economy."

"What! to save your horses coming again?"

"No; but that I may not weary my friends quite out."

"Oh, your friends are the best judges for themselves," said Mrs. Thrale; "do you think you can go anywhere that your company will be more desired?"

"Nay, nay," cried Dr. Johnson, "after such an excuse as that, your friends have a right to practise Irish hospitality, and lock up your bridle."

The matter was still undecided when Mrs. Thrale called him to walk out with her. . . .

At dinner, accordingly, he returned, and is now to stay till Tuesday. . . .

I have very often, though I mention them not, long and melancholy discourses with Dr. Johnson, about our dear deceased master, whom, indeed, he regrets incessantly;[1] but I love not to dwell on subjects of sorrow when I can drive them away, especially to you, upon this account, as you were so much a stranger to that excellent friend, whom you only lamented for the sake of those who survived him.

At dinner[2] we had a large party of old friends of Mrs. Thrale. Lady Frances Burgoyne, a mighty erect old lady of the last age, lofty, ceremonious, stiff, and condescending.

---

[1] On April 5, he wrote to Mrs. Thrale, "No death since that of my wife has ever oppressed me like this." (*Letters*, 2. 209.)
[2] July 30.

Montague Burgoyne, her son, and as like any other son as ever you saw.

Mrs. Burgoyne, his wife, a sweet, pretty, innocent, simple young girl, just married to him.

Miss Burgoyne, his eldest sister, a good, sensible, prating old maid.

Miss Kitty Burgoyne, a younger sister, equally prating, and *not* equally sensible.

Mr. Ned Hervey, brother to the bride.

To these were added Mr. Pepys and Sophy Streatfield; the former as entertaining, the latter as beautiful, as ever. We had a very good day, but not of a writing sort.

Dr. Johnson, whom I had not seen since his Sunninghill expedition,[1] as he only returned from town to-day, gave me almost all his attention, which made me of no little consequence to the Burgoynes, who all stared again when they saw him make up to me the moment I entered the room, and talk to me till summoned to dinner.

Mr. Pepys had desired this meeting, by way of a sort of reconciliation after the Lyttelton quarrel; and Dr. Johnson now made amends for his former violence, as he advanced to him as soon as he came in, and holding out his hand to him, received him with a cordiality he had never shown him before. Indeed, he told me himself, that "he thought the better of Mr. Pepys for all that had passed." He is as great a *souled* man as a *bodied* one, and, were

---

[1] Johnson and Mrs. Thrale had been visiting Mr. Crutchley at his home, Sunninghill. (*Diary,* 2. 22.)

he less furious in his passions, he would be demi-divine.

Mr. Pepys also behaved extremely well, politely casting aside all reserve or coldness that might be attributed to a lurking ill-will for what had passed.

Streatham.—My poor journal is now so in arrears, that I forget wholly the date of what I sent you last. I have, however, minutes by me of things, though not of times, and, therefore, the chronology not being very important, take them, my dear girls, promiscuously. I am still, I know, in August, *et voilà tout.*

We have now a new character added to our set, and one of no small diversion,—Mr. Musgrave,[1] an Irish gentleman of fortune, and member of the Irish Parliament. He is tall, thin, and agreeable in his face and figure; is reckoned a good scholar, has travelled, and been very well educated. His manners are impetuous and abrupt; his language is high-flown and hyperbolical; his sentiments are romantic and tender; his heart is warm and generous; his head hot and wrong! And the whole of his conversation is a mixture the most uncommon, of knowledge and triteness, simplicity and fury, literature and folly!

Keep this character in your mind, and, contradictory as it seems, I will give you, from time to time, such specimens as shall remind you of each of these six epithets.

He was introduced into this house by Mr. Seward,

---

[1] Afterwards Sir Richard. He appears once in Mrs. Piozzi's 'Anecdotes,' *Miscellanies,* 1. 342, but is not mentioned by name in the *Life;* cf., however, 4. 323, note.

with whom, and Mr. Graves of Worcester, he travelled into Italy: and some years ago he was extremely
intimate here. But, before my acquaintance was made
at Streatham, he had returned to Ireland; where,
about a year since, he married Miss Cavendish.
They are now, by mutual consent, parted. She is
gone to a sister in France, and he is come to spend
some time in England by vay of diverting his chagrin.

Mrs. Thrale who, though open-eyed enough to his
absurdities, thinks well of the goodness of his heart,
has a real regard for him; and he quite adores her,
and quite worships Dr. Johnson—frequently declaring (for what he once says, he says continually), that
he would spill his blood for him,—or clean his shoes,
—or go to the East Indies to do him any good! " I
am never," says he, " afraid of him; none but a fool
or a rogue has any need to be afraid of him. What
a fine old lion (looking up at his picture) [1] he is!
Oh! I love him,—I honour him,—I reverence him!
I would black his shoes for him. I wish I could give
him my night's sleep! " [2]

These are exclamations which he is making continually. Mrs. Thrale has extremely well said that
he is a caricature of Mr. Boswell,[3] who is a caricature,
I must add, of all other of Dr. Johnson's admirers.

---

[1] The well-known portrait by Reynolds, now in the National
Gallery, then owned by Mrs. Thrale.
[2] He was at this time troubled with insomnia; see below, p. 142.
[3] Boswell has been mentioned but once before in the *Diary*
(1.467); he was present at a dinner in Grosvenor Square which
was also attended by Miss Burney and Dr. Johnson. Since Miss
Burney always disliked him, her descriptions are to be taken
cum grano salis.

The next great favourite he has in the world to
our Doctor, and the person whom he talks *next most*
of, is Mr. Jessop, who was his schoolmaster, and
whose praise he is never tired of singing in terms the
most vehement,—quoting his authority for every
other thing he says, and lamenting our misfortune
in not knowing him.

His third favourite topic, at present, is *The Life of
Louis XV*. in 4 vols. 8vo, lately translated from the
French; and of this he is so extravagantly fond, that
he talks of it as a man might talk of his mistress;
provided he had so little wit as to talk of her
at all.

Painting, music, all the fine arts in their turn, he
also speaks of in raptures. He is himself very accomplished, plays the violin extremely well, is a very
good linguist, and a very decent painter. But no subject in his hands fails to be ridiculous, as he is sure,
by the abruptness of its introduction, the strange turn
of his expressions, or the Hibernian twang of his
pronunciation, to make everything he says, however
usual or common, seem peculiar and absurd.

When he first came here, upon the present renewal
of his acquaintance at Streatham, Mrs. Thrale sent
a summons to her daughter and me to come downstairs. We went together; I had long been curious
to see him, and was glad of the opportunity. The
moment Mrs. Thrale introduced me to him, he began a warm *éloge* of my father, speaking so fast, so
much, and so Irish, that I could hardly understand
him.

That over, he began upon this book, entreating Mrs. Thrale and all of us to read it, assuring us nothing could give us equal pleasure, minutely relating all its principal incidents with vehement expressions of praise or abhorrence, according to the good or bad he mentioned; and telling us that he had devoted three days and nights to making an index to it himself!

Then he touched upon his dear schoolmaster, Mr. Jessop, and then opened upon Dr. Johnson, whom he calls " the old lion," and who lasted till we left him to dress.

When we met again at dinner, and were joined by Dr. Johnson, the incense he paid him, by his solemn manner of listening, by the earnest reverence with which he eyed him, and by a theatric start of admiration every time he spoke, joined to the Doctor's utter insensibility to all these tokens, made me find infinite difficulty in keeping my countenance during the whole meal. His talk, too, is incessant; no female, however famed, can possibly excel him for volubility.

He told us a thousand strange staring stories, of noble deeds of valour and tender proofs of constancy, interspersed with extraordinary, and indeed incredible accidents, and with jests, and jokes, and bon-mots, that I am sure must be in Joe Miller.[1] And in the midst of all this jargon he abruptly called out, " Pray,

---

[1] *Joe Miller's Jests; or the Wit's Vade-Mecum.* Being a Collection of the most Brilliant Jests; the Politest Repartees; the most Elegant Bon-Mots, and the most pleasant short Stories in the English Language . . . London, 1739.

Mrs. Thrale, what is the Doctor's opinion of the American war?"

Opinion of the American war at this time of day![1] We all laughed cruelly; yet he repeated his question to the Doctor, who, however, made no other answer but by laughing too. But he is never affronted with Dr. Johnson, let him do what he will; and he seldom ventures to speak to him till he has asked some other person present for advice how he will *take* such or such a question.

We have had[2] some *extra* diversion from two queer letters. The first of these was to Dr. Johnson, dated from the Orkneys, and costing him 1*s*. 6*d*. The contents, were, to beg the Doctor's advice and counsel upon a very embarrassing matter; the writer, who signs his name and place of abode, says he is a clergyman, and labours under a most peculiar misfortune, for which he can give no account; and which is,—that though he very often writes letters to his friends and others, he never gets any answers; he entreats, therefore, that Dr. Johnson will take this into consideration, and explain to him to what so strange a thing may be attributed.

He then gives his direction.

The other of these curious letters is to myself; it is written upon fine French-glazed and gilt paper.

---

[1] Johnson had expressed his opinion of the American situation with unfortunate fulness as early as 1775 in *Taxation no Tyranny*.
[2] August 27.

"*Miss F. Burney,*
     "*At Lady Thrale's,*
          "*Streatham, Surrey.*

"*Madam*—I lately have read the three elegant volumes of *Evelina,* which were penned by you; and am desired by my friends, which are very numerous, to entreat the favour of you to oblige the public with a fourth.[1]

"Now, if this desire of mine should meet with your approbation, and you will honour the public with another volume (for it will not be ill-bestowed time), it will greatly add to the happiness of,—Honoured madam, a sincere admirer of you and *Evelina.*

"*Snow Hill.*"[2]

Now don't our two epistles vie well with each other for singular absurdity? Which of them shows least meaning, who can tell? This is the third queer anonymous letter I have been favoured with. The date is more curious than the contents; one would think the people on Snow Hill might think three volumes enough for what they are the better, and not desire a fourth to celebrate more Smiths and Branghtons.

At dinner,[3] Dr. Johnson returned, and Mr. Musgrave came with him. I did not see them till dinner was upon the table; and then Dr. Johnson, more in

---

[1] Perhaps this ardent correspondent recalled Richardson's continuation of *Pamela.*
[2] This address is perhaps taken from *Evelina.*
[3] September 3.

earnest than in jest, reproached me with not coming
to meet him, and afterwards with not speaking to
him, which, by the way, across a large table, and before company, I could not do, were I to be reproached
ever so solemnly. It is requisite to speak so loud in
order to be heard by him, and everybody listens so
attentively for his reply, that not all his kindness
will ever, I believe, embolden me to discourse with
him willingly except *tête-à-tête,* or only with his
family or my own.

Mr. Crutchley, who has more odd spite in him
than all the rest of the world put together, enjoyed
this call upon me, at which Mr. Musgrave no less
wondered! He seemed to think it an honour that
raised me to the highest pinnacle of glory, and started,
and lifted up his hands in profound admiration.

This, you may imagine, was no great inducement
to me to talk more; and when in the evening we all
met again in the library, Dr. Johnson still continuing
his accusation, and vowing I cared nothing for him,
to get rid of the matter, and the grinning of Mr.
Crutchley, and the theatrical staring of Mr. Musgrave, I proposed to Miss Thrale, as soon as tea was
over, a walk round the grounds.

The next morning, the instant I entered the library
at breakfast-time, where nobody was yet assembled
but Messrs. Musgrave and Crutchley, the former
ran up to me the moment I opened the door with a
large folio in his hand, calling out,

"See here, Miss Burney, you know what I said
about the Racks——"

"The what, sir?" cried I, having forgot it all.

"Why, the Racks; and here you see is the very same account. I must show it to the Doctor presently; the old lion hardly believed it."

He then read to me I know not how much stuff, not a word of which I could understand, because Mr. Crutchley sat laughing slyly, and casting up his eyes exactly before me, though unseen by Mr. Musgrave.

As soon as I got away from him, and walked on to the other end of the room, Mr. Crutchley followed me, and said,

"You went to bed too soon last night; you should have stayed a little longer, and then you would have heard such a panegyric as never before was spoken."

"So I suppose," quoth I, not knowing what he drove at.

"Oh yes!" cried Mr. Musgrave, "Dr. Johnson pronounced such a panegyric upon Miss Burney as would quite have intoxicated anybody else; not *her,* indeed, for she can bear it, but nobody else could."

"Oh! such praise," said Mr. Crutchley, "never did I hear before. It kept *me* awake, even *me,* after eleven o'clock, when nothing else could,—poor drowsy wretch that I am!"

They then both ran on praising this praise (*à qui mieux mieux*), and trying which should distract me most with curiosity to hear it; but I know Mr. Crutchley holds *all* panegyric in such infinite contempt and ridicule, that I felt nothing but mortification in finding he had been an auditor to my dear Dr. Johnson's partiality.

"Woe to him," cried he at last, " of whom no one speaks ill! Woe, therefore, to *you* in this house, I am sure!"

"No, no," cried I, "*you*, I believe, will save me from *that* woe."

In the midst of this business entered Miss Thrale. Mr. Musgrave, instantly flying up to her with the folio, exclaimed, "See, Miss Thrale, here's all that about the origin of Racks, that——"

"Of *what?*" cried she. "Of *rats?*"

This set us all grinning; but Mr. Crutchley, who had pretty well recovered his spirits, would not rest a moment from plaguing me about this praise, and began immediately to tell Miss Thrale what an oration had been made the preceding evening.

The moment Mrs. Thrale came in, all this was again repeated, Mr. Musgrave almost blessing himself with admiration while he talked of it, and Mr. Crutchley keeping me in a perpetual fidget, by never suffering the subject to drop.

When they had both exhausted all they had to say in a general manner of this *éloge,* and Dr. Johnson's fondness for me, for a little while we were allowed to rest; but scarce had I time to even hope the matter would be dropped, when Mr. Crutchley said to Mr. Musgrave,

"Well, sir, but now we have paved the way, I think you might as well go on."

"Yes," said Miss Thrale, never backward in promoting mischief, "methinks you might now disclose some of the particulars."

" Ay, do," said Mr. Crutchley, " pray repeat what he said."

" Oh! it is not in my power," cried Mr. Musgrave; " I have not the Doctor's eloquence. However, as well as I can remember, I will do it. He said that her manners were extraordinarily pleasing, and her language remarkably elegant; that she had as much virtue of mind as knowledge of the world; that with all her skill in human nature, she was at the same time as pure a little creature——"

This phrase, most comfortably to me, helped us to a laugh, and carried off in something like a joke praise that almost carried *me* off, from very shame not better to deserve it.

" Go on, go on! " cried Mr. Crutchley; " you have not said half."

" I am sensible of that," said he, very solemnly; " but it really is not in my power to do him justice, else I would say on, for Miss Burney I know would not be intoxicated."

" No, no; more, more," cried that tiresome creature; " at it again."

" Indeed, sir; and upon my word I would if I could; but only himself can do the old lion justice." . . .

We had half done breakfast before he came down; he then complained he had had a bad night and was not well.

" I could not sleep," said he, laughing; " no, not a wink, for thinking of Miss Burney; her cruelty destroys my rest."

" Mercy, sir! " cried Mrs. Thrale; " what, beginning already?—why, we shall all assassinate her.
Late at night, and early at morn,—no wonder you
can't sleep! "

" Oh! what would I give," cried he, " that Miss
Burney would come and tell me stories all night long!
—if she would but come and talk to me! "

" That would be delightful, indeed! " said I; " but
when, then, should I sleep? "

" Oh, that's *your* care! I should be happy enough
in keeping you awake."

" I wish, sir," cried Mr. Musgrave, with vehemence, " I could give you my own night's sleep! "

" I would have you," continued Dr. Johnson to me
(taking no notice of this flight), " come and talk to
me of *Mr. Smith,* and then tell me stories of old
Branghton, and then of his son, and then of your sea-
captain."

" And pray, sir," cried Mrs. Thrale, " don't forget *Lady Louisa,* for I shall break my heart if you
do."

" Ay," answered he, " and of *Lady Louisa,* and of
Evelina herself as much as you please, but not of
Mr. Macartney [1]—no, not a word of him! "

" I assure you, ma'am," said Mr. Musgrave, " the
very person who first told me of that book was Mr.
Jessop,[2] my schoolmaster. Think of that!—was it
not striking? ' A daughter,' says he, ' of your friend
Dr. Burney has written a book; and it does her much

---

[1] Because he was Scotch.
[2] See above, p. 135.

credit.' Think of that! (lifting up his hands to en-
force his admiration) ; and he desired me to read it—
he recommended it to me;—a man of the finest taste,
—a man of great profundity,—an extraordinary
scholar,—living in a remote part of Ireland,—a man
I esteem, upon my word! "

" But, sir," cried Mrs. Thrale to Dr. Johnson,
" why, these men tell such wonders of what you said
last night! Why, you spoke quite an oration in favour of Miss Burney."

" Ay," said Mr. Crutchley, " the moment it was
over I went to bed. I stayed to hear the panegyric;
but I thought I could bear nothing after it, and made
off."

" I would you were off now," cried I, " and in your
phaeton in the midst of this rain! "

" Oh, sir! " cried Mr. Musgrave, " the Doctor
went on with it again after you went; I had the
honour to hear a great deal more."

" Why, this is very fine indeed! " said Mrs.
Thrale; " why, Dr. Johnson,—why, what is all
this? "

" These young fellows," answered he, " play me
false; they take me in; they start the subject, and
make me say something of that Fanny Burney, and
then the rogues know that when I have once begun I
shall not know when to leave off."

" We are glad, sir," said Mr. Crutchley, " to
hear our own thoughts expressed so much better than
we can express them ourselves."

I could only turn up my eyes at him.

" Just so," said Mrs. Thrale,

" ' What oft was thought, but ne'er so well
express'd.' "

Here, much to my satisfaction, the conversation
broke up.

Dr. Johnson [1] has been very unwell indeed. Once
I was quite frightened about him; but he continues
his strange discipline—starving, mercury, opium; and
though for a time half demolished by its severity, he
always, in the end, rises superior both to the disease
and the remedy,—which commonly is the most alarming of the two. His kindness for me, I think, if
possible, still increased: he actually *bores* everybody
so about me that the folks even complain of it. I
must, however, acknowledge I feel but little pity for
their fatigue.

I went [2] to dear Dr. Johnson's, *rassegnarlo la solita
servitù*, but at one o'clock he was not up, and I did
not like to disturb him. I am very sorry about him—
exceeding sorry! When I parted from you on Monday, and found him with Dr. Lawrence,[3] I put my
nose into the old man's wig and shouted; but got none
except melancholy answers,—*so* melancholy, that I
was forced to crack jokes for fear of crying.

" There is gout at the bottom, madam," says Lawrence.

---

[1] September 14.   [2] February.
[3] His physician. He was at this time over seventy; Johnson
outlived him.

" I wish it were at the bottom! " replied saucebox,
as loud as she could bawl, and pointing to the
pedestals.

" He complains of a general *gravedo*," [1] cries the
Doctor; " but he speaks too good Latin for *us*."

" Do you take care, at least, that it does not
increase long," quoth I. (The word *gravedo*, you
know, makes *gravedinis*, and is, therefore, said to
" increase long in the genitive case.") I thought this
a good, stupid, scholarlike pun, and Johnson seemed
to like that Lawrence was pleased.

This morning I was with him again.

Oct. 15, 1782.

I am very sorry you [2] could not come to Streatham
at the time Mrs. Thrale hoped to see you, for when
shall we be likely to meet there again? You would
have been much pleased, I am sure, by meeting with
General Paoli,[3] who spent the day there, and was
extremely communicative and agreeable. I had seen
him in large companies, but was never made known
to him before; nevertheless, he conversed with me as
if well acquainted not only with myself, but my connections,—inquiring of me when I had last seen Mrs.
Montagu? and calling Sir Joshua Reynolds, when he
spoke of him, my friend. He is a very pleasing man,
tall and genteel in his person, remarkably well bred,
and very mild and soft in his manners.

---

[1] See *Letters*, 2. 229. " Gravedo, a cold in the head." (*N. E. D.*)
[2] This is an extract from a letter to Mr. Crisp.
[3] Johnson's friend, the Corsican patriot, who took refuge in England in 1769. (See *Life*, 2. 71.)

Fanny Burney in 1782
(After a portrait by Edward Burney)

I will try to give you a little specimen of his conversation, because I know you love to hear particulars
of all out-of-the-way persons. His English is blunder-
ing, but not unpretty. Speaking of his first acquaintance with Mr. Boswell,[1]

"He came," he said, "to my country, and he
fetched me some letter of recommending him; but
I was of the belief he might be an impostor, and I
supposed, in my minte, he was an espy; for I look
away from him, and in a moment I look to him again,
and I behold his tablets.[2] Oh! he was to the work
of writing down all I say! Indeed I was angry. But
soon I discover he was no impostor and no espy; and I
only find I was myself the monster he had come to
discern. Oh, —— is a very good man; I love him
indeed; so cheerful! so gay! so pleasant! but at the
first, oh! I was indeed angry."

After this he told us a story of an expectation he
had had of being robbed, and of the protection he
found from a very large dog that he is very fond of.

"I walk out," he said, "in the night; I go towards the field; I behold a man—oh, ugly one! I
proceed—he follow; I go on—he address me, 'You
have one dog,' he says. 'Yes,' say I to him. 'Is a
fierce dog?' he says; 'is he fiery?' 'Yes,' reply I,
'he can bite.' 'I would not attack in the night,' says
he, 'a house to have such dog in it.' Then I con-
clude he was a breaker; so I turn to him—oh, very

---

[1] Boswell scraped acquaintance with General Paoli during his
tour in Corsica, 1765.
[2] An interesting illustration of Boswell's biographical methods.

rough! not gentle—and I say, very fierce, ' He shall destroy you, if you are ten!'"

Afterwards, speaking of the Irish giant, who is now shown in town, he said,

" He is so large I am as a baby! I look at him—oh! I find myself so little as a child! Indeed, my indignation it rises when I see him hold up his hand so high. I am as nothing; and I find myself in the power of a man who fetches from me a half a crown."

This language, which is all spoke very pompously by him, sounds comical from himself, though I know not how it may read.

Adieu, my dear and kind daddy, and believe me your ever obliged and ever affectionate,

F. B.

Brighthelmstone,[1] *October 26.*—My journey was incidentless; but the moment I came into Brighthelmstone I was met by Mrs. Thrale, who had most eagerly been waiting for me a long while, and therefore I dismounted, and walked home with her. It would be very superfluous to tell you how she received me, for you cannot but know, from her impatient letters, what I had reason to expect of kindness and welcome.

I was too much tired to choose appearing at dinner, and therefore eat my eat upstairs, and was then decorated a little, and came forth to tea.

Mr. Harry Cotton and Mr. Swinerton were both

[1] Johnson's visit to Brighthelmstone is mentioned in the *Life,* 4. 159.

here. Mrs. Thrale said they almost lived with her,
and therefore were not to be avoided, but declared she
had refused a flaming party of blues, for fear I
should think, if I met them just after my journey, she
was playing Mrs. Harrel.[1]

Dr. Johnson received me too with his usual goodness, and with a salute so loud, that the two young
beaus, Cotton and Swinerton, have never done laughing about it.

Mrs. Thrale spent two or three hours in my room,
talking over all her affairs, and then we wished each
other *bon repos,* and—retired. *Grandissima* conclusion.

Oh, but let me not forget that a fine note came from
Mr. Pepys, who is here with his family, saying he
was *pressé de vivre,* and entreating to see Mrs. and
Miss T., Dr. Johnson, and Cecilia, at his house the
next day. I hate mightily this method of naming me
from my heroines, of whose honour I think I am more
jealous than of my own.

Oct. 27.—The Pepyses came to visit me in form,
but I was dressing; in the evening, however, Mrs. and
Miss T. took me to them. Dr. Johnson would not
go; he told me it was my day, and I should be
crowned, for Mr. Pepys was wild about *Cecilia.*

" However," he added, " do not hear too much of
it; but when he has talked about it for an hour
or so, tell him to have done. There is no other
way."

---

[1] A character in *Cecilia.*

A mighty easy way, this! however, 'tis what he literally practises for himself.

At dinner [1] we had Dr. Delap and Mr. Selwyn,[2] who accompanied us in the evening to a ball; as did also Dr. Johnson, to the universal amazement of all who saw him there;—but he said he had found it so dull being quite alone the preceding evening, that he determined upon going with us; " for," he said, " it cannot be worse than being alone." [3]

Strange that he should think so! I am sure I am not of his mind. . . .

Dr. Johnson was joined by a friend of his own, Mr. Metcalf,[4] and did tolerably well.

Poor Mr. Pepys had, however, real cause to bemoan my escape; [5] for the little set was broken up by my retreat, and he joined Dr. Johnson, with whom he entered into an argument upon some lines of Gray, and upon Pope's definition of wit, in which he was so roughly confuted, and so severely ridiculed, that he was hurt and piqued beyond all power of disguise,

---

[1] October 28.

[2] Dr. Delap is described at some length in the *Diary*, 1. 222; and Mr. Selwyn in the same, 1. 299.

[3] " Any company, any employment, whatever, he preferred to being alone. The great business of his life (he said) was to escape from himself; this disposition he considered as the disease of his mind which nothing cured but company." (Sir Joshua Reynolds, quot. *Life*, 1. 144-145.) On January 10, 1783, he wrote to John Nichols, " Sickness and solitude make tedious evenings. Come sometimes, and see, Sir, Your humble servant." (*Letters*, 2. 281.)

[4] For Mr. Metcalf see *Life*, 4. 160, and below, pp. 157, 165.

[5] October 29. The party at which this dispute occurred was given by Mrs. Thrale at Brighthelmstone. Cf. the similar quarrel above, pp. 124 ff.

OLD WISDOM.
Blinking at the Stars

A caricature of Johnson, dated 1782

and, in the midst of this discourse, suddenly turned from him, and, wishing Mrs. Thrale good-night, very abruptly withdrew.

Dr. Johnson was certainly right with respect to the argument and to reason; but his opposition was so warm, and his wit so satirical and exulting, that I was really quite grieved to see how unamiable he appeared, and how greatly he made himself dreaded by all, and by many abhorred. What pity that he will not curb the vehemence of his love of victory and superiority!

The sum of the dispute was this. Wit being talked of, Mr. Pepys repeated,—

" True wit is Nature to advantage dress'd,
  What oft was thought, but ne'er so well express'd."

" That, sir," cried Dr. Johnson, " is a definition both false and foolish. Let wit be dressed how it will, it will equally be wit, and neither the more nor the less for any advantage dress can give it."

Mr. P.—But, sir, may not wit be so ill expressed, and so obscure, by a bad speaker, as to be lost?

Dr. J.—The fault, then, sir, must be with the hearer. If a man cannot distinguish wit from words, he little deserves to hear it.

Mr. P.—But, sir, what Pope means——

Dr. J.—Sir, what Pope means, if he means what he says, is both false and foolish. In the first place, " what oft was thought," is all the worse for being often thought, because to be wit, it ought to be newly thought.

Mr. P.—But, sir, 'tis the expression makes it new.

Dr. J.—How can the expression make it new? It may make it clear, or may make it elegant; but how new? You are confounding words with things.

Mr. P.—But, sir, if one man says a thing very ill, may not another man say it so much better that——

Dr. J.—That other man, sir, deserves but small praise for the amendment; he is but the tailor to the first man's thoughts.

Mr. P.—True, sir, he may be but the tailor; but then the difference is as great as between a man in a gold lace suit and a man in a blanket.

Dr. J.—Just so, sir, I thank you for that: the difference is precisely such, since it consists neither in the gold lace suit nor the blanket, but in the man by whom they are worn.

This was the summary; the various contemptuous sarcasms intermixed would fill, and very unpleasantly, a quire.

Thursday, Oct. 31.—A note came this morning to invite us all, except Dr. Johnson, to Lady Rothes's. Dr. Johnson has tortured poor Mr. Pepys so much that I fancy her ladyship omitted him in compliment to her brother-in-law.

Saturday, Nov. 2.—We went to Lady Shelley's. Dr. Johnson, again, excepted in the invitation. He is almost constantly omitted, either from too much respect or too much fear. I am sorry for it, as he hates being alone, and as, though he scolds the others,

he is well enough satisfied himself; and, having given
vent to all his own occasional anger or ill-humour, he
is ready to begin again, and is never aware that those
who have so been " downed " by him, never can much
covet so triumphant a visitor. In contests of wit, the
victor is as ill off in future consequences as the van-
quished in present ridicule.

Monday, Nov. 4.—This was a grand and busy
day. Mr. Swinerton [1] has been some time arranging
a meeting for all our house, with Lady De Ferrars.[2] . . .

I happened to be standing by Dr. Johnson when
all the ladies came in; but, as I dread him before
strangers, from the staring attention he attracts both
for himself and all with whom he talks, I endeavoured
to change my ground. However, he kept prating a
sort of comical nonsense that detained me some minutes whether I would or not; but when we were all
taking places at the breakfast-table I made another
effort to escape. It proved vain; he drew his chair
next to mine, and went rattling on in a humorous sort
of comparison he was drawing of himself to me,—
not one word of which could I enjoy, or can I remember, from the hurry I was in to get out of his way.
In short, I felt so awkward from being thus marked
out, that I was reduced to whisper a request to Mr.
Swinerton to put a chair between us, for which I
presently made a space: for I have often known him
stop all conversation with me, when he has ceased to

¹ The young beau mentioned above, pp. 148-49.
² For account of Lady De Ferrars, see *Diary,* 2. 124 ff.

have me for his next neighbour. Mr. Swinerton, who is an extremely good-natured young man, and so intimate here that I make no scruple with him, instantly complied, and placed himself between us.

But no sooner was this done, than Dr. Johnson, half seriously, and very loudly, took him to task.

"How now, sir! what do you mean by this? Would you separate me from Miss Burney?"

Mr. Swinerton, a little startled, began some apologies, and Mrs. Thrale winked at him to give up the place; but he was willing to oblige me, though he grew more and more frightened every minute, and coloured violently as the Doctor continued his remonstrance, which he did with rather unmerciful raillery, upon his taking advantage of being in his own house to thus supplant him, and *crow;* but when he had borne it for about ten minutes, his face became so hot with the fear of hearing something worse, that he ran from the field, and took a chair between Lady De Ferrars and Mrs. Thrale.

I think I shall take warning by this failure, to trust only to my own expedients for avoiding his public notice in future. However it stopped here; for Lord De Ferrars came in, and took the disputed place without knowing of the contest, and all was quiet.

All that passed afterwards was too general and too common to be recollected. . . .

"Ay," cried Dr. Johnson, "some people want to make out some credit to me from the little rogue's book. I was told by a gentleman this morning, that it was a very fine book, if it was all her own. 'It is all her own,' said I, 'for me, I am sure, for I never saw one word of it before it was printed.' "[1]

This gentleman I have good reason to believe is Mr. Metcalf. . . . He is much with Dr. Johnson, but seems to have taken an unaccountable dislike to Mrs. Thrale, to whom he never speaks. I have seen him but once or twice myself; and as he is dry, and I am shy, very little has passed between us. . . .

While we were debating this matter, a gentleman suddenly said to me,—" Did you walk far this morning, Miss Burney? " And, looking at him, I saw Mr. Metcalf, whose graciousness rather surprised me, for he only made to Mrs. Thrale a cold and distant bow, and it seems he declares, aloud and around, his aversion to literary ladies. That he can endure, and even seek me, is, I presume, only from the general perverseness of mankind, because he sees I have always turned from him; not, however, from disliking him, for he is a shrewd, sensible, keen, and very clever man; but merely from a dryness on his own side that has excited retaliation.

" Yes," I answered, " we walked a good way."

" Dr. Johnson," said he, " told me in the morning you were no walker; but I informed him that I had had the pleasure of seeing you upon the Newmarket Hill."

" Oh, he does not know," cried I, " whether I am a walker or not—he does not see me walk, because he never walks himself."

---

[1] And yet Lord Macaulay could intimate, in his essay on Mme. D'Arblay, that Johnson had a hand in " correcting " *Cecilia!*

" He has asked me," said he, " to go with him to Chichester, to see the cathedral,[1] and I told him I would certainly go if he pleased; but why, I cannot imagine, for how shall a blind man see a cathedral? "

" I believe," quoth I, " his blindness is as much the effect of absence as of infirmity, for he sees wonderfully at times." [2]

" Why, he has assured me he cannot see the colour of any man's eyes, and does not know what eyes any of his acquaintances have."

" I am sure, however," cried I, " he can see the colour of a lady's top-knot, for he very often finds fault with it."

" Is that possible? "

" Yes, indeed; and I was much astonished at it at first when I knew him, for I had concluded that the utmost of his sight would only reach to tell him whether he saw a cap or a wig."

Here he was called away by some gentleman.

Thursday.[3]—Mr. Metcalf called upon Dr. Johnson, and took him out an airing. Mr. Hamilton [4] is gone, and Mr. Metcalf is now the only person out of this house that voluntarily communicates with the Doctor. He has been in a terrible severe humour

---

[1] Johnson had already visited many, if not most, of the English cathedrals. In 1777 Boswell wrote to him, " You have, I believe, seen all the cathedrals in England, except that of Carlisle." For the whole matter, see Hill's *Appendix B* to the *Life*, 3. The proposed visit to Chichester was made. (See *Life*, 4. 160.)

[2] See above, p. 3.

[3] November 7.

[4] For Miss Burney's account of Hamilton, see *Diary*, 1. 308.

of late, and has really frightened all the people, till they almost ran from him. To me only I think he is now kind, for Mrs. Thrale fares worse than anybody. 'Tis very strange and very melancholy that he will not a little more accommodate his manners and language to those of other people. He likes Mr. Metcalf, however, and so do I, for he is very clever and entertaining when he pleases. Capt. Phillips [1] will remember that was not the case when we saw him at Sir Joshua's. He has, however, all the *de quoi*.

Poor Dr. Delap confessed to us that the reason he now came so seldom, though he formerly almost lived with us when at this place, was his being too unwell to cope with Dr. Johnson. And the other day Mr. Selwyn having refused an invitation from Mr. Hamilton to meet the Doctor, because he preferred being here upon a day when he was out, suddenly rose at the time he was expected to return, and said he must run away, " for fear the Doctor should call him to account."

We spent this evening [2] at Lady De Ferrars, [3] where Dr. Johnson accompanied us, for the first time he has been invited of our parties since my arrival.

Monday and *Tuesday*.[4]—I have no time, except to tell you a comical tale which Mrs. Thrale ran to

---

[1] Fanny's brother-in-law, husband of the " Susan " to whom much of the *Diary* is addressed.
[2] November 12.
[3] Cf. above, p. 153.
[4] November 18 and 19.

acquaint me with. She had been calling upon Mr. Scrase, an old and dear friend, who is confined with the gout; and while she was inquiring about him of his nurse and housekeeper, the woman said,

" Ah, madam, how happy are you to have Minerva in the house with you ! "

" Oh," cried Mrs. Thrale, "you mean my dear Miss Burney, that wrote *Cecilia*. So you have read it; and what part did you like ? "

" Oh, madam, I liked it all better than anything I ever saw in my life; but most of all I liked that good old gentleman, Mr. Albany, that goes about telling people their duty, without so much as thinking of their fine clothes."

When Mrs. Thrale told us this at dinner, Dr. Johnson said,

" I am all of the old housekeeper's mind; Mr. Albany I have always stood up for; he is one of my first favourites. Very fine indeed are the things he says."

My dear Dr. Johnson!—what condescension is this! He fully, also, enters into all my meaning in the high-flown language of Albany, from his partial insanity and unappeasable remorse.

So here concludes Brighthelmstone for 1782.

Dec. 8.—Now for Miss Monckton's assembly. . . .

I was presently separated from Mrs. Thrale, and entirely surrounded by strangers, all dressed superbly, and all looking saucily; and as nobody's names were

spoken, I had no chance to discover any acquaintances. Mr. Metcalf, indeed, came and spoke to me
the instant I came in, and I should have been very
happy to have had him for my neighbour; but he
was engaged in attending to Dr. Johnson, who was
standing near the fire, and environed with listeners.

Some new people now coming in, and placing
themselves in a regular way, Miss Monckton exclaimed,—" My whole care is to prevent a circle ";[1]
and hastily rising, she pulled about the chairs, and
planted the people in groups, with as dexterous a disorder as you would desire to see. . . .

Then came in Sir Joshua Reynolds, and he soon
drew a chair near mine, and from that time I was
never without some friend at my elbow.

" Have you seen," he said, " Mrs. Montagu
lately? "

" No, not very lately."

" But within these few months? "

" No, not since last year."

" Oh, you must see her, then. You ought to see
and to hear her—'twill be worth your while. Have
you heard of the fine long letter she has written? "

" Yes, but I have not met with it."

" I have."

" And who is it to? "

" The old Duchess of Portland.[2] She desired Mrs.

---

[1] The circle was the fashionable arrangement of guests at a
levee or conversazione.

[2] An aged Bluestocking, a relic of the former age. In her
childhood Prior addressed to her his charming *Letter to the Honourable Lady Miss Margaret-Cavendish-Holles-Harley.*

Montagu's opinion of *Cecilia,* and she has written it
at full length. I was in a party at Her Grace's, and
heard of nothing but you. She is so delighted, and
so sensibly, so rationally, that I only wish you could
have heard her. And old Mrs. Delany [1] had been
forced to begin it, though she had said she should
never read any more; however, when we met, she was
reading it already for the third time."

Pray tell my daddy [2] to rejoice for me in this conquest of the Duchess, his old friend, and Mrs.
Delany, his sister's.

Sir Joshua is extremely kind; he is always picking
up some anecdote of this sort for me; yet, most delicately, never lets me hear his own praises but through
others. He looks vastly well, and as if he had never
been ill.

After this Mrs. Burke saw me, and, with much
civility and softness of manner, came and talked with
me, while her husband, without seeing me, went behind my chair to speak to Mrs. Hampden.

Miss Monckton, returning to me, then said,

" Miss Burney, I had the pleasure yesterday of
seeing Mrs. Greville." [3]

I suppose she concluded I was very intimate with
her.

" I have not seen her," said I, " many years."

---

[1] Mrs. Delany was the intimate friend of the Duchess of Portland; she was now in her eighty-third year. In earlier times she
had corresponded with Dean Swift. Miss Burney met her some
months later; it was Mrs. Delany who introduced Miss Burney
to the king and queen.
[2] Mr. Crisp.
[3] See below, pp. 209 ff.

Dear Madam   Edinburgh
                                          20 Decr. 1782

It is strange that I am not yet old enough not to give credit to what I read in the newspapers. I did beleive that you was gone or just going abroad; and I was selfish enough to be sorry for it. But a letter from our most respected Freind Dr. Johnson has informed me that you and three nieces are in Argyll Street. I hope to have the pleasure of finding you there in March. In the mean time, may I again intreat to hear from you how Dr. Johnson does, from time to time. I express myself inelegantly. But I trust you think me worthy of that attention; and I know I am grateful for your goodness.

Every body here is running after Cecilia; and I am vain of telling that I have had the pleasure of being frequently in Miss Burney's company

An unpublished letter of Boswell's, referring to Johnson and Miss Burney

company at Mrs. Thrale's.

I am

Dear Madam

your obliged and

faithful humble servant

James Boswell

"I know, however," cried she, looking surprised, "she is your godmother."

"But she does not do her duty and answer for me, for I never see her."

"Oh, you have answered very well for yourself! But I know by that your name is Fanny."

She then tripped to somebody else, and Mr. Burke very quietly came from Mrs. Hampden, and sat down in the vacant place at my side. I could then wait no longer, for I found he was more near-sighted than myself; I therefore, turned towards him and bowed: he seemed quite amazed, and really made me ashamed, however delighted, by the expressive civility and distinction with which he instantly rose to return my bow, and stood the whole time he was making his compliments upon seeing me, and calling himself the blindest of men for not finding me out sooner. And Mrs. Burke, who was seated near me, said, loud enough for me to hear her,

"See, see! what a flirtation Mr. Burke is beginning with Miss Burney! and before my face too!"

These ceremonies over, he sate down by me, and began a conversation which you, my dearest Susy, would be glad to hear, for my sake, word for word; but which I really could not listen to with sufficient ease, from shame at his warm eulogiums, to remember with any accuracy. The general substance, however, take as I recollect it.

After many most eloquent compliments upon the book, too delicate either to shock or sicken the nicest ear, he very emphatically congratulated me upon its most universal success; said " he was now too late to speak of it, since he could only echo the voice of the whole nation "; and added, with a laugh, " I had hoped to have made some merit of my enthusiasm; but the moment I went about to hear what others say, I found myself merely one in a multitude."

He then told me that, notwithstanding his admiration, he was the man who had dared to find some faults with so favourite and fashionable a work. I entreated him to tell me what they were, and assured him nothing would make me so happy as to correct them under his direction. He then enumerated them. . . .

" But," said he, when he had finished his comments, " what excuse must I give for this presumption? I have none in the world to offer but the real, the high esteem I feel for you; and I must at the same time acknowledge it is all your own doing that I am able to find fault; for it is your general perfection in writing that has taught me to criticise where it is not quite uniform."

Here's an orator, dear Susy!

Then, looking very archly at me, and around him, he said,

" Are you sitting here for characters? Nothing, by the way, struck me more in reading your book than the admirable skill with which your ingenious characters make themselves known by their own words."

He then went on to tell me that I had done the most wonderful of wonders in pleasing the old wits, particularly the Duchess of Portland and Mrs. Delany, who resisted reading the book till they were teased into it, and, since they began, could do nothing else; and he failed not to point out, with his utmost eloquence, the difficulty of giving satisfaction to those who piqued themselves upon being past receiving it.

"But," said he, " I have one other fault to find, and a far more material one than I have mentioned."

" I am more obliged to you. What is it? "

" The disposal of this book. I have much advice to offer to you upon that subject. Why did not you send for your own friend out of the city? he would have taken care you should not part with it so much below par." [1]

He meant Mr. Briggs.[2]

Sir Joshua Reynolds now joined us.

" Are you telling her," said he, " of our conversation with the old wits? I am glad you hear it from Mr. Burke, Miss Burney, for he can tell it so much better than I can, and remember their very words."

" Nothing else would they talk of for three whole hours," said he, " and we were there at the third reading of the bill."

" I believe I was in good hands," said I, " if they talked of it to you? "

" Why, yes," answered Sir Joshua, laughing, " we

[1] " She had £250 for it from Payne and Cadell. Most people say she ought to have had a thousand. It is now going into the third edition, tho' Payne owns that they printed 2,000 at the first edition, and Lowndes told me five hundred was the common number for a novel." (Charlotte Burney in the *Early Diary,* 2. 307.)
[2] A character in *Cecilia,* a miser.

joined in from time to time.   Gibbon says he read the whole five volumes in a day."

" 'Tis impossible," cried Mr. Burke, " it cost me three days; and you know I never parted with it from the time I first opened it."

Here are laurels, Susy! My dear daddy and Kitty, are you not doubly glad you so kindly hurried me upstairs to write when at Chessington?

Mr. Burke then went to some other party, and Mr. Swinerton took his place, with whom I had a dawdling conversation upon dawdling subjects; and I was not a little enlivened, upon his quitting the chair to have it filled by Mr. Metcalf, who, with much satire, but much entertainment, kept chattering with me till Dr. Johnson found me out, and brought a chair opposite to me.

Do you laugh, my Susan, or cry at your F. B.'s honours?

" So," said he to Mr. Metcalf, " it is you, is it, that are engrossing her thus? "

" He's jealous," said Mr. Metcalf drily.

" How these people talk of Mrs. Siddons! " [1] said the Doctor. " I came hither in full expectation of hearing no name but the name I love and pant to hear,—when from one corner to another they are talking of that jade Mrs. Siddons! till, at last wearied out, I went yonder into a corner, and repeated to myself Burney! Burney! Burney! Burney! "

[1] Mrs. Siddons's success had begun in the winter of 1776, but had been confined to the provinces. Her first successful appearance in London had been made on the tenth of October, 1782; she had thus been less than two months before the public when this conversation took place.

" Ay, sir," said Mr. Metcalf, " you should have
carved it upon the trees."

" Sir, had there been any trees, so I should; but,
being none, I was content to carve it upon my
heart." . . .

Miss Monckton now came to us again, and I congratulated her upon her power in making Dr. Johnson
sit in a group; upon which she immediately said to him,

" Sir, Miss Burney says you like best to sit in a
circle ! " [1]

" Does she ? " said he, laughing. " Ay, never mind
what she says.   Don't you know she is a writer of
romances ? "

" Yes, that I do, indeed! " said Miss Monckton,
and every one joined in a laugh that put me horribly
out of countenance.

" She may write romances and speak truth," said
my dear Sir Joshua, who, as well as young Burke, and
Mr. Metcalf, and two strangers, joined now in our
little party.

" But, indeed, Dr. Johnson," said Miss Monckton, " you *must* see Mrs. Siddons.   Won't you see her
in some fine part? "

" Why, if I *must,* madam, I have no choice." [2]

" She says, sir, she shall be very much afraid of
you."

---

[1] See above, p. 159, note 1.
[2] There is no record that Johnson ever saw Mrs. Siddons act.
Mrs. Siddons called on him, however, in October, 1783, at which
time he promised her that whenever she should act the part of
Katharine (*sic*) in *Henry VIII* he would " once more hobble out
to the theatre." (*Life,* 4. 242; cf. *Letters,* 2. 345.)   She did not act
Katharine until after his death.

" Madam, that cannot be true."

" Not true," cried Miss Monckton, staring, " yes it is."

" It *cannot* be, madam."

" But she said so to me; I heard her say it my-self."

" Madam, it is not *possible!* remember, therefore, in future, that even fiction should be supported by probability."

Miss Monckton looked all amazement, but in-sisted upon the truth of what she had said.

" I do not believe, madam," said he warmly, " she knows my name."

" Oh, that is rating her too low," said a gentle-man stranger.

" By not knowing my name," continued he, " I do not mean so literally; but that, when she sees it abused in a newspaper, she may possibly recollect that she has seen it abused in a newspaper before."

" Well, sir," said Miss Monckton, " but you must see her for all this."

" Well, madam, if you desire it, I will go. See her I shall not, nor hear her; but I'll go, and that will do. The last time I was at a play, I was ordered there by Mrs. Abington, or Mrs. Somebody, I do not well remember who, but I placed myself in the middle of the first row of the front boxes, to show that when I was called I came."

The talk upon this matter went on very long, and with great spirit; but I have time for no more of it. I felt myself extremely awkward about going away, not choosing, as it was my first visit, to take French leave, and hardly knowing how to lead the way alone among so many strangers.

At last, and with the last, I made my attempt. A large party of ladies arose at the same time, and I tripped after them; Miss Monckton, however, made me come back, for she said I must else wait in the other room till those ladies' carriages drove away.

When I returned, Sir Joshua came and desired he might convey me home; I declined the offer, and he pressed it a good deal, drolly saying,

" Why, I am old enough, a'n't I? "

And when he found me stout, he said to Dr. Johnson,

" Sir, is not this very hard? Nobody thinks me very young, yet Miss Burney won't give me the privilege of age in letting me see her home? She says I a'n't old enough."

I had never said any such thing.

" Ay, sir," said the doctor, " did I not tell you she was a writer of romances? "

Again I tried to run away, but the door stuck, and Miss Monckton prevented me, and begged I would stay a little longer. She then went and whispered something to her mother, and I had a notion from her manner, she wanted to keep me to supper, which I did not choose, and, therefore, when her back was turned, I prevailed upon young Burke to open the door for me, and out I went. Miss Monckton ran after me, but I would not come back. I was, however, and

I am, much obliged by her uncommon civility and attentions to me. She is far better at her own house than elsewhere.

Now, to return to Tuesday,[1] one of my outdays.

I went in the evening to call on Mrs. Thrale, and tore myself away from her to go to Bolt Court to see Dr. Johnson, who is very unwell. He received me with great kindness, and bade me come oftener, which I will try to contrive. He told me he heard of nothing but me, call upon him who would; and, though he pretended to growl, he was evidently delighted for me. His usual set, Mrs. Williams and Mrs. De Mullins, were with him; and some queer man of a parson who, after grinning at me some time, said,

"Pray, Mrs. De Mullins, is the fifth volume of *Cecilia* at home yet? Dr. Johnson made me read it, ma'am."

"Sir, he did it much honour——"

"*Made* you, sir?" said the Doctor; "you give an ill account of your own taste or understanding, if you wanted any *making* to read such a book as *Cecilia*."

"Oh, sir, I don't mean that; for I am sure I left everything in the world to go on with it."

A shilling was now wanted for some purpose or other, and none of them happened to have one; I begged that I might lend one.

"Ay, do," said the Doctor, "I will borrow of

[1] Probably December 17.

you; [1] authors are like privateers, always fair game for one another."

" True, sir," said the parson, " one author is always robbing another."

" I don't know that, sir," cried the Doctor; " there sits an author who, to my knowledge, has robbed nobody. I have never once caught her at a theft. The rogue keeps her resources to herself! "

Friday.[2]—I dined with Mrs. Thrale and Dr. Johnson, who was very comic and good-humoured. Susan Thrale had just had her hair turned up, and powdered, and has taken to the womanly robe. Dr. Johnson sportively gave her instructions how to increase her consequence, and to " take upon her " properly.

" Begin," said he, " Miss Susy, with something grand—something to surprise mankind! Let your first essay in life be a warm censure of *Cecilia.* You can no way make yourself more conspicuous. Tell the world how ill it was conceived, and how ill executed. Tell them how little there is in it of human nature, and how well your knowledge of the world enables you to judge of the failings in that book. Find fault without fear; and if you are at a loss for any to find, invent whatever comes into your mind, for you may say what you please, with little fear of

---

[1] " He has now and then borrowed a shilling of me; and when I asked for it again, seemed to be rather out of humour. A droll little circumstance once occurred: as if he meant to reprimand my minute exactness as a creditor, he thus addressed me;—' Boswell, *lend* me sixpence—*not to be repaid.*' " (*Life*, 4. 191.)

[2] December 27.

detection, since of those who praise *Cecilia* not half
have read it, and of those who have read it, not half
remember it.   Go to work, therefore, boldly; and
particularly mark that the character of Albany is extremely unnatural, to your own knowledge, since you
never met with such a man at Mrs. Cummyn's
School."

This stopped his exhortation, for we laughed so
violently at this happy criticism that he could not
recover the thread of his harangue.

Mrs. Thrale, who was to have gone with me to
Mrs. Ord's, gave up her visit in order to stay with
Dr. Johnson; Miss Thrale, therefore, and I went to-
gether.

Friday, 4th Jan.—We had an invited party at
home, both for dinner and the evening. . . .

Dr. Johnson came so very late, that we had all
given him up: he was, however, very ill, and only
from an extreme of kindness did he come at all.
When I went up to him, to tell how sorry I was to
find him so unwell,—

"Ah!" he cried, taking my hand and kissing it,
"who shall ail anything when ' Cecilia ' is so near?
Yet you do not think how poorly I am!"

This was quite melancholy, and all dinner-time he
hardly opened his mouth but to repeat to me,—
"Ah! you little know how ill I am."   He was ex-
cessively kind to me, in spite of all his pain, and
indeed I was so sorry for him, that I could talk no
more than himself.   All our comfort was from Mr.

Seward, who enlivened us as much as he possibly
could by his puns and his sport. But poor Dr. Johnson was so ill, that after dinner he went home.

I made a visit to poor Dr. Johnson,[1] to inquire
after his health. I found him better, yet extremely
far from well. One thing, however, gave me infinite
satisfaction. He was so good as to ask me after
Charles,[2] and said, " I shall be glad to see him; pray
tell him to call upon me." I thanked him very much,
and said how proud he would be of such a permission.

" I should be glad," said he, still more kindly,
" to see him, if he were not your brother; but were
he a dog, a cat, a rat, a frog, and belonged to you,
I must needs be glad to see him! "[3]

Mr. Seward has sent me a proof plate, upon silver
paper, of an extremely fine impression of this dear
Doctor, a mezzotinto, by Doughty,[4] from Sir Joshua's
picture, and a very pretty note to beg my acceptance
of it. I am much obliged to him, and very glad to
have it.

Thursday, Feb. 23. . . . He [Mr. Cambridge[5]]
began talking of Dr. Johnson, and asking after his
present health.

---

[1] January 10.
[2] Her younger brother, a schoolteacher, who afterwards became
famous as a Greek scholar.
[3] Cf. below, p. 177.
[4] The best-known of the engravings of Johnson; taken from Sir
Joshua's portrait now in the National Gallery.
[5] The Rev. Richard Owen Cambridge, of Twickenham. The
conversation here recorded is said to have taken place during a
journey to London (*Diary*, 2.203-204), but cf. the following note.

" He is very much recovered," I answered, " and out of town, at Mr. Langton's.[1] And there I hope he will entertain him with enough of Greek."

" Yes," said Mr. Cambridge, " and make his son repeat the Hebrew alphabet to him." [2]

" He means," said I, " to go, when he returns, to Mr. Bowles, in Wiltshire.[1] I told him I had heard that Mr. Bowles was very much delighted with the expectation of seeing him, and he answered me,— ' He is so delighted, that it is shocking!—it is really shocking to see how high are his expectations.' I asked him why; and he said,—' Why, if any man is expected to take a leap of twenty yards, and does actually take one of ten, everybody will be disappointed, though ten yards may be more than any other man ever leaped! ' "

Thursday, June 19.—We heard to-day that Dr.

---

[1] There is some strange confusion in dates at this point in the *Diary*. Johnson's visit to Langton took place in July, not in February, and the visit to Mr. Bowles in the following August and September. (See *Life*, 4.233 ff.) Hill in his edition of the *Letters* (2.317, note), quotes this passage, with the remark that Miss Burney has certainly misdated the entry, but it is more likely that a page of her MS. has been misplaced and incorrectly dated, not improbably by her first editor, Mrs. Barrett. Color is given to this supposition by the fact that in July of this same year Miss Burney and her parents dined with the Cambridges at Twickenham (*Diary*, 2.218), at which time the conversation here recorded may very well have taken place. It is also noticeable that in this entry of July 15 a passage seems to be missing (page 221). It is therefore possible to assume that the conversation under discussion originally occupied this place, and for some reason not obvious was transferred from its original position. Dobson in his edition of the *Diary* seems not to have noticed this discrepancy in dates.

[2] See above, p. 26.

Johnson had been taken ill,[1] in a way that gave a dreadful shock to himself, and a most anxious alarm to his friends. Mr. Seward brought the news here, and my father and I instantly went to his house. He had earnestly desired me, when we lived so much together at Streatham, to see him frequently if he should be ill. He saw my father, but he had medical people with him, and could not admit me upstairs, but he sent me down a most kind message, that he thanked me for calling, and when he was better should hope to see me often. I had the satisfaction to hear from Mrs. Williams that the physicians had pronounced him to be in no danger, and expected a speedy recovery.

The stroke was confined to his tongue. Mrs. Williams told me a most striking and touching circumstance that attended the attack. It was at about four o'clock in the morning: he found himself with a paralytic affection; he rose, and composed in his own mind a Latin prayer to the Almighty, "that whatever were the sufferings for which he must prepare himself, it would please Him, through the grace and mediation of our blessed Saviour, to spare his intellects, and let them all fall upon his body." When he had composed this, internally, he endeavoured to speak it aloud, but found his voice was gone.

Wednesday, July 1.—I was again at Mrs. Vesey's

---

[1] The story of this illness, told in Johnson's own words, may be read in a series of letters to Mrs. Thrale (*Letters*, 2. 300 ff.), where the Latin prayer mentioned in the text may also be found. (Cf. *Life,* 4. 227 ff.)

where again I met Mr. Walpole, Mr. Pepys, Miss
Elliott, Mr. Burke, his wife and son, Sir Joshua
Reynolds, and some others. . . .

I had the satisfaction to hear from Sir Joshua that
Dr. Johnson had dined with him at the Club. I
look upon him, therefore, now, as quite recovered.
I called the next morning to congratulate him, and
found him very gay and very good-humoured.[1]

Thursday, Oct, 29.—This morning, at breakfast,
Mr. Hoole [2] called. I wanted to call upon Dr. Johnson, and it is so disagreeable to me to go to him
alone, now poor Mrs. Williams is dead,[3] on account
of the quantity of men always visiting him,[4] that I
most gladly accepted, almost asked, his 'squireship.

We went together. The dear Doctor received me
with open arms.

" Ah, dearest of all dear ladies! " he cried, and
made me sit in his best chair.

He had not breakfasted.

" Do you forgive my coming so soon? " said I.

" I cannot forgive your not coming sooner," he
answered.

---

[1] On this same day Dr. Johnson wrote to Mrs. Thrale, " This
morning I took the air by a ride to Hampstead, and this afternoon
I dined with the club—I hope that I recover by degrees, but my
nights are restless." (*Letters,* 2. 311 ff.)

[2] The Rev. Samuel Hoole. He was the one who read the Litany
to the dying Johnson. (See *Life,* 4. 409.)

[3] For the death of Mrs. Williams, which occurred September 6,
see *Letters,* 2. 331 and *Life,* 4. 235.

[4] " About twelve o'clock I commonly visited him, and frequently found him in bed, or declaiming over his tea, which he
drank very plentifully. He generally had a levee of morning
visitors, chiefly men of letters . . . and sometimes learned ladies."
(Dr. Maxwell's account of Johnson, *Life,* 2. 118.)

I asked if I should make his breakfast, which I
have done since we left Streatham; he readily con-
sented.

"But, sir," quoth I, "I am in the wrong chair."
For I was away from the table.

"It is so difficult," said he, "for anything to be
wrong that belongs to you, that it can only be I am
in the wrong chair, to keep you from the right one."
And then we changed.

You will see by this how good were his spirits
and his health.

I stayed with him two hours, and could hardly get
away; he wanted me to dine with him, and said he
would send home to excuse me; but I could not possibly do that.   Yet I left him with real regret.

Wednesday, Nov. 19.—I received a letter from Dr.
Johnson, which I have not by me, but will try to
recollect.

"To Miss Burney [1]

"*Madam*—You have now been at home this long
time, and yet I have neither seen nor heard from you.
Have we quarrelled?

"I have met with a volume of the *Philosophical*

---

[1] The letter, as Miss Burney intimates, is not a literally accurate copy of the original (which may be found in the *Letters,*
2. 353); but is so nearly a reproduction of it as to make the
original not worth quoting here.   The most important difference
is the absence of the title of the newly-found volume in the
original letter.   This is, therefore, an interesting proof of the reliability of Miss Burney's verbal memory, and may serve to give
us confidence in her record of Johnson's conversation.

Transactions, which I imagine to belong to Dr. Burney.[1] Miss Charlotte [2] will please to examine.

" Pray send me a direction where Mrs. Chapone [3] lives; and pray, some time, let me have the honour of telling you how much I am, madam, your most humble servant,   " SAM. JOHNSON." [4]

Now if ever you read anything more dry, tell me. I was shocked to see him undoubtedly angry, but took courage, and resolved to make a serious defence; therefore thus I answered,

" TO DR. JOHNSON

" *Dear Sir*—May I not say dear? for quarrelled I am sure we have not. The bad weather alone has

---

[1] Johnson was very careless with borrowed books. A number of those which he borrowed while writing the *Dictionary* were never returned. In her *Memoirs of Dr. Burney,* Mme. D'Arblay gives the following account of Garrick's imitation of Johnson: "He took off the voice, sonorous, impressive, and oratorical, of Dr. Johnson, in a short dialogue with himself that had passed the preceding week. 'David!—will you lend me your Petrarca?' 'Y-e-s, Sir!....' 'David! you sigh?' 'Sir—you shall have it, certainly.' 'Accordingly,' Mr. Garrick continued, 'the book—stupendously bound—I sent to him that very evening. But scarcely had he taken the noble quarto in his hands, when—as Boswell tells, he poured forth a Greek ejacuation, and a couplet or two from Horace; and then, in one of those fits of enthusiasm which always seem to require that he should spread his arms aloft in the air, his haste was so great to debarrass them for that purpose, that he suddenly pounces my poor Petrarca over his head upon the floor! Russia leather, gold border, and all! And then, standing for several minutes erect, he forgot probably that he had ever seen it; and left my poor dislocated Beauty to the mercy of the housemaid's morning mop!'" (*Memoirs,* 1. 352-353.)
[2] Fanny's sister.
[3] Formerly Miss Mulso, the friend of Richardson, and later author of the famous *Letters.*
[4] According to Hill (*Letters,* 2. 354), Miss Burney wrote at the foot of this letter, " F. B. flew to him instantly and most gratefully."

kept me from waiting upon you; but now you have condescended to give me a summons, no lion shall stand in the way of my making your tea this afternoon, unless I receive a prohibition from yourself, and then I must submit; for what, as you said of a certain great lady, signifies the barking of a lap-dog, if once the lion puts out his paw?[1]

" The book was very right. Mrs. Chapone lives at either No. 7 or 8 in Dean Street, Soho.

" I beg you, sir, to forgive a delay for which I can only ' tax the elements with unkindness,' and to receive, with your usual goodness and indulgence, your ever most obliged and most faithful humble servant,   " F. BURNEY.

" *St. Martin's Street, Nov. 19, 1783.*"

My dear father spared me the coach, and to Bolt Court, therefore, I went, and with open arms was I received. Nobody was there but Charles [2] and Mr. Sastres,[3] and Dr. Johnson was, if possible, more instructive, entertaining, good-humoured, and exquisitely fertile, than ever. He thanked me repeatedly for coming, and was so kind I could hardly ever leave him.

Just then [4] my father came in: and then Mr. G. C.[5] came, and took the chair half beside me.

---

[1] " This bore reference to an expression of Dr. Johnson's, upon hearing that Mrs. Montagu resented his *Life of Lord Lyttelton.*" (MME. D'ARBLAY, *Memoirs,* 2. 357, note.)

[2] Her brother. (See above, p. 171.)

[3] An Italian master, to whom Johnson left a bequest.

[4] This conversation took place at an assembly of Mrs. Vesey's, on December 9. (*Diary,* 2. 231.)

[5] The younger Mr. Cambridge, the Rev. George Owen Cambridge, a frequent character in the pages of the *Diary.*

I told him of some new members for Dr. Johnson's club.[1]

"I think," said he, "it sounds more like some club that one reads of in the *Spectator*,[2] than like a real club in these times; for the forfeits of a whole year will not amount to those of a single night in other clubs. Does Pepys belong to it?"

"Oh no! he is quite of another party! He is head man on the side of the defenders of Lord Lyttelton. Besides, he has had enough of Dr. Johnson; for they had a grand battle upon the *Life of Lyttelton*, at Streatham."[3]

"And had they really a serious quarrel? I never imagined it had amounted to that."

"Oh yes, serious enough, I assure you. I never saw Dr. Johnson really in a passion but then: and dreadful, indeed, it was to see. I wished myself away a thousand times. It was a frightful scene. He so red, poor Mr. Pepys so pale!"

"But how did it begin? What did he say?"

"Oh, Dr. Johnson came to the point without much

[1] The Essex Head Club, not the more famous Literary Club. For an account of its foundation and members, see *Life*, 4. 253-255 and 436-438. Mme. D'Arblay gives an inferior account of it, under the title "Sam's Club" in *Memoirs*, 2. 261 ff.

[2] See No. 9, for March 10, 1710. The first and third rules of the Two-Penny Club described in this paper were, "Every member at his first coming in shall lay down his Two-Pence," and "If any member absents himself he shall forfeit a Penny for the Use of the Club . . ."; the fifth rule of the Essex Head Club was "Every member present at the Club shall spend at least sixpence; and every member who stays away shall forfeit three-pence."

[3] See above, pp. 124 ff.

ceremony. He called out aloud, before a large company, at dinner, ' What have you to say, sir, to me or
of me? Come forth, man! I hear you object to my
Life of Lord Lyttelton. What are your objections?
If you have anything to say, let's hear it. Come
forth, man, when I call you! "

"What a call, indeed! Why then, he fairly bullied
him into a quarrel! "

"Yes. And I was the more sorry, because Mr.
Pepys had begged of me, before they met, not to let
Lord Lyttelton be mentioned. Now I had no more
power to prevent it than this macaroon cake in my
hand."

"It was behaving ill to Mrs. Thrale, certainly, to
quarrel in her house."

"Yes; but he never repeated it; though he wished
of all things to have gone through just such another
scene with Mrs. Montagu,[1] and to refrain was an act
of heroic forbearance."

"Why, I rather wonder he did not; for she was
the head of the set of Lytteltonians."

"Oh, he knows that; he calls Mr. Pepys only her
prime minister."

"And what does he call her? "

" ' Queen,' to be sure; ' Queen of the Blues! '
She came to Streatham one morning, and I saw he was
dying to attack her. But he had made a promise to
Mrs. Thrale to have no more quarrels in her house,
and so he forced himself to forbear. Indeed he was
very much concerned, when it was over, for what had

[1] See above, p. 123.

passed; and very candid and generous in acknowledging it. He is too noble to adhere to wrong."

" And how did Mrs. Montagu herself behave? "

" Very stately, indeed, at first. She turned from
him stiffly, and with a most distant air, and without
even courtesying to him, and with a firm intention to
keep to what she had publicly declared—that she
would never speak to him more! However, he went
up to her himself, longing to begin! and very roughly
said,—' Well, madam, what's become of your fine
new house? I hear no more of it.' "

" But how did she bear this? "

" Why, she was obliged to answer him; and she
soon grew so frightened—as everybody does—that
she was as civil as ever."

He laughed heartily at this account. But I told
him Dr. Johnson was now much softened. He had
acquainted me, when I saw him last, that he had
written to her upon the death of Mrs. Williams,[1] because she had allowed her something yearly, which
now ceased.

" ' And I had a very kind answer from her,' said
he.

" ' Well then, sir,' cried I, ' I hope peace now
will be again proclaimed.'

" ' Why, I am now,' said he, ' come to that time
when I wish all bitterness and animosity to be at an
end. I have never done her any serious harm—nor

---

[1] This beautiful and touching letter (*Letters,* 2. 336), ends, " That
I have not written sooner, you may impute to absence, to ill-
health, to any thing rather than want of regard to the benefactress
of my departed friend."

would I; though I could give her a bite!—but she
must provoke me much first.   In volatile talk, indeed,
I may have spoken of her not much to her mind; for
in the tumult of conversation malice is apt to grow
sprightly; and there, I hope, I am not yet decrepid!' "
He quite laughed aloud at this characteristic
speech.

I most readily assured the Doctor that I had
never yet seen him limp!

Tuesday.[1]—I spent the afternoon with Dr. Johnson, who indeed is very ill,[2] and whom I could hardly
tell how to leave.   But he is rather better since,
though still in a most alarming way.   Indeed, I am
very much afraid for him!   He was very, very kind!
—Oh, what a cruel, heavy loss will he be!

Tuesday, Dec. 30.—I went to Dr. Johnson, and
spent the evening with him.   He was very indifferent,
indeed.   There were some very disagreeable people
with him; and he once affected me very much, by
turning suddenly to me, and grasping my hand, and
saying,

" The blister I have tried for my breath [3] has betrayed some very bad tokens; but I will not terrify
myself by talking of them: ah, *priez Dieu pour
moi!* "

You may believe I promised that I would!—Good

---

[1] December 16.
[2] See the letters to Mrs. Thrale (December 13) and Dr. Taylor
(December 20), *Letters,* 2. 364 ff.
[3] See *Letters,* 2. 369.

and excellent as he is, how can he so fear death?[1]
—Alas, my Susy, how awful is that idea!—He was
quite touchingly affectionate to me. How earnestly I
hope for his recovery!

Tuesday, Jan. 6.—I spent the afternoon with Dr.
Johnson, and had the great satisfaction of finding
him better.

Monday, April 19.—I went in the evening to see
dear Dr. Johnson. He received me with open arms,
scolded me with the most flattering expressions for
my absence, but would not let me come away without making me promise to dine with him next day,
on a salmon from Mrs. Thrale.[2] This I did not dare
refuse, as he was urgent, and I had played truant so
long; but, to be sure, I had rather have dined first, on
account of poor Blacky.[3] He is amazingly recovered,

---

[1] In a letter to Mrs. Thrale, dated December 31 (*Letters,* 2. 369)
he describes himself as "looking back with sorrow, and forward
with terrour." In considering Johnson's dread of death, two
things must always be remembered: (1) he feared not the physical
pangs of dissolution, but the fate of his soul. Boswell says (*Life,*
2. 298), "His fear . . . was the result of philosophical and re-
ligious consideration. He feared death, but he feared nothing else,
not even what might occasion death." (2) He was resigned and
hopeful at the end. (*Life,* 4. 416 ff.)

[2] On this day Johnson wrote to Mrs. Thrale, "I received in the
morning your magnificent fish, and in the afternoon your apology
for not sending it. . . . Since I was sick I know not if I have
not had more delicacies sent me than I had ever seen till I saw
your table." (*Letters,* 2. 390 ff.)

[3] Mr. Dobson (*Diary,* 2. 252, note) is undoubtedly correct in
assuming that this is a reference to Frank Barber, Johnson's negro
servant. He quotes from the *Life,* 2. 215, "Foote, I remember, in
allusion to Francis, the *negro,* was willing to suppose that our
repast was *black broth.*"

and perfectly good-humoured and comfortable, and smilingly alive to idle chat.

At Dr. Johnson's we had Mr. and Mrs. Hoole and their son, and Mrs. Hall,[1] a very good Methodist, and sister of John Wesley. The day was tolerable, but Dr. Johnson is never his best when there is nobody to draw him out;[2] but he was much pleased with my coming, and very kind indeed.

Norbury Park,[3] *Sunday, Nov. 28.*—Last Thursday, Nov. 25, my father set me down at Bolt Court, while he went on upon business. I was anxious to again see poor Dr. Johnson, who has had terrible health since his return from Lichfield.[4] He let me in, though very ill. He was alone, which I much rejoiced at; for I had a longer and more satisfactory conversation with him than I have had for many months. He was in rather better spirits, too, than I have lately seen him; but he told me he was

---

[1] "Sister of the Rev. Mr. John Wesley, and resembling him, as I thought, both in figure and manner" (*Life,* 4. 92 ff.), which passage see also for a conversation between her and Dr. Johnson. Mrs. Hall was a Methodist preacher.

[2] See above, p. 3.

[3] The residence of her friends, Mr. and Mrs. Locke. Mrs. Locke took Mrs. Thrale's place as Miss Burney's dear friend, companion, and hostess. See *Diary,* 2, *passim.*

[4] "In July I went to Lichfield, and performed the journey with very little fatigue in the common vehicle, but found no help from my native air. I then removed to Ashbourn, in Derbyshire, where for some time I was oppressed very heavily by the asthma; and the dropsy had advanced so far, that I could not without great difficulty button me at my knees." (*Letters,* 2. 423.) Towards the end of September, he returned to Lichfield. The symptoms of his illness may be found in the series of painful letters which he wrote to various friends from there. This was the last visit that Johnson made; he returned to London on November 16.

going to try what sleeping out of town might do for him.

"I remember," said he, "that my wife, when she was near her end,[1] poor woman, was also advised to sleep out of town; and when she was carried to the lodgings that had been prepared for her, she complained that the staircase was in very bad condition—for the plaster was beaten off the walls in many places. 'Oh,' said the man of the house, 'that's nothing but by the knocks against it of the coffins of the poor souls that have died in the lodgings!'"

He laughed, though not without apparent secret anguish, in telling me this. I felt extremely shocked, but, willing to confine my words at least to the literal story, I only exclaimed against the unfeeling absurdity of such a confession.

"Such a confession," cried he, "to a person then coming to try his lodging for her health, contains, indeed, more absurdity than we can well lay our account for."

I had seen Miss T.[2] the day before.

"So," said he, "did I."

I then said, "Do you ever, sir, hear from her mother?"

"No," cried he, "nor write to her. I drive her quite from my mind. If I meet with one of her letters, I burn it instantly. I have burnt all I can find. I never speak of her, and I desire never to hear of

---

[1] She died in 1752.
[2] Miss Thrale, who had separated from her mother at the time of the latter's marriage to Piozzi.

her more.   I drive her, as I said, wholly from my mind."

Yet, wholly to change this discourse, I gave him a history of the Bristol milk-woman [1] and told him the tales I had heard of her writing so wonderfully, though she had read nothing but Young and Milton; "though those," I continued, "could never possibly, I should think, be the first authors with anybody. Would children understand them? and grown people who have not read are children in literature."

"Doubtless," said he; "but there is nothing so little comprehended among mankind as what is genius.   They give to it all, when it can be but a part.   Genius is nothing more than knowing the use of tools; [2] but there must be tools for it to use: a man who has spent all his life in this room will give a very poor account of what is contained in the next."

[1] The poems of this woman, after having been submitted to the correction of Miss Hannah More, appeared in a handsome quarto, towards the end of 1784 (dated ahead 1785), entitled, *Poems on Several Occasions* by Ann Yearsley, a Milkwoman of Bristol. An enormous list of distinguished subscribers contains the names of Miss Burney and her father.   Later Mrs. Yearsley lost the patronage of Miss More, and having no adventitious appeal, like that of her townsman Chatterton, sank gradually from public view.

[2] Johnson, like Carlyle later, believed genius to be an inborn power or insight which might be turned by education into almost any channel.   "One man has more mind than another.   He may direct it differently; he may, by accident, see the success of one kind of study, and take a desire to excel in it.   I am persuaded that had Sir Isaac Newton applied to poetry, he would have made a very fine epic poem.   I could as easily apply to law as to tragic poetry.   BOSWELL. Yet, Sir, you did apply to tragic poetry, not to law.   JOHNSON. Because, Sir, I had not money to study law. Sir, the man who has vigour, may walk to the east just as well as to the west, if he happens to turn his head that way." (*Life*, 5.35.)   Cf. *Life*, 2.437, note, for a comparison of various passages on this subject.

" Certainly, sir; yet there is such a thing as invention? Shakespeare could never have seen a Caliban."

" No; but he had seen a man, and knew, therefore, how to vary him to a monster. A man who would draw a monstrous cow, must first know what a cow commonly is; or how can he tell that to give her an an ass's head or an elephant's tusk will make her monstrous? Suppose you show me a man who is a very expert carpenter; another will say he was born to be a carpenter—but what if he had never seen any wood? Let two men, one with genius, the other with none, look at an overturned waggon:—he who has no genius, will think of the waggon only as he sees it, overturned, and walk on; he who has genius, will paint it to himself before it was overturned,—standing still, and moving on, and heavy loaded, and empty; but both must see the waggon, to think of it at all."

How just and true all this, my dear Susy! He then animated, and talked on, upon this milk-woman, upon a once as famous shoemaker,[1] and upon our immortal Shakespeare, with as much fire, spirit, wit, and truth of criticism and judgment, as ever yet I have heard him. How delightfully bright are his faculties,

---

[1] " He spoke with much contempt of the notice taken of Woodhouse, the poetical shoemaker. He said it was all vanity and childishness: and that such subjects were, to those who patronised them, mere mirrours of their own superiority. ' They had better (said he), furnish the man with good implements for his trade, then raise subscriptions for his poems. He may make an excellent shoemaker, but can never make a good poet. A schoolboy's exercise may be a pretty thing for a schoolboy; but it is no treat for a man.' " (*Life*, 2. 127; cf. 1. 520.)

though the poor and infirm machine that contains them seems alarmingly giving way.

Yet, all brilliant as he was, I saw him growing worse, and offered to go, which, for the first time I ever remember, he did not oppose; but, most kindly pressing both my hands,

" Be not," he said, in a voice of even tenderness, " be not long in coming again for my letting you go now."

I assured him I would be the sooner, and was running off, but he called me back, in a solemn voice, and, in a manner the most energetic, said,

" Remember me in your prayers! "

I longed to ask him to remember me, but did not dare. I gave him my promise, and, very heavily indeed, I left him. Great, good, and excellent that he is, how short a time will he be our boast! Ah, my dear Susy, I see he is going! This winter will never conduct him to a more genial season here! Elsewhere, who shall hope a fairer? I wish I had bid him pray for me; but it seemed to me presumptuous, though this repetition of so kind a condescension might, I think, have encouraged me.

St. Martin's Street, Wednesday, Dec. 10.—I went in the evening to poor Dr. Johnson. Frank told me he was very ill, but let me in. He would have taken me upstairs, but I would not see him without his direct permission. I desired Frank to tell him I called to pay my respects to him, but not to disturb him if he was not well enough to see me. Mr.

Strahan,[1] a clergyman, he said, was with him alone.

In a few minutes, this Mr. Strahan came to me himself. He told me Dr. Johnson was very ill, very much obliged to me for coming, but so weak and bad he hoped I would excuse his not seeing me. . . .

Dear, dear, and much-reverenced Dr. Johnson! how ill or how low must he be, to decline seeing a creature he has so constantly, so fondly, called about him! If I do not see him again I shall be truly afflicted. And I fear, I almost know, I cannot!

At night my father brought us the most dismal tidings of dear Dr. Johnson. Dr. Warren had seen him, and told him to take what opium he pleased![2] He had thanked and taken leave of all his physicians. Alas!—I shall lose him, and he will take no leave of me! My father was deeply depressed; he has himself tried in vain for admission this week. Yet some people see him—the Hooles, Mr. Sastres, Mr. Langton;—but then they must be in the house, watching for one moment, whole hours. I hear from every one he is now perfectly resigned to his approaching fate, and no longer in terror of death.[3] I am thankfully happy in hearing that he speaks himself now of the change his mind has undergone, from its dark horror, and says—" He feels the irradiation of hope! "

---

[1] See *Life*, 4. 415 ff.

[2] He did not avail himself of this permission. When he realized that he was beyond medical aid, he said, " I will take no more physic, not even my opiates; for I have prayed that I may render up my soul to God unclouded." Boswell adds, " In this resolution he persevered." (*Life*, 4. 415.)

[3] Cf. *Life*, 4. 416.

Good, and pious, and excellent Christian—who shall feel it if not he?

Thursday morning.[1]—I am told by Mr. Hoole,[2] that he inquired of Dr. Brocklesby if he thought it likely he might live six weeks? and the Doctor's hesitation saying—No—he has been more deeply depressed than ever. Fearing death as he does, no one can wonder. Why he should fear it, all may wonder.

He sent me down yesterday, by a clergyman who was with him,[3] the kindest of messages, and I hardly know whether I ought to go to him again or not; though I know still less why I say so, for go again I both must and shall. One thing, his extreme dejection of mind considered, has both surprised and pleased me; he has now constantly an amanuensis with him, and dictates to him such compositions, particularly Latin and Greek, as he has formerly made, but repeated to his friends without ever committing to paper.[4] This, I hope, will not only gratify his survivors, but serve to divert him.

[1] This extract from a letter to Mrs. Locke, begun Sunday, December 7, but not completed till Thursday, December 11, actually precedes the entry for December 10 in the original *Diary;* but as it relates to the same visit (though written a day later), it is here given in its proper chronological position. Hill (*Life,* 4. 439) incorrectly assumes that the date should be December 9.

[2] See above, p. 174, note.

[3] Mr. Strahan.

[4] "He was able, in the course of his restless nights, to make translations of Greek epigrams from the *Anthologia;* and to compose a Latin epitaph for his father, his mother, and his brother Nathaniel. He meditated at the same time, a Latin inscription to the memory of Garrick, but his vigour was exhausted." Murphy, in *Miscellanies,* 1. 445. Boswell records that he repeated to his attendants the verses on Sir John Lade referred to above, p. 33, note. (*Life,* 4. 411.)

The good Mr. Hoole and equally good Mr. Sastres attend him, rather as nurses than friends, for they sit whole hours by him, without even speaking to him. He will not, it seems, be talked to—at least very rarely. At times, indeed, he reanimates; but it is soon over, and he says of himself, " I am now like Macbeth,—question enrages me." [1]

My father saw him once while I was away, and carried Mr. Burke with him,[2] who was desirous of paying his respects to him once more in person. He rallied a little while they were there; and Mr. Burke, when they left him, said to my father—" His work is almost done; and well has he done it! "

Dec. 11.—We had a party to dinner, by long appointment, for which, indeed, none of us were well disposed, the apprehension of hearing news only of death being hard upon us all. The party was, Dr. Rose, Dr. Gillies, Dr. Garthshore, and Charles.[3]

The day could not be well—but mark the night.

---

[1] Mr. Hoole, in his ' Narrative,' records this utterance under date, November 28. (*Miscellanies,* 2. 151.) It is therefore hardly to be thought of as one of his dying utterances.

[2] Langton told Boswell that "one day he found Mr. Burke and four or five more friends sitting with Johnson. Mr. Burke said to him, 'I am afraid, Sir, such a number of us may be oppressive to you.' 'No, sir (said Johnson), it is not so; and I must be in a wretched state, indeed, when your company would not be a delight to me.' Mr. Burke, in a tremulous voice expressive of being very tenderly affected, replied, 'My dear Sir, you have always been too good to me.' Immediately afterwards he went away. This was the last circumstance in the acquaintance of these two eminent men." (*Life,* 4. 407.)

[3] Dr. Rose and Dr. Gillies were distinguished classical scholars; Dr. Garthshore was a physician. Dr. Rose was master of Chiswick School, where Charles Burney was an instructor.

My father, in the morning, saw this first of men!
I had not his account till bedtime; he feared over-
exciting me. He would not, he said, but have seen
him for worlds! He happened to be better, and admitted him. He was up, and very composed. He
took his hand very kindly, asked after all his family,
and then, in particular, how Fanny did?

" I hope," he said, " Fanny did not take it amiss
that I did not see her? I was very bad! "

Amiss!—what a word! Oh that I had been present to have answered it! My father stayed, I suppose, half an hour, and then was coming away. He
again took his hand, and encouraged him to come
again to him; and when he was taking leave, said—
" Tell Fanny to pray for me! "

Ah! dear Dr. Johnson! might I but have *your*
prayers! After which, still grasping his hand, he
made a prayer himself,—the most fervent, pious,
humble, eloquent, and touching, my father says, that
ever was composed. Oh, would I had heard it! He
ended it with Amen! in which my father joined, and
was echoed by all present. And again, when my
father was leaving him, he brightened up, something
of his arch look returned, and he said—" I think I
shall throw the ball at Fanny yet! " [1]

Little more passed ere my father came away, decided, most tenderly, not to tell me this till our party
was gone.

This most earnestly increased my desire to see him;

[1] Probably, begin a conversation with; from the old phrase
" To take up the ball: to take one's turn in conversation, etc."
(*N. E. D.*)

this kind and frequent mention of me melted me
into double sorrow and regret. I would give the
world I had but gone to him that day! It was, however, impossible, and the day was over before I knew
he had said what I look upon as a call to me. This
morning, after church time, I went. Frank said he
was very ill, and saw nobody; I told him I had
understood by my father the day before that he meant
to see me. He then let me in. I went into his room
upstairs; he was in his bedroom. I saw it crowded,
and ran hastily down. Frank told me his master had
refused seeing even Mr. Langton. I told him merely
to say I had called, but by no means to press my admission. His own feelings were all that should be
consulted; his tenderness, I knew, would be equal,
whether he was able to see me or not.

I went into the parlour, preferring being alone in
the cold, to any company with a fire. Here I waited
long, here and upon the stairs, which I ascended and
descended to meet again with Frank, and make inquiries; but I met him not. At last upon Dr. Johnson's ringing his bell, I saw Frank enter his room,
and Mr. Langton follow. " Who's that? " I heard
him say; they answered, " Mr. Langton," and I
found he did not return.

Soon after, all the rest went away but a Mrs.
Davis, a good sort of woman,[1] whom this truly

---

[1] On September 16, 1783, Johnson wrote to Frank, " I purpose to
be with [you] on Thursday before dinner. As Thursday is my
birthday, I would have a little dinner got, and would have you
invite Mrs. Desmoulins, Mrs. Davis that was about Mrs. Williams,
and Mr. Allen and Mrs. Gardiner."

charitable soul had sent for to take a dinner at his
house. I then went and waited with her by the fire:
it was, however, between three and four o'clock before I got any answer. Mr. Langton then came himself. He could not look at me, and I turned away
from him. Mrs. Davis asked how the Doctor was?
"Going on to death very fast!" was his mournful
answer. "Has he taken," she said, "anything?"
"Nothing at all! We carried him some bread and
milk—he refused it, and said—'*The less the better.*'"
She asked more questions, by which I found his
faculties were perfect, his mind composed, and his
dissolution was quick drawing on.

.   .   .   .

I could not immediately go on, and it is now long
since I have written at all; but I will go back to this
afflicting theme, which I can now better bear.

Mr. Langton was, I believe, a quarter of an
hour in the room before I suspected he meant to
speak to me, never looking near me. At last
he said,

"This poor man, I understand, ma'am, desired
yesterday to see you."

"My understanding that, sir, brought me to-
day."

"Poor man! it is pity he did not know himself
better, and that you should have had this trouble."

"Trouble!" cried I; "I would come a hundred
times to see him the hundredth and first!"

"He hopes, now, you will excuse him; he is very

sorry not to see you; but he desired me to come and speak to you myself, and tell you he hopes you will excuse him, he feels himself too weak for such an interview."

I hastily got up, left him my most affectionate respects, and every good wish I could half utter, and ran back to the coach. Ah, my Susy! I have never been to Bolt Court since!

Dec. 20.—This day was the ver-honoured, everlamented Dr. Johnson committed to the earth. Oh, how sad a day to me! My father attended, and so did Charles. I could not keep my eyes dry all day; nor can I now, in the recollecting it; but let me pass over what to mourn is now so vain!

I long to know [1] what you think of our dear Dr. Johnson's meditations,[2] and if you do not, in the midst of what you will wish unpublished, see stronger than ever the purity of his principles and character, and only lament that effusions should be given to the world that are too artless to be suited to it.

[1] From a letter to Dr. Burney, dated September 24, 1785.
[2] *Prayers and Meditations,* Composed by Samuel Johnson, LL.D., and published from his manuscripts by George Strahan . . . London, 1785. Strahan was the clergyman mentioned above, p. 188, who attended the dying Johnson. This work may be most easily consulted in the *Miscellanies,* 1. 1 ff. It is significant of the popular interest in Johnson that, within two years of his death, there appeared from the press, not only the work mentioned above, but also anonymous *Memoirs,* a biographical sketch in the *Gentleman's Magazine, The Beauties of Samuel Johnson, Table-Talk, Last Words of Dr. Johnson, More Last Words of Dr. Johnson,* Mme. Piozzi's *Anecdotes,* and Boswell's *Journal of a Tour to the Hebrides.* The official *Life,* by Sir John Hawkins, appeared in 1787. Boswell's *Life* did not appear till 1791.

Tuesday, Dec. 20.[1]—1st, summons; 2ndly, entrée.
" Miss Burney, have you heard that Boswell is
going to publish a life of your friend Dr. Johnson? "[2]

" No, ma'am."

" I tell you as I heard. I don't know for the truth
of it, and I can't tell what he will do. He is so
extraordinary a man, that perhaps he will devise
something extraordinary."[3]

He[4] had lately, he told me, had much conversation concerning me with Mr. Boswell. I feel sorry
to be named or remembered by that biographical,
anecdotical memorandummer, till his book of poor
Dr. Johnson's life is finished and published. What
an anecdote, however, did he tell me of that most
extraordinary character! He is now an actual
admirer and follower of Mrs. Rudd![5]—and
avows it, and praises her extraordinary attractions
aloud!

The King came into the room during coffee, and
talked over Sir John Hawkins's *Life of Dr. Johnson*

---

[1] The conversation with Queen Charlotte here recorded took
place at the house of Mrs. Delany (above, p. 160), where Miss
Burney happened to be visiting.

[2] Boswell announced his intention of publishing a *Life of Johnson*
in his *Journal of a Tour to the Hebrides,* which was published in
this year.

[3] Her sarcasm proved greater wisdom than she could have
suspected.

[4] Miss Burney had recently become, as a result of the meeting
with the king and queen mentioned above, one of Queen Charlotte's Dressers. The " he " of the first sentence is one of her
fellow-slaves, the Queen's French reader, whom Miss Burney always
calls " Mr. Turbulent," for whom see *Diary,* 3, *passim.*

[5] See above, p. 47, note 3.

and with great candour and openness. I have not yet read it.

Once before, when I lived in the world,[1] I had met with Dr. Beattie,[2] but he then spoke very little, the company being large; and for myself, I spoke not at all. Our personal knowledge of each other therefore sunk not very deep. It was at the house of Miss Reynolds. My ever-honoured Dr. Johnson was there, and my poor Mrs. Thrale, her 'aughter, Mrs. Ord, Mrs. Horneck, Mrs. Gwynn,[3] the Bishop of Dromore,[4] and Mrs. Percy, and Mr. Boswell, and Mr. Seward, with some others.

Many things I do recollect of that evening, particularly one laughable circumstance. I was coming away at night, without having been seen by Dr. Johnson, but knowing he would reproach me afterwards, I begged my father to tell him I wished him good-night. He instantly called me up to him, took both my hands, which he extended as far asunder as they would go, and just as I was unfortunately curtseying to be gone, he let them loose and dropped both his own on the two sides of my hoop, with so ponderous a weight, that I could not for some time rise from the inclined posture into which I had put myself, and in which, though quite unconscious of what he was about, he seemed forcibly holding me.

---

[1] That is, before she became one of the queen's attendants. Her life at court was a species of slavery slowly undermining her health and spirits.

[2] It is not recorded elsewhere in the *Diary*.

[3] Goldsmith's "Jessamy Bride," formerly Mary Horneck.

[4] Dr. Percy.

Wednesday, January 9.—To-day Mrs. Schwellenberg [1] did me a real favour, and with real good-nature; for she sent me the letters of my poor lost friends, Dr. Johnson and Mrs. Thrale,[2] which she knew me to be almost pining to procure. The book belongs to the Bishop of Carlisle, who lent it to Mr. Turbulent, from whom it was again lent to the Queen, and so passed on to Mrs. Schwellenberg. It is still unpublished.

With what a sadness have I been reading! what scenes has it revived!—what regrets renewed! These letters have not been more improperly published in the whole, than they are injudiciously displayed in their several parts. She has given all—every word [3] —and thinks that, perhaps, a justice to Dr. Johnson, which, in fact, is the greatest injury to his memory.[4]

The few she has selected of her own do her, indeed, much credit: she has discarded all that were trivial and merely local, and given only such as contain something instructive, amusing, or ingenious.

About four of the letters, however, of my ever-revered Dr. Johnson are truly worthy his exalted

[1] This was the old German woman, Miss Burney's fellow-attendant on the queen, whom Macaulay genially describes as "a hateful old toad-eater, as illiterate as a chambermaid, as proud as a whole German chapter, rude, peevish, unable to bear solitude, unable to conduct herself with common decency in society."

[2] Mrs. Thrale was not lost to her by death, but only by her marriage with Piozzi, which Miss Burney, like Johnson, never really forgave; cf. above, p. 184.

[3] This is not literally true.

[4] Miss Burney, like Hannah More, who implored Boswell to "mitigate the asperities" of Johnson's character, had small confidence in the advisability of telling the whole truth. To what ridiculous results her theory of clipping and adorning the facts led her may be seen in her *Memoirs of Dr. Burney.*

powers: one is upon Death,[1] in considering its approach as we are surrounded, or not, by mourners; another, upon the sudden and premature loss of poor Mrs. Thrale's darling and only son.[2]

Our name once occurs: how I started at its sight!—'Tis to mention the party that planned the first visit to our house:[3] Miss Owen, Mr. Seward, Mrs. and Miss Thrale, and Dr. Johnson. How well shall we ever, my Susan, remember that morning!

He loved Dr. Johnson,[4]—and Dr. Johnson returned his affection. Their political principles and connections were opposite, but Mr. Wyndham respected his venerable friend too highly to discuss any points that could offend him; and showed for him so true a regard, that, during all his late illnesses, for the latter part of his life, his carriage and himself were alike at his service, to air, visit, or go out, whenever he was disposed to accept them.

Nor was this all; one tender proof he gave of warm and generous regard, that I can never forget, and that rose instantly to my mind when I heard his name, and gave him a welcome in my eyes when they met his face: it is this: Dr. Johnson, in his last visit to Lichfield, was taken ill, and waited to recover strength for travelling back to town in his usual

---

[1] No. 302, *Letters*, 1.212.
[2] No. 465, *Letters*, 1.381.
[3] No. 512, *Letters*, 2.4-5. See above, p. 1.
[4] This is an extract from the entry for February 13, descriptive of the trial of Warren Hastings. "Mr. Wyndham I had seen twice before . . . he is one of the most agreeable, spirited, well-bred, and brilliant conversers I have ever spoken with." (*Diary*, 3.419.) He attended the dying Johnson. (*Life*, 4.407.)

The Ghost of Johnson Haunting Mrs. Thrale

(A caricature, dated 1788)

vehicle, a stage-coach;—as soon as this reached the ears of Mr. Wyndham, he set off for Lichfield in his own carriage, to offer to bring him back to town in it, and at his own time.

For a young man of fashion, such a trait towards an old, however dignified philosopher, must surely be a mark indisputable of an elevated mind and character; and still the more strongly it marked a noble way of thinking, as it was done in favour of a person in open opposition to all his own party, and declared prejudices. . . .

I reminded him of the airings, in which he gave his time with his carriage for the benefit of Dr. Johnson's health. "What an advantage!" he cried, "was all that to myself! I had not merely an admiration, but a tenderness for him,—the more I knew him, the stronger it became. We never disagreed; even in politics I found it rather words than things in which we differed."

"And if you could so love him," cried I, "knowing him only in a general way, what would you have felt for him had you known him at Streatham?"

I then gave him a little history of his manners and way of life there,—his good humour, his sport, his kindness, his sociability, and all the many excellent qualities that, in the world at large, were by so many means obscured.

He was extremely interested in all I told him, and regrettingly said he had only known him in his worst days, when his health was upon its decline, and infirmities were crowding fast upon him.

" Had he lived longer," he cried, " I am satisfied
I should have taken him to my heart! have looked
up to him, applied to him, advised with him in the
most essential occurrences of my life? I am sure
too,—though it is a proud assertion,—he would have
liked me, also, better, had we mingled more. I felt
a mixed fondness and reverence growing so strong
upon me, that I am satisfied the closest union would
have followed his longer life "

I then mentioned how ki.`dly he had taken his
visit to him at Lichfield during a severe illness.
" And he left you," I said, " a book? " [1]

" Yes," he answered, " and he gave me one, also,
just before he died. ' You will look into this sometimes,' he said, ' and not refuse to remember whence
you had it.' "

And then he added he had heard him speak of
me,—and with so much kindness, that I was forced
not to press a recapitulation: yet now I wish I had
heard it.

Just before we broke up, " There is nothing," he
cried, with energy, " for which I look back upon myself with severer discipline than the time I have
thrown away in other pursuits, that might else have
been devoted to that wonderful man! "

And now for a scene a little surprising.

The beautiful chapel of St. George, repaired and
finished by the best artists at an immense expense,
which was now opened after a very long shutting up

[1] Copies of a work in Greek, and of the *New Testament*. (*Life,*
4. 402, note; 440.)

for its preparations, brought innumerable strangers to Windsor, and, among others, Mr. Boswell.

This I heard, in my way to the chapel, from Mr. Turbulent,[1] who overtook me, and mentioned having met Mr. Boswell at the Bishop of Carlisle's the evening before. He proposed bringing him to call upon me; but this I declined, certain how little satisfaction would be given here by the entrance of a man so famous for compiling anecdotes. But yet I really wished to see him again, for old acquaintance' sake, and unavoidable amusement from his oddity and good humour, as well as respect for the object of his constant admiration, my revered Dr. Johnson. I therefore told Mr. Turbulent I should be extremely glad to speak with him after the service was over.

Accordingly, at the gate of the choir, Mr. Turbulent brought him to me. We saluted with mutual glee: his comic-serious face and manner have lost nothing of their wonted singularity; nor yet have his mind and language, as you will soon confess.

" I am extremely glad to see you indeed," he cried, "but very sorry to see you here. My dear ma'am, why do you stay?—it won't do, ma'am! you must resign![2]—we can put up with it no longer. I told my good host the Bishop so last night; we are all grown quite outrageous! "

---

[1] See above, p. 198, note 4.

[2] So close was Miss Burney's confinement as "Dresser" that her health had begun to give way. Boswell was not the only one who complained of the treatment which she was patiently enduring. "Walpole asked whether her talents were given to be buried in obscurity. Wyndham . . . threatened to set the Literary Club on her father." Dobson's *Fanny Burney,* p. 172.

Whether I laughed the most, or stared the most, I am at a loss to say; but I hurried away from the cathedral, not to have such treasonable declarations overheard, for we were surrounded by a multitude.

He accompanied me, however, not losing one moment in continuing his exhortations: " If you do not quit, ma'am, very soon, some violent measures, I assure you, will be taken. We shall address Dr. Burney in a body; I am ready to make the harangue myself. We shall fall upon him all at once."

I stopped him to inquire about Sir Joshua;[1] he said he saw him very often, and that his spirits were very good. I asked about Mr. Burke's book.[2] " Oh," cried he, " it will come out next week: 'tis the first book in the world, except my own, and that's coming out also very soon; only I want your help."

" My help?"

" Yes, madam; you must give me some of your choice little notes of the Doctor's; we have seen him long enough upon stilts; I want to show him in a new light. Grave Sam, and great Sam, and solemn Sam, and learned Sam,—all these he has appeared over and over. Now I want to entwine a wreath of the graces across his brow; I want to show him as gay Sam, agreeable Sam, pleasant Sam; so you must help me with some of his beautiful billets to yourself."

I evaded this by declaring I had not any stores at hand. He proposed a thousand curious expedients to get at them, but I was invincible.

---

[1] His eyesight had recently begun to fail; he had lost the sight of one eye entirely, and apprehended total blindness.
[2] *Reflections on the Revolution in France.*

The Bust of Johnson Frowning at Boswell,
Courtenay, and Mrs. Thrale

(A caricature, dated 1786)

Then I was hurrying on, lest I should be too late.
He followed eagerly, and again exclaimed, " But,
ma'am, as I tell you, this won't do—you must resign
off-hand! Why, I would farm you out myself for
double, treble the money! I wish I had the regula-
tion of such a farm,—yet I am no farmer general.
But I should like to farm you, and so I will tell Dr.
Burney. I mean to address him; I have a speech
ready for the first opportunity."

He then told me his *Life of Dr. Johnson* was
nearly printed, and took a proof-sheet out of his
pocket to show me; with crowds passing and repass-
ing, knowing me well, and staring well at him; for
we were now at the iron rails of the Queen's Lodge.

I stopped; I could not ask him in: I saw he expected it, and was reduced to apologize, and tell him
I must attend the Queen immediately.

He uttered again stronger and stronger exhortations for my retreat, accompanied by expressions
which I was obliged to check in their bud. But finding he had no chance for entering, he stopped me
again at the gate, and said he would read me a page
of his work.

There was no refusing this; and he began, with a
letter of Dr. Johnson's to himself. He read it in
strong imitation of the Doctor's manner, very well,
and not caricature.[1] But Mrs. Schwellenberg was at

[1] Boswell was one of the best of the numerous mimics of Johnson, even rivalling Garrick. Hannah More tells how she was
once " the umpire in a trial of skill between Garrick and Boswell,
which could most nearly imitate Dr. Johnson's manner. I remember I gave it for Boswell in familiar conversation, and for
Garrick in reciting poetry." (*Miscellanies*, 2.195.)

her window, a crowd was gathering to stand round the rails, and the King and Queen and Royal family now approached from the Terrace. I made a rather quick apology, and, with a step as quick as my now weakened limbs have left in my power, I hurried to my apartment.

You may suppose I had inquiries enough, from all around, of " Who was the gentleman I was talking to at the rails? " And an injunction rather frank not to admit him beyond those limits.

However, I saw him again the next morning, in coming from early prayers, and he again renewed his remonstrance, and his petition for my letters of Dr. Johnson.

I cannot consent to print private letters, even of a man so justly celebrated, when addressed to myself; no, I shall hold sacred those revered and but too scarce testimonies of the high honour his kindness conferred upon me. One letter I have from him that is a masterpiece of elegance and kindness united. 'Twas his last.[1]

June 5.—Mr. Turbulent[2] at this time outstayed the tea-party one evening, not for his former rho-domontading, but to seriously and earnestly advise me to resign. My situation, he said, was evidently death to me.

---

[1] The famous letter reading, " Mr. Johnson who came home last night, sends his respects to Dear Doctor Burney, and all the dear Burneys little and great. Nov. 17th 1784." It was his last letter to the Burneys, not, as has been often inferred, the last he ever wrote.

[2] See above, p. 195. He prided himself upon being a wag.

He was eager to inquire of me who was Mrs. Lenox? He had been reading, like all the rest of the world, Boswell's *Life of Dr. Johnson,* and the preference there expressed of Mrs. Lenox to all other females [1] had filled him with astonishment, as he had never even heard her name.

These occasional sallies of Dr. Johnson, uttered from local causes and circumstances, but all retailed verbatim by Mr. Boswell, are filling all sort of readers with amaze, except the small party to whom Dr. Johnson was known, and who, by acquaintance with the power of the moment over his unguarded conversation, know how little of his solid opinion was to be gathered from his accidental assertions. [2]

The King, who was now also reading this work, [3] applied to me for explanations without end. Every night at this period he entered the Queen's dressing room, and delayed Her Majesty's proceedings by a length of discourse with me upon this subject. All that flowed from himself was constantly full of the goodness and benevolence of his character; and I was never so happy as in the opportunity thus

[1] "I dined yesterday at Mrs. Garrick's, with Mrs. Carter, Miss Hannah More, and Miss Fanny Burney. Three such women are not to be found: I know not where I could find a fourth, except Mrs. Lennox, who is superior to them all." (*Life*, 4. 275.) See also above, p. 49.

[2] It is of course the proud distinction of Boswell's *Life* that it records not only the solid opinions but the accidental assertions, not only the general and the impersonal, but the peculiar and distinguishing. Had Miss Burney but realized it, her own *Diary* was at its best when it most nearly resembled Boswell's greater work.

[3] Among the passages that must have interested King George is the description of his own conversation with Johnson. (*Life*, 2. 33 ff.)

graciously given me of vindicating, in instances almost innumerable, the serious principles and various excellences of Dr. Johnson from the clouds so frequently involving and darkening them, in narrations so little calculated for any readers who were strangers to his intrinsic worth, and therefore worked upon and struck by what was faulty in his temper and manners.

I regretted not having strength to read this work to Her Majesty myself. It was an honour I should else have certainly received; for so much wanted clearing! so little was understood! However, the Queen frequently condescended to read over passages and anecdotes which perplexed or offended her; and there were none I had not a fair power to soften or to justify. Dear and excellent Dr. Johnson! I have never forgot nor neglected his injunction given me when he was ill—to stand by him and support him, and not hear him abused when he was no more, and could not defend himself! but little—little did I think it would ever fall to my lot to vindicate him to his King and Queen.

This day had been long engaged for breakfasting with Mrs. Dickenson and dining with Mrs. Ord.

The breakfast guests were Mr. Langton, Mr. Foote, Mr. Dickenson, jun., a cousin, and a very agreeable and pleasing man; Lady Herries, Miss Dickenson, another cousin, and Mr. Boswell.

This last was the object of the morning. I felt a strong sensation of that displeasure which his lo-

quacious communications of every weakness and infirmity of the first and greatest good man of these
times have awakened in me at his first sight; and
though his address to me was courteous in the extreme, and he made a point of sitting next me, I felt
an indignant disposition to a nearly forbidding reserve and silence. How many starts of passion and
prejudice has he blackened into record, that else might
have sunk, for ever forgotten, under the preponder-
ance of weightier virtues and excellences!

Angry, however, as I have long been with him, he
soon insensibly conquered, though he did not soften
me: there is so little of ill design or ill nature in him,
he is so open and forgiving for all that is said in return that he soon forced me to consider him in a less
serious light, and change my resentment against his
treachery into something like commiseration of his
levity; and before we parted, we became good friends.
There is no resisting great good-humour,[1] be what
will in the opposite scale.

He entertained us all as if hired for that purpose,
telling stories of Dr. Johnson, and acting them with
incessant buffoonery. I told him frankly that if he
turned him into ridicule by caricature, I should fly
the premises: he assured me he would not, and indeed,
his imitations, though comic to excess, were so far
from caricature that he omitted a thousand gesticu-
lations which I distinctly remember.

Mr. Langton told some stories himself [2] in imita-

---

[1] See above, pp. 201 ff.
[2] He was one of Boswell's most fertile sources of Johnsonian information. See *Life*, 4. 1-2.

tion of Dr. Johnson; but they became him less than
Mr. Boswell, and only reminded of what Dr. Johnson himself once said to me—" Every man has some
time in his life, an ambition to be a wag." If Mr.
Langton had repeated anything from his truly great
friend quietly, it would far better have accorded with
his own serious and respectable character.

The proof of the frontispiece to Boswell's *Life,* with MS.
note in Boswell's handwriting

(First state of an engraving by Heath, from a portrait by Reynolds)

Second Impression of D. Johnson's Portrait
after the Plate had been improved by Sir
Joshua Reynolds's suggestions. Mr. Heath
afterwards gave it a few additional
touches.

Second state of Heath's engraving, with note by Boswell

EXTRACTS FROM THE MEMOIRS OF DR. BURNEY [1]

A few months [2] after the Streathamite morning
visit to St. Martin's-street that has been narrated,[3]
an evening party was arranged by Dr. Burney, for
bringing thither again Dr. Johnson and Mrs. Thrale,
at the desire of Mr. and Mrs. Greville and Mrs.
Crewe; [4] who wished under the quiet roof of Dr.
Burney, to make acquaintance with these celebrated
personages.

The party consisted of Dr. Johnson, Mr. and Mrs.
Greville, Mrs. Crewe, Mr., Mrs., and Miss Thrale;
Signor Piozzi, Mr. Charles Burney, the Doctor, his
wife and four of his daughters.

---

[1] These *Memoirs,* published in 1832, when Mme. D'Arblay was
eighty years old, repose largely upon her diaries and letters, and
often repeat—invariably in inferior form—the material of those
earlier works. Much of the work on Johnson in the *Memoirs*
is therefore not given here, because the superior version has already
been given. At times Mme. D'Arblay seems to be using material in the diaries that she destroyed or material that has never
been reprinted; sometimes she seems to be writing largely from
memory; at all times she is careful to dress up her material in a
style that Macaulay stigmatized as a "new Euphuism," a style that
reminds us now of Johnson at his worst, and now of Mr. Wilkins
Micawber. It is needless to point out that these reminiscences
are far less reliable than the strictly contemporary records that
have here preceded them.

[2] I have ventured to condense the following account, which is
unusually tumid, even for Mme. D'Arblay.

[3] See above, p. 1. Mme. D'Arblay had retold the story in the
Memoirs.

[4] Mr. Greville was the representative of a distinguished family
and the author of *Maxims, Characters, and Reflections,* a book
praised by Boswell. His wife was a poetess in a small way, the
author of an *Ode to Indifference.* Mrs. Crewe was their daughter.

Mr. Greville, in manner, mien, and high personal presentation, was still the superb Mr. Greville of other days.

The first step taken by Dr. Burney for social conciliation, which was calling for a cantata from Signor Piozzi, turned out, on the contrary, the herald to general discomfiture; for it cast a damp of delay upon the mental gladiators.

Piozzi, a first-rate singer, whose voice was deliciously sweet, and whose expression was perfect, sung in his very best manner, from his desire to do honour to *il Capo di Casa*[1]; but *il Capo di Casa* and his family alone did justice to his strains: neither the Grevilles nor the Thrales heeded music beyond what belonged to it as fashion: the expectations of the Grevilles were all occupied by Dr. Johnson.

Mr. Greville, who had been curious to see, and who intended to examine this leviathan of literature, as Dr. Johnson was called in the current pamphlets of the day, considered it to be his proper post to open the campaign of the *conversazione*. But he had heard so much, from his friend Topham Beauclerk, whose highest honour was classing himself as one of the friends of Dr. Johnson, that he was cautious how to encounter so tremendous a literary athletic. He thought it, therefore, most consonant to his dignity to leave his own character as author in the background; and to take the field with the aristocratic armour of pedigree and distinction. Aloof, therefore, he kept from all; and assuming his most supercilious air of

---

[1] Dr. Burney.

distant superiority, planted himself, immovable as a noble statue, upon the hearth, as if a stranger to the whole set.

Mrs. Greville would willingly have entered the lists herself, but that she naturally concluded Dr. Johnson would make the advances.

And Mrs. Crewe, to whom all this seemed odd and unaccountable, but to whom, also, from her love of anything unusual, it was secretly amusing, sat perfectly passive in silent observance.

Dr. Johnson, himself, had come with the full intention of passing two or three hours, with well-chosen companions, in social elegance. His own expectations, indeed, were small—for what could meet their expansion? his wish, however, to try all sorts and conditions of persons, as far as belonged to their intellect, was unqualified and unlimited; and gave to him nearly as much desire to see others, as his great fame gave to others to see his eminent self. But his signal peculiarity in regard to society, could not be surmised by strangers; and was as yet unknown even to Dr. Burney. This was that, notwithstanding the superior powers with which he followed up every given subject, he scarcely ever began one himself; [1] though the masterly manner in which, as soon as any topic was started, he seized it in all its bearings, had so much the air of belonging to the leader of the discourse, that this singularity was unnoticed and unsuspected, save by the experienced observation of long years of acquaintance.

[1] See above, pp. 3, 183.

Not, therefore, being summoned to hold forth, he remained silent; composedly at first, and afterwards abstractedly.

Dr. Burney now began to feel considerably embarrassed; though still he cherished hopes of ultimate relief from some auspicious circumstance. Vainly, however, he sought to elicit some observations that might lead to disserting discourse; all his attempts received only quiet, acquiescent replies, "signifying nothing." Every one was awaiting some spontaneous opening from Dr. Johnson.

Mrs. Thrale, of the whole coterie, was alone at her ease. She grew tired of the music, and yet more tired of remaining a mere cipher in the company. Her spirits rose rebelliously above her control; and, in a fit of utter recklessness of what might be thought of her by her fine new acquaintance, she suddenly, but softly, arose, and stealing on tip-toe behind Signor Piozzi; who was accompanying himself on the pianoforte to an animated *arria parlante,* with his back to the company, and his face to the wall; she ludicrously began imitating him by squaring her elbows, elevating them with ecstatic shrugs of the shoulders, and casting up her eyes, while languishingly reclining her head; as if she were not less enthusiastically, though somewhat more suddenly, struck with the transports of harmony than himself.

This grotesque ebullition of ungovernable gaiety was not perceived by Dr. Johnson, who faced the fire, with his back to the performer and the instrument. But the amusement which such an unlooked for exhibition caused to the party, was momentary; for Dr. Burney, shocked lest the poor Signor should observe, and be hurt by, this mimicry, glided gently round to Mrs. Thrale, and, with something between pleasantry and severity, whispered to her, " Because, Madam, you have no ear for music, will you destroy the attention of all who, in that one point, are otherwise gifted? "

It was now that shone the brightest attribute of Mrs. Thrale, sweetness of temper. She took this rebuke with a candour, and a sense of its justice the most amiable: she nodded her approbation of the admonition; and, returning to her chair, quietly sat down, as she afterwards said, like a pretty little miss, for the remainder of one of the most humdrum evenings that she had ever passed.

Strange, indeed, strange and most strange, the event considered, was the opening intercourse between Mrs. Thrale and Signor Piozzi. Little could she imagine that the person whom she was thus called away from holding up to ridicule, would become but a few years afterwards, the idol of her fancy and the lord of her destiny!

The most innocent person of all that went forward was the laurelled chief of the little association, Dr. Johnson; who, though his love for Dr. Burney made it a pleasure to him to have been included in the invitation, marvelled, probably, by this time, since uncalled upon to distinguish himself, why he had been bidden to the meeting. But as the evening advanced, he wrapt himself up in his own thoughts, in a manner it was frequently less difficult to him to do than to let alone, and became completely absorbed in silent rumination: sustaining, nevertheless, a grave and composed demeanour, with an air by no means wanting in dignity any more than in urbanity.

Very unexpectedly, however, ere the evening closed, he shewed himself alive to what surrounded him, by one of those singular starts of vision, that made him seem at times,—though purblind to things in common, and to things inanimate,—gifted with an eye of instinct for espying any action or position that he thought merited reprehension: for, all at once, looking fixedly on Mr. Greville, who, without much self-denial, the night being very cold, pertinaciously kept his station before the chimney-piece, he exclaimed: " If it were not for depriving the ladies of the fire,— I should like to stand upon the hearth myself! " [1]

A smile gleamed upon every face at this pointed speech. Mr. Greville tried to smile himself, though faintly and scoffingly. He tried, also, to hold to his post, as if determined to disregard so cavalier a liberty: but the sight of every eye around him cast down, and every visage struggling vainly to appear serious, disconcerted him; and though, for two or three minutes, he disdained to move, the awkwardness of the general pause impelled him, ere long, to glide back to his chair; but he rang the bell with force as he passed it, to order his carriage.

It is probable that Dr. Johnson had observed the

[1] Cf. Charlotte Burney's account of the same event, given below, p. 245.

high air and mien of Mr. Greville, and had purposely brought forth that remark to disenchant him from his self-consequence.

The party then broke up.[1]

While this charming work [2] was in progress, when only the Thrale family and its nearly adopted guests, the two Burneys, were assembled, Dr. Johnson, would frequently produce one of its proof-sheets to embellish [3] the breakfast table, which was always in the library; and was, certainly, the most sprightly and agreeable meeting of the day; for then, as no strangers were present to stimulate exertion, or provoke rivalry, argument was not urged on by the mere spirit of victory; it was instigated only by such truisms as could best bring forth that conflict of pros and cons which elucidates opposing opinions. Wit was not flashed with the keen sting of satire; yet it elicited not less gaiety from sparkling with an unwounding brilliancy, which brightened without inflaming, every eye, and charmed without tingling, every ear.

These proof-sheets Mrs. Thrale was permitted to read aloud; and the discussions to which they led were in the highest degree entertaining. Dr. Burney wistfully desired to possess one of them; but left to his daughter the risk of the petition. A hint, however,

---

[1] Johnson, it appears, met Greville again in 1780 at Dr. Burney's (*Letters*, 2. 146), but no account of the meeting has been preserved.

[2] Johnson's *Lives of the Poets*.

[3] Of Mme. D'Arblay's later style, Sir Leslie Stephen well says (*D.N.B.*): "In the *Memoirs of Dr. Burney* she adopted a peculiar magniloquence which may be equally regarded as absurd or delicious."

proved sufficient, and was understood not alone with compliance, but vivacity. Boswell, Dr. Johnson said, had engaged Frank Barber, his negro servant, to collect and preserve all the proof-sheets;[1] but though it had not been without the knowledge, it was without the order[1] or the interference of their author; to the present solicitor, therefore, willingly and without scruple, he now offered an entire life; adding, with a benignant smile, " Choose your poet! "

Without scruple, also, was the acceptance; and, without hesitation, the choice was Pope. And that not merely because, next to Shakespeare himself, Pope draws human characters the most veridically, perhaps, of any poetic delineator; but for yet another reason. Dr. Johnson composed with so ready an accuracy, that he sent his copy to the press unread;[2] reserving all his corrections for the proof-sheets: and, consequently, as not even Dr. Johnson could read twice without ameliorating some passages, his proof-sheets were at times liberally marked with changes; and, as the Museum copy of Pope's Translation of the Iliad, from which Dr. Johnson has given many examples, contains abundant emendations by Pope, the Memorialist[3] secured at once, on the same page, the marginal alterations and second thoughts of that great author, and of his great biographer.[4]

---

[1] *Life,* 3.371. There Boswell distinctly says that Johnson has *permitted* him to preserve the proof-sheets.
[2] An old habit. (Cf. *Life,* 1.203, 3.42, and above, p. 71, note.)
[3] Mme. D'Arblay's unostentatious way of referring to herself.
[4] This book is now in the possession of Mr. R. B. Adam, of Buffalo, N. Y.

[1]

POPE.

ALEXANDER POPE was born in London, May 22, 1688, of parents whofe rank or ftation was never afcertained : we are informed that they were of *gentle blood*; that his father was of a family of which the Earl of. Downe was the head, and that his mother was the daughter of William Turner, Efquire, of York, who had like-. wife three fons, one of whom had the. honour of being killed and the other of dying in the fervice of Charles the Firft;

A   the

First page of the proof-sheets of Johnson's *Life of Pope*, with correction in Johnson's handwriting, and a note by Miss Burney

When the book was published, Dr. Johnson brought to Streatham a complete set, handsomely bound, of the Works of the Poets, as well as his own Prefaces, to present to Mr. and Mrs. Thrale. And then, telling this Memorialist that to the King, and to the chiefs of Streatham alone he could offer so large a tribute, he most kindly placed before her a bound copy of his own part of the work; in the title page of which he gratified her earnest request by writing her name, and " From the Author."

After which, at her particular solicitation, he gave her a small engraving of his portrait from the picture of Sir Joshua Reynolds.[1] And while, some time afterwards, she was examining it at a distant table, Dr. Johnson, in passing across the room, stopt to discover by what she was occupied; which he no sooner discerned, than he began see-sawing for a moment or two in silence; and then with a ludicrous half laugh, peeping over her shoulder, he called out: " Ah ha!—Sam Johnson!—I see thee!—and an ugly dog thou art! "

He even extended his kindness to a remembrance of Mr. Bewley, the receiver and preserver of the wisp of a Bolt-court hearth-broom,[2] as a relic of the

[1] As Sir Joshua painted at least six different portraits of Johnson, many of which were engraved before the death of Johnson this is no adequate description, as Mme. D'Arblay ought to have known. It is probable that she refers to the frontispiece used in the edition of the *Lives*, which is reproduced herewith.

[2] This occurred in 1760. I quote the account of it from the first volume of the *Memoirs*, p. 127. " While awaiting the appearance of his revered host, Mr. Burney recollected a supplication from the philosopher of Massingham [Mr. Bewley] to be indulged with some token, however trifling or common, of his friend's admission

Author of the *Rambler;* which anecdote Dr. Burney
had ventured to confess: and Dr. Johnson now, with
his compliments, sent a set of the Prefaces to St.
Martin's-street, directed,

"From the Broom Gentleman":

which Mr. Bewley received with rapturous gratitude.

Dr. Johnson, in compliment to his friend Dr. Burney, and by no means incurious himself to see the
hermit of Chessington,[1] immediately descended to
meet Mr. Crisp; and to aid Mrs. Thrale, who gave
him a vivacious reception, to do the honours of
Streatham.

The meeting, nevertheless, to the great chagrin of
Dr. Burney, produced neither interest nor pleasure:
for Dr. Johnson, though courteous in demeanour and
looks, with evident solicitude to shew respect to Mr.

to the habitation of this great man. Vainly, however, Mr. Burney
looked around the apartment for something that he might in-
noxiously purloin. Nothing but coarse and necessary furniture
was in view; nothing portable—not even a wafer, the cover of
a letter, or a split pen, was to be caught; till at length, he had
the happiness to espie an old hearth broom in the chimney-corner.
From this, with hasty glee, he cut off a bristly wisp, which he
hurried into his pocket-book; and afterwards formally folded in
silver paper, and forwarded, in a frank to Lord Oxford, for Mr.
Bewley; by whom the burlesque offering was hailed with good-
humoured acclamation, and preserved through life."
     I suspect that this delightfully inflated bit of narrative reposes
entirely upon the following brief entry in Miss Burney's *Early
Diary,* "Mr. Bewley accepted as a present or relic, a tuft of his
hearth-broom, which my father secretly cut off, and sent to him
in a frank. He thinks it more precious than pearls." (I. 169.)
     [1] "Chessington Hall, a rambling and ruinous old house between
Kingston and Epsom. At this date, though on high ground, it
stood in the middle of a wild and almost trackless common, which
separated it effectually from the passing stranger." (Dobson,
Fanny Burney, 13.)

SAMUEL JOHNSON L.L.D.

Frontispiece to the *Lives of the Poets,* 1781

Crisp, was grave and silent; and whenever Dr. Johnson did not make the charm of conversation, he only
marred it by his presence; from the general fear he
incited, that if he spoke not, he might listen; and
that if he listened—he might reprove.

Ease, therefore, was wanting; without which nothing in society can be flowing or pleasing. The Chessingtonian conceived, that he had lived too long away
from the world [1] to start any subject that might not,
to the Streathamites, be trite and out of date; and
the Streathamites believed that they had lived in it so
much longer, that the current talk of the day might,
to the Chessingtonian, seem unintelligible jargon:
while each hoped that the sprightly Dr. Burney would
find the golden mean by which both parties might be
brought into play.

But Dr. Burney, who saw in the kind looks and
complacency of Dr. Johnson intentional good-will to
the meeting, flattered himself that the great philolo-
gist was but waiting for an accidental excitement, to
fasten upon some topic of general use or importance,
and then to describe or discuss it, with the full powers
of his great mind.

Dr. Johnson, however, either in health or in spirits,
was, unfortunately, oppressed; and, for once, was
more desirous to hear than to be heard. [2]

Mr. Crisp, therefore, lost, by so unexpected a
taciturnity, this fair and promising opportunity for

---

[1] He had retired to Chessington nearly thirty years before.

[2] Miss Burney herself, however, has repeatedly observed (above,
pp. 3, 183, 211) that if Johnson was to talk with brilliancy, it was
necessary that he be " drawn out."

developing and enjoying the celebrated and extraordinary colloquial abilities of Dr. Johnson and finished the visit with much disappointment; lowered also, and always, in his spirits by parting from his tenderly attached young companion.

Dr. Burney had afterwards, however, the consolation to find that Mr. Crisp had impressed even Dr. Johnson with a strong admiration of his knowledge and capacity; for in speaking of him in the evening to Mr. Thrale, who had been absent, the Doctor emphatically said, "Sir, it is a very singular thing to see a man with all his powers so much alive, when he has so long shut himself up from the world. Such readiness of conception, quickness of recollection, facility of following discourse started by others, in a man who has so long had only the past to feed upon, are rarely to be met with. Now, for my part," added he, laughing, "that *I* should be ready or even universal, is no wonder; for my dear little mistress here," turning to Mrs. Thrale, "keeps all my faculties in constant play."

Mrs. Thrale then said that nothing, to her, was so striking, as that a man who had so long retired from the world, should so delicately have preserved its forms and courtesies, as to appear equally well bred with any elegant member of society who had not quitted it for a week.

Inexpressibly gratifying to Dr. Burney was the award of such justice, from such judges, to his best and dearest loved friend.

From this time forward, Dr. Burney could scarcely

recover his daughter from Streatham, even for a few days, without a friendly battle. A sportively comic exaggeration of Dr. Johnson's upon this flattering hostility was current at Streatham, made in answer to Dr. Burney's saying, upon a resistance to her departure for St. Martin's-street in which Dr. Johnson had strongly joined, " I must really take her away, Sir, I must indeed; she has been from home so long."

" Long? no, Sir! I do not think long," cried the Doctor, see-sawing, and seizing both her hands, as if purporting to detain her: " Sir! I would have her Always come—and Never go!——"

When next, after this adjuration, Dr. Burney took the Memorialist back to Streatham,[1] he found there, recently arrived from Scotland, Mr. Boswell; whose sprightly Corsican tour, and heroic, almost Quixotic pursuit of General Paoli, joined to the tour to the Hebrides with Dr. Johnson, made him an object himself of considerable attention.

He spoke the Scotch accent strongly,[2] though by no means so as to affect, even slightly, his intelligibility to an English ear. He had an odd mock solemnity of tone and manner, that he had acquired imperceptibly from constantly thinking of and imitating Dr. Johnson; whose own solemnity, nevertheless, far from mock, was the result of pensive rumina-

---

[1] If Mme. D'Arblay's reminiscences are chronologically arranged, this event probably took place on Monday, March 29, 1779. (See *Life,* 3. 377.) Miss Burney's *Diary* has but one entry for March, 1779, but at that time she was at Streatham. (*Diary,* 1. 211.)
[2] Boswell was particularly proud that he did not.

tion. There was, also, something slouching in the gait and dress of Mr. Boswell, that wore an air, ridiculously enough, of purporting to personify the same model. His clothes were always too large for him; his hair, or wig, was constantly in a state of negligence; and he never for a moment sat still or upright upon a chair. Every look and movement displayed either intentional or involuntary imitation. Yet certainly it was not meant as caricature; for his heart, almost even to idolatry, was in his reverence of Dr. Johnson.

Dr. Burney was often surprised that this kind of farcical similitude escaped the notice of the Doctor; but attributed his missing it to a high superiority over any such suspicion, as much as to his near-sightedness; for fully was Dr. Burney persuaded, that had any detection of such imitation taken place, Dr. Johnson, who generally treated Mr. Boswell as a schoolboy,[1] whom, without the smallest ceremony, he pardoned or rebuked, alternately, would so indignantly have been provoked, as to have instantaneously inflicted upon him some mark of his displeasure. And equally he was persuaded that Mr. Boswell, however shocked and even inflamed in receiving it, would soon, from his deep veneration, have thought it justly incurred;[2]

[1] In 1779 Boswell was in his thirty-ninth year, Johnson in his seventieth.
[2] This is unfair; Boswell was not servile in his quarrels and reconciliations with Johnson. (See, in particular, *Life,* 3. 338.) Altogether too much sport has been made of Boswell's devotion to Johnson. It is wrong to consider him as having foisted himself repeatedly upon Johnson, especially when we remember Johnson's pathetic appeals to his friends to keep him in mind, and to be near him as often as possible.

and, after a day or two of pouting and sullenness, would have compromised the matter by one of his customary simple apologies, of " Pray, Sir, forgive me ! "

Dr. Johnson, though often irritated by the officious importunity of Mr. Boswell, was really touched by his attachment. It was indeed surprising, and even affecting, to remark the pleasure with which this great man accepted personal kindness, even from the simplest of mankind; and the grave formality with which he acknowledged it even to the meanest. Possibly it was what he most prized, because what he could least command; for personal partiality hangs upon lighter and slighter qualities than those which earn solid approbation; but of this, if he had least command, he had also least want; his towering superiority of intellect elevating him above all competitors, and regularly establishing him, wherever he appeared, as the first Being of the society.

As Mr. Boswell was at Streatham only upon a morning visit, a collation was ordered, to which all were assembled. Mr. Boswell was preparing to take a seat that he seemed, by prescription, to consider as his own, next to Dr. Johnson; but Mr. Seward, who was present, waived his hand for Mr. Boswell to move further on, saying, with a smile, " Mr. Boswell, that seat is Miss Burney's."

He stared, amazed: the asserted claimant was new and unknown to him, and he appeared by no means pleased to resign his prior rights. But, after looking round for a minute or two, with an important air of demanding the meaning of this innovation, and receiving no satisfaction, he reluctantly, almost resentfully, got another chair; and placed it at the back of the shoulder of Dr. Johnson; while this new and unheard of rival quietly seated herself as if not hearing what was passing; for she shrunk from the explanation that she feared might ensue, as she saw a smile stealing over every countenance, that of Dr. Johnson himself not excepted, at the discomfiture and surprise of Mr. Boswell.

Mr. Boswell, however, was so situated as not to remark it in the Doctor; and of every one else, when in that presence, he was unobservant, if not contemptuous. In truth when he met with Dr. Johnson, he commonly forbore even answering anything that was said, or attending to anything that went forward, lest he should miss the smallest sound from that voice to which he paid such exclusive, though merited homage. But the moment that voice burst forth, the attention which it excited in Mr. Boswell amounted almost to pain. His eyes goggled with eagerness; he leant his ear almost on the shoulder of the Doctor; and his mouth dropt open to catch every syllable that might be uttered: nay, he seemed not only to dread losing a word, but to be anxious not to miss a breathing; as if hoping from it, latently, or mystically, some information.

But when, in a few minutes, Dr. Johnson, whose eye did not follow him, and who had concluded him to be at the other end of the table, said something gaily and good-humouredly, by the appellation of

Bozzy; and discovered, by the sound of the reply,
that Bozzy had planted himself, as closely as he
could, behind and between the elbows of the new
usurper and his own, the Doctor turned angrily
round upon him, and clapping his hand rather
loudly upon his knee, said, in a tone of displeasure,
"What do you do there, Sir?—Go to the table,
Sir!"

Mr. Boswell instantly, and with an air of affright,
obeyed: and there was something so unusual in such
humble submission to so imperious a command, that
another smile gleamed its way across every mouth,
except that of the Doctor and of Mr. Boswell; who
now, very unwillingly, took a distant seat.

But, ever restless when not at the side of Dr. Johnson, he presently recollected something that he wished
to exhibit, and, hastily rising, was running away in
its search; when the Doctor, calling after him, au-
thoritatively said: "What are you thinking of, Sir?
Why do you get up before the cloth is removed?—
Come back to your place, Sir!"

Again, and with equal obsequiousness, Mr. Boswell did as he was bid; when the Doctor, pursing
his lips, not to betray rising risibility, muttered half
to himself: "Running about in the middle of meals!
—One would take you for a Branghton!—"

"A Branghton, Sir?" repeated Mr. Boswell, with
earnestness; "what is a Branghton, Sir?"

"Where have you lived, Sir," cried the Doctor,
laughing, "and what company have you kept, not to
know that?"

Mr. Boswell now, doubly curious, yet always apprehensive of falling into some disgrace with Dr. Johnson, said, in a low tone, which he knew the Doctor could not hear, to Mrs. Thrale: " Pray, Ma'am, what's a Branghton?—Do me the favour to tell me?—Is it some animal hereabouts? "

Mrs. Thrale only heartily laughed, but without answering: as she saw one of her guests uneasily fearful of an explanation. But Mr. Seward cried, " I'll tell you, Boswell,—I'll tell you!—if you will walk with me into the paddock; only let us wait till the table is cleared; or I shall be taken for a Branghton, too! "

They soon went off together; and Mr. Boswell, no doubt, was fully informed of the road that had led to the usurpation by which he had thus been annoyed. But the Branghton fabricator took care to mount to her chamber [1] ere they returned; and did not come down till Mr. Boswell was gone.

Dr. Burney, when the Cecilian [2] business was arranged, again conveyed the Memorialist to Streatham. No further reluctance on his part, nor exhortations on that of Mr. Crisp, sought to withdraw her from that spot, where, while it was in its glory, they had so recently, and with pride, seen her distinguished. And truly eager was her own haste, when mistress of

---

[1] Miss Burney, like Evelina, was for ever "mounting to her chamber."
[2] *Cecilia* was published in July, 1782.

her time, to try once more to soothe those sorrows and chagrins in which she had most largely participated, by answering to the call, which had never ceased tenderly to pursue her, of return.

With alacrity, therefore, though not with gaiety, they re-entered the Streatham gates—but they soon perceived that they found not what they had left!

Changed, indeed, was Streatham! Gone its chief,[1] and changed his relict! unaccountably, incomprehensibly, indefinably changed! She was absent and agitated; not two minutes could she remain in a place; she scarcely seemed to know whom she saw; her speech was so hurried it was hardly intelligible; her eyes were assiduously averted from those who sought them, and her smiles were faint and forced.

The Doctor, who had no opportunity to communicate his remarks, went back, as usual, to town; where soon also, with his tendency, as usual, to view everything cheerfully, he revolved in his mind the new cares and avocations by which Mrs. Thrale was perplexed; and persuaded himself that the alteration which had struck him, was simply the effect of her new position.

Too near, however, were the observations of the Memorialist for so easy a solution. The change in her friend was equally dark and melancholy; yet not personal to the Memorialist was any alteration. No affection there was lessened; no kindness cooled; on the contrary, Mrs. Thrale was more fervent in both; more touchingly tender; and softened in disposition

---

[1] See above, p. 122, note.

beyond all expression, all description: but in everything else,—in health, spirits, comfort, general looks,
and manner, the change was at once universal and
deplorable. All was misery and mystery: misery the
most restless; mystery the most unfathomable.

The mystery, however, soon ceased; the solicita-
tions of the most affectionate sympathy could not long
be urged in vain;—the mystery passed away—not so
the misery! That, when revealed, was but to both
parties doubled, from the different feelings set in
movement by its disclosure.

The astonishing history of the enigmatical attachment which impelled Mrs. Thrale to her second marriage, is now as well known as her name; but its
details belong not to the history of Dr. Burney;
though the fact too deeply interested him, and was
too intimately felt in his social habits, to be passed
over in silence in any memoirs of his life.

But while ignorant yet of its cause, more and more
struck he became at every meeting, by a species of
general alienation which pervaded all around at
Streatham. His visits, which, heretofore, had seemed
galas to Mrs. Thrale, were now begun and ended almost without notice; and all others,—Dr. Johnson not
excepted,—were cast into the same gulph of general
neglect, or forgetfulness;—all,—save singly this
Memorialist!—to whom, the fatal secret once acknowledged, Mrs. Thrale clung for comfort; [1] though

---

[1] The fact that Mrs. Thrale communicated the story of her passion for Piozzi to Miss Burney under pledge of secrecy undoubtedly
accounts for the absence from the *Diary* of any account parallel to
this.

she saw, and generously pardoned, how wide she was from meeting approbation.[1]

In this retired, though far from tranquil manner, passed many months; during which, with the acquiescent consent of the Doctor, his daughter, wholly devoted to her unhappy friend, remained uninterruptedly at sad and altered Streatham; sedulously avoiding what at other times she most wished, a *tête-à-tête* with her father. Bound by ties indissoluble of honour not to betray a trust that, in the ignorance of her pity, she had herself unwittingly sought, even to him she was as immutably silent, on this subject, as to all others—save, singly, to the eldest daughter of the house; whose conduct, through scenes of dreadful difficulty, notwithstanding her extreme youth, was even exemplary; and to whom the self-beguiled, yet generous mother, gave full and free permission to confide every thought and feeling to the Memorialist.

And here let a tribute of friendship be offered up to the shrine of remembrance, due from a thousand ineffaceably tender recollections. Not wildly, and with male and headstrong passions, as has currently been asserted, was this connection brought to bear on the part of Mrs. Thrale. It was struggled against at time with even agonizing energy; and with efforts so vehement, as nearly to destroy the poor machine they were exerted to save. But the subtle poison had

---

[1] A modern reader finds difficulty in discovering any adequate reason why Mrs. Thrale should not have married Piozzi with the full approbation of her friends. See Broadley's *Dr. Johnson and Mrs. Thrale*, London, 1910. In 1782 Mrs. Thrale was in her forty-second year.

glided into her veins so unsuspectedly, and, at first, so unopposedly, that the whole fabric was infected with its venom; which seemed to become a part, never to be dislodged, of its system.

It was, indeed, the positive opinion of her physician and friend, Sir Lucas Pepys, that so excited were her feelings, and so shattered, by their early indulgence, was her frame, that the crisis which might be produced through the medium of decided resistance, offered no other alternative but death or madness.

A few weeks earlier, the Memorialist had passed a nearly similar scene with Dr. Johnson.[1] Not, however, she believes, from the same formidable species of surmise; but from the wounds inflicted upon his injured sensibility, through the palpably altered looks, tone, and deportment, of the bewildered lady of the mansion; who, cruelly aware what would be his wrath, and how overwhelming his reproaches against her projected union, wished to break up their residing under the same roof before it should be proclaimed.

This gave to her whole behaviour towards Dr. Johnson, a sort of restless petulancy, of which she was sometimes hardly conscious; at others, nearly reckless; but which hurt him far more than she purposed, though short of the point at which she aimed, of precipitating a change of dwelling that would elude its being cast, either by himself or the world, upon a passion that her understanding blushed to own; even while she was sacrificing to it all of

[1] She has just described her father's adieu to Streatham.

inborn dignity that she had been bred to hold most sacred.

Dr. Johnson, while still uninformed of an entanglement it was impossible he should conjecture, attributed her varying humours to the effect of wayward health meeting a sort of sudden wayward power: and imagined that caprices, which he judged to be partly feminine, and partly wealthy, would soberize themselves away in being unnoticed. He adhered, therefore, to what he thought his post, in being the ostensible guardian protector of the relict and progeny of the late chief of the house; taking no open or visible notice of the alteration in the successor—save only at times, and when they were *tête-à-tête*, to this Memorialist; to whom he frequently murmured portentous observations on the woeful, nay alarming deterioration in health and disposition of her whom, so lately, he had signalized as the gay mistress of Streatham.

But at length, as she became more and more dissatisfied with her own situation, and impatient for its relief, she grew less and less scrupulous with regard to her celebrated guest; she slighted his counsel; did not heed his remonstrances; avoided his society; was ready at a moment's hint to lend him her carriage when he wished to return to Bolt Court; but awaited a formal request to accord it for bringing him back.

The Doctor then began to be stung; his own aspect became altered; and depression, with indignant uneasiness, sat upon his venerable front.

It was at this moment that, finding the Memorialist

was going one morning to St. Martin's Street, he desired a cast thither in the carriage, and then to be set down at Bolt Court.

Aware of his disturbance, and far too well aware how short it was of what it would become when the cause of all that passed should be detected, it was in trembling that the Memorialist accompanied him to the coach, filled with dread of offending him by any reserve, should he force upon her any inquiry; and yet impressed with the utter impossibility of betraying a trusted secret.

His look was stern, though dejected, as he followed her into the vehicle; but when his eye, which, however short-sighted, was quick to mental perception, saw how ill at ease appeared his companion, all sternness subsided into an undisguised expression of the strongest emotion, that seemed to claim her sympathy, though to revolt from her compassion; while, with a shaking hand, and pointing finger, he directed her looks to the mansion from which they were driving; and, when they faced it from the coach window, as they turned into Streatham Common, tremulously exclaiming: " That house . . . is lost to *me*—for ever ! " [1]

During a moment he then fixed upon her an interrogative eye, that impetuously demanded: " Do you not perceive the change I am experiencing? "

[1] For Johnson's final farewell to Streatham, which occurred on Oct 6, 1782, see *Life*, 4.158 ff. This of course did not mean the end of his friendship with Mrs. Thrale, with whom he still corresponded (*Letters*, 2. *passim*); the revelation of the cause of Mrs. Thrale's coldness and distrust came much later (July, 1784). See below, and *Letters*, 2.404 ff.

A sorrowing sigh was her only answer.

Pride and delicacy then united to make him leave her to her taciturnity.

He was too deeply, however, disturbed to start or to bear any other subject; and neither of them uttered a single word till the coach stopt in St. Martin's Street, and the house and the carriage door were opened for their separation! He then suddenly and expressively looked at her, abruptly grasped her hand, and, with an air of affection, though in a low, husky voice, murmured rather than said: " Good-morning, dear lady!" but turned his head quickly away, to avoid any species of answer.

She was deeply touched by so gentle an acquiescence in her declining the confidential discourse upon which he had indubitably meant to open, relative to this mysterious alienation. But she had the comfort to be satisfied, that he saw and believed in her sincere participation in his feelings; while he allowed for the grateful attachment that bound her to a friend so loved; who, to her at least, still manifested a fervour of regard that resisted all change; alike from this new partiality, and from the undisguised, and even strenuous opposition of the Memorialist to its indulgence.

The " Adieu, Streatham!" that had been uttered figuratively by Dr. Burney, without any knowledge of its nearness to reality, was now fast approaching to becoming a mere matter of fact; for, to the almost equal grief, however far from equal loss, of Dr. Johnson and Dr. Burney, Streatham, a short time afterwards, though not publicly relinquished, was quitted by Mrs. Thrale and her family.

A latent,[1] but most potent reason, had, in fact, some share in abetting the elements in the failure of the Memorialist of paying her respects in Bolt Court at this period; except when attending thither her father. Dr. Burney feared her seeing Dr. Johnson alone; dreading, for both their sakes, the subject to which the Doctor might revert, if they should chance to be *tête-à-tête*. Hitherto, in the many meetings of the two Doctors and herself that had taken place after the paralytic stroke of Dr. Johnson,[2] as well as during the many that had more immediately followed the retreat of Mrs. Thrale to Bath, the name of that

---

[1] Mme. D'Arblay appears here to have confused two visits to Johnson, one made in November, 1783, the other in November, 1784. The letter to which she refers below, reproaching her for not calling (see above, p. 175), was sent November 19, 1783; but the conversation which she here records as having occurred at the subsequent visit could hardly have taken place at that time. There is no evidence that Johnson's feelings toward Mrs. Thrale were so bitter in the year 1783 as Mme. D'Arblay here represents them. As late as March 10, 1784, he wrote her, "Do not reject me from your thoughts. Shall we ever exchange confidence by the fireside again?" (*Letters,* 2.381); on the twenty-fifth of the same month, Mrs. Thrale is still his "mistress," and he complains that he does not understand her "disorder." On the other hand, during Miss Burney's visit to him in November, 1784, a conversation quite in keeping with the spirit of the one here recorded took place (above, pp. 184-85.) He drives Mrs Piozzi from his mind and burns her letters. There, as here, Miss Burney is in haste to change the subject of the conversation.

If, in spite of the evidence against it, this scene be an authentic occurrence of November, 1783 (long, it will be remembered, before Mrs. Thrale had ceased struggling against her passion for Piozzi), we can only feel that Johnson is selfish and unreasonable, finding no other excuse for his burst of wrath than his own words, "Illness makes a man a scoundrel." (*Diary,* 3.399.)

[2] June 16, 1783. (See above, p. 173, and *Letters,* 2.300 ff.)

lady had never once been mentioned by any of the three.

Not from any difference of opinion was the silence; it was rather from a painful certainty that their opinions must be in unison, and, consequently, that in unison must be their regrets. Each of them, therefore, having so warmly esteemed one whom each of them, now, so afflictingly blamed, they tacitly concurred that, for the immediate moment, to cast a veil over her name, actions, and remembrance, seemed what was most respectful to their past feelings, and to her present situation.

But, after the impressive reproach of Dr. Johnson [1] to the Memorialist relative to her absence; and after a seizure which caused a constant anxiety for his health, she could no longer consult her discretion at the expense of her regard; and, upon ceasing to observe her precautions, she was unavoidably left with him, one morning, by Dr. Burney, who had indispensable business further on in the city, and was to call for her on his return.

Nothing yet had publicly transpired, with certainty or authority, relative to the projects of Mrs. Thrale, who had now been nearly a year at Bath; though nothing was left unreported, or unasserted, with respect to her proceedings. Nevertheless, how far Dr. Johnson was himself informed, or was ignorant on the subject, neither Dr. Burney nor his daughter could tell; and each equally feared to learn.

Scarcely an instant, however, was the latter left

---

[1] The letter referred to p. 234, note 1.

alone in Bolt Court, ere she saw the justice of her long apprehensions; for while she planned speaking upon some topic that might have a chance to catch the attention of the Doctor, a sudden change from kind tranquility to strong austerity took place in his altered countenance; and, startled and affrighted, she held her peace.

A silence almost awful succeeded, though, previously to Dr. Burney's absence, the gayest discourse had been reciprocated.

The Doctor, then see-sawing violently in his chair, as usual when he was big with any powerful emotion whether of pleasure or of pain, seemed deeply moved; but without looking at her, or speaking, he intently fixed his eyes upon the fire; while his panic-struck visitor, filled with dismay at the storm which she saw gathering over the character and conduct of one still dear to her very heart, from the furrowed front, the laborious heaving of the ponderous chest, and the roll. of the large penetrating, wrathful eye of her honoured, but just then, terrific host, sate mute, motionless, and sad; tremblingly awaiting a mentally demolishing thunderbolt.

Thus passed a few minutes, in which she scarcely dared breathe; while the respiration of the Doctor, on the contrary, was of asthmatic force and loudness; then, suddenly turning to her, with an air of mingled wrath and woe, he hoarsely ejaculated: " Piozzi! "

He evidently meant to say more; but the effort with which he articulated that name robbed him of any voice for amplification, and his whole frame grew tremulously convulsed.

His guest, appalled, could not speak; but he soon discerned that it was grief from coincidence, not distrust from opposition of sentiment, that caused her taciturnity.

This perception calmed him, and he then exhibited a face " in sorrow more than anger." His see-sawing abated of its velocity, and, again fixing his looks upon the fire, he fell into pensive rumination.

From time to time, nevertheless, he impressively glanced upon her his full fraught eye, that told, had its expression been developed, whole volumes of his regret, his disappointment, his astonished indignancy; but, now and then, it also spoke so clearly and so kindly, that he found her sight and her stay soothing to his disturbance, that she felt as if confidentially communing with him, although they exchanged not a word.

At length, and with great agitation, he broke forth with: " She cares for no one! You, only—You, she loves still!—but no one—and nothing else!—You she still loves——"

A half smile now, though of no very gay character, softened a little the severity of his features, while he tried to resume some cheerfulness in adding: " As she loves her little finger! "

It was plain by this burlesque, or, perhaps, playfully literal comparison, that he meant now, and tried, to dissipate the solemnity of his concern.

The hint was taken; his guest started another subject; and this he resumed no more. He saw how distressing was the theme to a hearer whom he ever wished to please, not distress; and he named Mrs. Thrale no more. Common topics took place, till they were rejoined by Dr. Burney, whom then, and indeed always, he likewise he spared upon this subject.

APPENDIX

EXTRACTS FROM THE JOURNALS OF SUSAN AND CHARLOTTE BURNEY

" I have *such* a thing to tell you," [1] said he [my father] " about poor Fan " [2]—

" Dear sir, what? " and I immediately suppos'd he had spoke to Mrs. Thrale.

" Why to-night, we were sitting at tea—only Johnson, Mrs. Thrale and me—' Madam,' cried Johnson *see saw-ing* on his chair—' Mrs. Chol'mley was talking to me last night of a new novel,[3] which she says has a very uncommon share of merit—*Evelina*— She says she has not been so much entertained this great while as in reading it—and that she shall go all over London in order to discover the author '—

" ' Good G—d ' cried Mrs. Thrale—' why somebody else mentioned that book to me—Lady Westcote it was I believe—*The modest writer of Evelina,* she talk'd to me of.'

" ' Mrs. Chol'mley says she never met so much modesty with so much *merit* before in any literary performance,' said Johnson.

[1] Extract from a letter of Susan Burney's, first printed in the *Early Diary,* London, 1889, from which all the subsequent extracts are taken.
[2] Before the publication of *Evelina,* Dr. Burney had been somewhat inclined to condescension toward his daughter Fanny, as one of the lesser members of the family.
[3] Cf. above, p. 10.

" ' Why,' said I, quite coolly and innocently—
' Somebody recommended it to *me* too—I read a little
of it, which indeed seem'd to be above the common
place works of this kind.'

" ' Well,' said Mrs. Thrale—' I'll get it certainly.'
' It will do ' said I, ' for your time of confinement I
think.'

" ' You *must* have it Madam,' cried Johnson,—
' for Mrs. Chol'mley says she shall keep it on her
table the whole summer, that everybody that knows
her may see it—for she says everybody ought to read
it ! ' "—

A tolerably agreeable conversation this, methinks—
It took away my breath, and made me skip about like
a mad creature—What effect it may have on you I
know not—But I think it will occasion you no less
consternation than you received from the Monthly
Review [1]—

" And how did *you* feel sir ? " cried I to my father.

" Feel ?   Why I *liked it, of all things!*—and I
wanted somebody else to introduce the book there too
—'Twas just what I wish'd—I am sure Mrs. Thrale
will be pleased with it."

Leicester Fields.
Chesington,[2] Sunday, Aug. 1, 1779.

We arrived at Streatham at a very little past eleven.
As a *place,* it surpassed all my expectations.   The

---

[1] An extremely laudatory notice of *Evelina* appeared in the
Monthly Review for April, 1778.
[2] A letter from Susan to Fanny Burney.

avenue to the house, plantations, &c. are beautiful;
worthy of the charming inhabitants. It is a little
Paradise, I think. Cattle, poultry, dogs, all running
freely about, without annoying each other. Sam [1]
opened the chaise-door, and told my father breakfast
was not quite over, and I had no sooner got out
than Mr. Thrale appeared at a window close to the
door,—and, indeed, my dear Fanny, you did not tell
me anything about him which I did not find *entirely*
just. With regard to his reception of me, it was
particularly polite. I followed my father into the
library, which was much such a room as I expected;—
a most charming one. There sat Mrs. Thrale and
Dr. Johnson, the latter finishing his breakfast [2] upon
peaches. Mrs. Thrale immediately rose to meet me
very sweetly, and to *welcome me to* Streatham. Dr.
Johnson, too, rose. *"How do, dear lady?"* My
father told him it was not *his* Miss [3]—but another of
his own bantlings. Dr. Johnson, however, looked at
me with great kindness, and not at all in a *discour-
aging* manner. . . . Dr. Johnson interrupted Mrs.
Thrale by telling my father Mrs. Thrale had desired
Mr. Potter [4] to translate some verses for him, which
he, (Dr. J.) had before undertaken to do. "How
so?" said my father. *"Why Mr. Potter?"* "Nay,

---

[1] "'Sam' was Samuel Greaves, an old servant of Mr. Thrale,
after whose death Dr. Johnson instituted 'Sam's Club.'" ELLIS.
(Cf. above, p. 178.)

[2] Eleven was no late hour for Johnson, who frequently lay abed
till noon.

[3] Fanny, of course. The mistake was due to defective eyesight.
(Cf. above, p. 3.)

[4] Johnson considered Potter's translation of Æschylus "verbiage."
(*Life*, 3. 256.)

Sir, I don't know. It was Mrs. Thrale's fancy."
Mrs. Thrale said she would go and fetch them. As
soon as she was gone, Dr. Johnson invited me to take
her seat, which was next to him. " Come, come here,
my little dear," said he, with great kindness, and took
my hand as I sat down, I took then courage to deliver
your respects. " Aye.—Why don't she come among
us? " said he. I said you were confined by a sick
sister, but that you were very sorry to be away. " A
rogue! " said he, laughing. " She don't mind *me!* "
And then I *up and spoke vast fine* [1] about you, for Dr.
Johnson looked so kind, and so good-humour'd I was
not afraid of the sound of my voice. Mr. Thrale
then came in,—and, by the way, during my whole
visit look'd at me with so much *curiosity,* tho' he behaved with the utmost politeness, that I could not
help thinking all the time of his having said he *had
not had fair play about that Miss Susan.* I am sorry
he had heard me puff'd; however, kinder and more
flattering attention could not be paid me from *all*
quarters than I received. Dr. Johnson insisted upon
my eating one of his peaches, and, when I had eat it,
took a great deal of pains to persuade me to take
another. " No," said Mr. Thrale, " they're good for
nothing. Miss Burney must have some better than
them." However, I was humble. They did for *me.*
Miss Thrale came in: coldly civil as usual, [2]—but was
very chatty with me, *for her,* before I went away.

Then came back Mrs. Thrale, with the *verses,*

---

[1] Susan falls instinctively into the language of the Branghtons.
[2] Cf. above, p. 1.

Anonymous engraving of Johnson in the last years
of his life

Anonymous engraving of Johnson in the last year of his life.

which she had been copying out. I rose, and took
a seat next Miss Thrale. However, she made me
return to that next Dr. Johnson, that *he might hear
what I had to say.* " But, if I have *nothing* to say,
Ma'am? " said I—" Oh, never fear," said she, laughing, " I'll warrant you'll find something to talk
about." The verses were then given to my father.
After he had read the first stanza, " Why, these are
none of Potter's! " said he, " these are *worse* than
Potter! They beat him at his own weapons." Dr.
Johnson and Mrs. Thrale laugh'd very much, and the
verses proved to be the former's, and were composed,
in a comical humour, the evening before, in derision
of Potter.[1] They are admirable, you will see them
at Streatham, and perhaps procure a copy, which my
father could not do. Dr. Johnson is afraid of having
them spread about as some other verses were he wrote
in the same way to redicule [*sic*] poor Dr. Percy;[2]
but Mrs. Thrale advised my father to make you attack Dr. Johnson about them, " for she can do what
she pleases with him." [3] . . .

My father then played over some songs from the
Olimpiade during which Dr. Johnson came in. He
had a book in his hand, and wanted to shew some pas-

---

[1] These verses have perhaps perished. They were probably not
dissimilar in spirit to those entitled *Parody of a Translation from
the Medea of Euripides, Works* (1787), II. 376, which Mme.
Piozzi intimates (' Anecdotes,' *Miscellanies,* I. 191) were done in
imitation of Gray's *Elegy.* It is, I think, not impossible that these
are the very verses referred to in the text.

[2] The verses ridiculing Percy, and one or two other similar
burlesques, may be found in the same place as the verses referred
to in the preceding note.

[3] There is no evidence that Fanny ever tried to get them.

sage to my father, but seeing him engaged, stopt close to me, who was standing near the piano-forte. He put his arm round me, and smiling very good-humouredly, said, " Now you don't expect that I shall ever love you so well as I do your sister? "—" Oh, no, Sir," said I—" I have no such hopes—I am not so presumptuous."—" I am glad you are *so modest,*" said he, laughing,—and so encouraged by his good humour, (and he kept *see-sawing* me backwards and forwards in his arms, as if he had taken me for *you*) that I told him I must make an interest with him *through you.* He again said he was glad I was *so modest,* and added—" but I believe *you're* a good little creature—I think one should love *you,* too, *if one did but know you!*"[1] There's for you!—I assure you I shall set this little conversation down among my first honours. It put me in good humour and spirits for the rest of the day. After this Mr. Thrale came in, and some very good conversation went about concerning *Count Manucci,*[2] Mr. and Mrs. Pepys,[3] and I don't know who besides. . . .

When we were to go, Dr. Johnson comically repeated his *"Don't expect me to love you so well as your sister,"* but added, as I left the room, a very good-natured farewell—*" Goodbye, my little love."*

[1] In 1781, Johnson wrote to Mrs. Thrale, of the Burney family, "I love all of that breed whom I can be said to know, and one or two whom I hardly know I love upon credit, and love them because they love each other." (*Letters,* 2. 237.)   Cf. above, p. 171.
[2] What is known of Johnson's relations with Count Manucci may be found in the *Life,* 2. 390, 394; 3. 89, 91, and *Letters,* 1. 392 ff.
[3] See above, pp. 123 ff.

He [Garrick] [1] took off Dr. Johnson most admirably. Indeed, I enjoyed it doubly from having
been in his company; his *see-saw,* his *pawing,* his very
look, and his voice! My *cot!* what an astonishing thing
it is he [Garrick] has not a good ear for music! He
took him off in a speech (that has *stuck in his gizzard*
ever since some friendly person was so obliging as
to repeat it to him). Indeed, I should much wonder
if it did not, for it would have been a severe speech
if it had been said upon who it would, much more
upon Garrick, indeed I think it must have been exaggerated, or if not that it was a very severe, ill-
natured, unjust thing. " Yes, yes, Davy has some
convivial pleasantries in him; but 'tis a futile Fellow." [2] A little while after he took him off in one
of his *own convivial pleasantries.* " No, Sir; I'm for
the musick of the ancients, it has been corrupted so." [3]

The gentlemen [4] were so kind and considerate as
to divert themselves by making a fire skreen to the
whole room—Dr. Johnson, made them all *make off,*
for when nobody would have imagined he had known
the gentlemen were in the room, he said that " if he
was not *ashamed* he would keep the fire from the

[1] A selection from Charlotte Burney's *Journal.*

[2] Boswell tells the same anecdote. (*Life,* 2. 326.) Cf. above, p. 8,
note, and *Life,* 2. 464.

[3] Mrs. Ellis, the editor of the *Early Diary,* points out that this
refers " to the controversy as to the relative value of ancient and
modern poetry, music, etc., etc., which raged from the end of
the seventeenth into the first quarter of the eighteenth century."
Garrick undoubtedly cites this instance of Johnson's conservatism
because he is in the presence of the daughter of a famous musician.

[4] This is a scrap from the *Journal* of Charlotte Burney, describing the disastrous conversazione recorded above, pp. 209 ff.

ladies too,"—this reproof (for a *reproof* it certainly was, altho' given in a very comical dry way) was productive of a scene as *good as a comedy,* for Mr. Suard [1] tumbled on to the sopha directly, Mr. Thrale on to a chair, Mr. Davenant sneaked off the *premises* seemingly in as great a fright and as much confounded as if he had done any bad action, ahd Mr. *Gruel,* [2] being left *solus* was obliged to stalk off in spight of his teeth, and it was pretty evidently against the grain. During one of the duets, Piozzi, fatigued I suppose with being encircled with strangers and having nobody to converse with, regaled himself with a short nap.

Dr. Johnson was immensely *smart,* for *him,*—for he had not only a very decent tidy suit of cloathes on, but his hands, face, and linnen were clean, and he treated us with his *worsted wig* which Mr. Thrale made him a present of, because it scarce ever got out of curl, and he generally diverts himself with laying [*sic*] down just after he has got a fresh wig on.

[1] Mr. Seward.
[2] " Mr. ' Gruel ' is the lofty Greville, this being one of Charlotte's puns." ELLIS.

INDEX